D0984061

Messiahs of 1933

Messiahs of 1933

*How American Yiddish Theatre
Survived Adversity Through Satire*

Joel Schechter

TEMPLE UNIVERSITY PRESS
Philadelphia

COVER ILLUSTRATION: *The Wonder Horse* with Litvak (Isidore Meltzer) on horse (Jack Goldman and Harry Bender) and unidentified actor in *We Live and Laugh,* New York, 1936. *Courtesy of the National Archives.*

TEMPLE UNIVERSITY PRESS
1601 North Broad Street
Philadelphia PA 19122
www.temple.edu/tempress

⊛ The paper used in this publication meets the requirements of the American National Standard for Information Sciences—Permanence of Paper for Printed Library Materials, ANSI Z39.48-1992

Library of Congress Cataloging-in-Publication Data

Schechter, Joel, 1947-
  Messiahs of 1933 : how American Yiddish theatre survived adversity through satire / Joel Schechter.
    p. cm.
  Includes bibliographical references and index.
  ISBN-13: 978-1-59213-872-2 (cloth : alk. paper)
  1. Theater, Yiddish—United States—History. 2. Satire, Yiddish—United States—History and criticism. 3. Yiddish drama—United States—History and criticism. 4. Jewish actors—United States. I. Title.

PN3035.S32 2008
792.089'92407—dc22   2007036744

2 4 6 8 9 7 5 3 1

Contents

Messiahs of 1933

1

Messiahs of 1933

*How Playwright Moishe Nadir and Artef Led
America Out of the Great Depression to a Future of
Full Employment, Justice, and Yiddish Satire for All*

One of the most radical cultural events in America could
have taken place during the Great Depression, if everyone
in the country spoke Yiddish: the public would have been
able to welcome a Yiddish-speaking messiah who arrived in New
York. With thirteen to fourteen million Americans unemployed,
thousands of banks closed permanently, and breadlines everywhere,
the nation needed a messiah. Not one, but two saviors arrived in New
York and spoke the language of East European Jews in May of 1933.
They could be seen in the company of actors at the Yiddish theatre
collective Artef (Arbeter Teater Farband, or Worker's Theatrical Alliance), when it staged Moishe Nadir's play, *Messiah in America*.[1]

Nadir's stage play begins with a comic portrait of theatre producers, and extends its satire to messianism. Broadway producer
Menachem Yosef and his assistant Jack the Bluffer announce that a
Yiddish-speaking messiah has arrived, and can be seen in their theatre for a price. Menachem knows his messiah is an impostor, but
the public welcomes the savior, much to the producer's delight.

The 1933 producers of Nadir's play were messianic too. Artef's
actors, their director, and Nadir took upon themselves the tasks
of a messiah, inaugurating in artistic form their visions of social
justice, peace, and redistributed wealth. Their Yiddish-language

responses to inequality and economic hardship in *Messiah in America* and other plays might now be regarded as scenes of a lost cause. The new, radical society their reveries anticipated never arrived. Their leftist political and artistic legacies remain outside mainstream American culture. Yet, this does not mean the work of these artists disappeared completely. The unions on strike, the anarchist peddler on Rivington Street, the tailor who won the lottery, and the false messiahs Artef presented on stage between 1928 and 1940 still can be found in play texts. Immodest proposals that Nadir and his theatre colleagues shaped into plays during that period survive with humor, daring, and imagination intact, as scenes of social change and satire born in a time of adversity.

The creations by Yiddish stage satirists like Nadir and his friend, puppeteer Yosl Cutler, differed from those of most other American artists who responded to the Great Depression. By the time the Hollywood cast of *Gold Diggers of 1933* sang "Brother Can You Spare a Dime?" in English, much of the United States was experiencing the economic insecurity and tests of will that Yiddish-speaking immigrants had known for decades, when they fled Eastern European pogroms and anti-Semitic governments. Artists like Nadir and Cutler, and their American Jewish artistic community, could bring their earlier education in poverty and survival, and their own forms of leftist politics and messianic tradition, into Yiddish theatre when responding to challenges of the period. In Yosl Cutler's 1936 puppet show parodying Ansky's classic play, *The Dybbuk*, a delirious Kabbalah student dreams of a "united front" formed by poor Jews within the "goyish" (or non-Jewish) crisis of the Depression.[2] But his vision of Yiddish activism and its culture uniting everyone for social change was only a dream.

The social consciousness and satire conveyed through theatre by Cutler, Nadir, and their associates did not find much of an audience in the English-speaking public, or "goyim" of America. Even Yiddish-speaking audiences generally preferred to see Second Avenue's other theatres—where famous actors performed melodramas and musicals, and provided theatrical escapes from national crisis rather than confrontations with it. Sharing the 1933 Yiddish theatre season (but not the Artef stage) with Nadir's play in New York were *Love for Sale*, featuring the popular actor and singer Aaron Lebedev; *A Mother's Struggle*, starring tearful, melodramatic Jennie Goldstein; *Getzel Becomes a Bridegroom*, with comedian Menasha Skulnik in the title role; renowned actor Boris

Thomashefsky's production of *Polish Wedding*; Joseph Rumshinsky's musical, *The Girl From Warsaw*; and the Yiddish Art Theatre's acclaimed adaptation of I. J. Singer's novel, *Yoshe Kalb*. These plays about the Old World of Jews in transition and about New World Jews in love differed substantially in subject and style from the satiric, politically engaged theatre repertoire to which Nadir contributed. He and his colleagues in Artef, in the puppet theatre Modicut, and in the Yiddish Unit of the Federal Theatre Project created a special, alternate arena of response to the Great Depression and fascism in the thirties, as they staged ebullient scenes of resistance to oppression and struggles for survival by working-class Jews in the most difficult of times, although more difficult times were to follow in Europe in the 1940s.

Nadir's collaborations with Artef, with Yosl Cutler and Zuni Maud's puppet theatre, Modicut, and with the Federal Theatre Project's Yiddish Unit were not commercial ventures; his stage work, as well as plays by his colleagues, depended on support from workers' clubs, and on federal subsidy in the case of the Yiddish Unit. *Messiah in America* satirizes a world of money-making theatre production and cutthroat business competition that leftist Yiddish theatre workers like Nadir rejected. In the first scene of Nadir's play, a scheme to profit from messianic longings begins in the office of Broadway theatre producer Menachem Yosef. Desperately seeking new stage acts that will attract spectators, Menachem mentions in passing that he works to make a living, not merely to pursue his ideals; he is not so pure or self-sacrificing that he could "bring on the Messiah" by himself.[3] Menachem's words inspire his assistant Jack the Bluffer.

> JACK: What did you just say: Messiah? Messiah. Quiet. Why not bring on the Messiah? . . .
> MENACHEM: Are you just talking, or do you mean business?
> JACK: I mean business. You understand, it's like this. In America we have so many and so many Jews. We have plenty of Jews in New York alone. Am I right, or not?
> MENACHEM: Right.
> JACK: Nu, good, figure it this way. Every Jew is waiting for the messiah to come. And every Jew that's waiting for the messiah to come can afford a ticket for, let's say, a dollar seventy-five. Am I right, or not?
> MENACHEM: Right.

JACK: So let's figure it this way. Two thousand people a night, at a dollar seventy-five each, makes 3,500 dollars a night. Am I right, or not?

MENACHEM: Right.

JACK: So figure it this way. (*Writing.*) Seven shows a week, plus two matinees, Saturday and Sunday, makes nine shows a week, at 3,500 a show, comes to . . .

MENACHEM: Wait a minute til I lock the door. (*Does so.*) All in all, I like it. It's a deal. But where do we get a messiah?

Not idealism, but profit motives speed the arrival of the first false messiah in Nadir's play. The "First Messiah Redemption Corporation" and other outrageously inventive plans for financial success take hold. Soon a battle for corporate control of the messiah market erupts. Through his stage satire, Nadir encourages the audience to laugh at the new messiahs of capitalism—men who promise to save everyone for a price, or let the market save them—in this case for the price of a theatre ticket. One measure of Artef's distance from capitalist art can be found in the thirty-five cent price of tickets it sold for Nadir's play in May 1933—far cheaper than Menachem Yosef's $1.75 ticket to see the same savior.[4]

Artef also differed from commercial theatre, according to David Lifson, in these ways:

It had no capital, no investors, no rich patrons. The students in Artef gave most of their income to sustain the studio and its teachers. Substantiating Artef's dedication to art, Lifshitz (Artef's treasurer) submitted that *200,000* [a Sholem Aleichem text which became one of Artef's most popular productions] played to 60,000 people, but was withdrawn at the height of its run because Artef believed it should give more than one play a season to its subscribers.[5]

Far more eager than Artef to profit from long-running attractions, the first commercial producer featured in Nadir's satire not only charges high prices for tickets but he also keeps his messiah's wages low. The alleged messiah arrives after Menachem Yosef's assistant, Jack, calls in his Uncle Simkhe, a bearded immigrant from Eastern Europe who looks pious enough to be mistaken for a holy man, and who needs a job. Yosef persuades Simkhe to sign a contract guaranteeing him $35 a week, a respectable weekly salary in 1933, but a sum that turns out to be a very small percentage of the company's profits. It is not known what the standard pay for messiahs was that year, but Menachem Yosef ensures that the messiah will not be overpaid.

No satire of messianic capitalism would be complete without market competition, and after word spreads of the first messiah's arrival, a rival producer joins the fray by introducing a second messiah in America. Zipkin, who directs and performs in a Coney Island sideshow, has this conversation with the sideshow barker, Charlie:

> ZIPKIN: Have you heard anything about what's doing with Menachem's messiah?
>
> CHARLIE: Rakes in barrels of gold, they say.
>
> ZIPKIN: Really? Gold? Barrels? He rakes it, hah? Quiet now, quiet, let me just think a minute. (*Hand to forehead*) You know what I'm going to tell you, Charlie . . . We'll come out with a messiah too—a better one than Menachem's.

Zipkin then introduces a new, younger, motorcycle-riding, English-speaking messiah to the world. The prospect of attracting an English-language audience means larger profits for the Yiddish-speaking Zipkin and his company. Looking back at the era in which Artef produced Nadir's play, it is tempting to ask whether the leftist collective should have followed Zipkin's example, and staged its satire about messiahs in English as well as Yiddish. That audience-expanding, profit-seeking idea was not part of Artef's 1933 repertoire, but in retrospect, Zipkin may have known more about economic and cultural survival in America than the artists satirizing his type. As seen in Chapter 4, a farsighted administrator in the Federal Theatre Project's Yiddish Unit initiated new translations of Yiddish plays into English in the thirties to reach a wider audience. Had the government-funded translations not stopped in 1939, innovative Yiddish plays might be more widely known to English-speaking Americans today. Unfortunately, Nadir's stage satire and others equally notable remain unpublished in English. Despite the 1933 hiring of a bilingual messiah who might have attracted *goyim* to his theatre, Zipkin and his comic life have been known primarily to those who can read Nadir's play in Yiddish.

Nadir himself took an interest in widely accessible and popular entertainment forms, as demonstrated by the boxing match with which he ends *Messiah in America*. After Zipkin and Menachem Yosef agree that they must either fiercely compete or merge their businesses, they come up with a perfect corporate solution. The rival businesses merge and promote a boxing match between their messiahs to determine which one is the true savior. The older, greenhorn messiah (Simkhe) wins the match, thanks to a horseshoe concealed in one of his boxing gloves. The innocent old man knocks out the younger messiah without knowing hidden weights are prohibited. He's simply told the horseshoe is a good-luck charm.

Both of the producers in Nadir's play herald the outcome of the boxing match as the start of a new age, a triumph for Jews of all nations, if not all of humanity. Holding the victor's hands up high, Jack the Bluffer announces that this "greatest fight of all time and all lands . . . [is] a credit to every American citizen in general and in particular to us, Israelites, whose history goes back to Jerusalem, to Zion, to the cedars of Lebanon, to the River Jordan, to the Wailing Wall." The new age's promise for the future is questionable, considering that it starts with the death of the younger messiah. The unfortunate man lies cold on the floor of the boxing ring as Jack delivers his laudatory speech. Everyone else on stage is oblivious to the death. Those in need of a messiah cheer their new world champion, and the producers secure their better world in the form of cash, jewelry, a new car, and a trip to Florida—profits from the public's offerings to their false messiahs.

The death in the ring that inaugurates the "new age" on stage had a grim counterpart in the militarism and fascism rising offstage, particularly in Europe during the thirties. Although Nadir could not have anticipated the rise of Hitler when he wrote his satire of messianism late in the twenties, the battle between the two theatrical producers to "corner the messiah market" speaks to a time when messiahs of one variety or another were wanted by nations, as well as individuals, and false messiahs might be accepted by desperate followers. On May 11, 1933, days before false messiahs walked across Artef's stage on the Lower East Side, the Yiddish newpaper *Morgn Frayhayt* reported that 100,000 people marched in New York City to protest against Hitler's fascism. Nadir's satire was not specifically directed at Hitler, but the political and economic conditions of the period rendered all the more timely his wariness of messiahs who would not save Jews, or anyone else. Jews had greeted false messiahs in earlier periods of history and literature, notably when Sabbati Zvi (1626-76) became "the Anointed One" and "King of

Figure 1.1

Nadir's *Messiah in America* comic strip illustrated by Spain Rodriguez. *Courtesy of the artist and* Jewish Currents.

the Jews." Nadir was by no means the first Yiddish author to write a play about a false messiah. Yiddish theatre pioneer Avrom Goldfaden's *Ben Ami*, a melodrama about a false messiah, opened in New York in December 1907. The famous actor Boris Thomashefsky produced the play, and Goldfaden in person watched its favorable reception. Nadir, aged 22 that year and already writing in New York, could have seen the play.[6] Sholem Asch wrote a play about Sabbati Zvi in 1908. The messiah's delayed arrival had been joked about by non-Yiddish authors too. Kafka once predicted, "The Messiah will come only when he is no longer necessary," and his ironic prognostication has so far proven accurate.[7]

However, no other Yiddish play featured a comic, Coney Island messiah before Nadir set his second, younger false messiah's arrival there. The new, English-speaking messiah joins the world of popular entertainment as a featured sideshow performer, and then as a boxing contestant. Although the stage directions don't say so, it would be appropriate for the fat lady, the bearded lady, the sword swallower, and the petrified man to cheer for the new arrival's victory in the ring. The impostor messiah's employer (Zipkin) is theirs, and their sideshow needs new attractions as much as Menachem Yosef does on Broadway. In this play's "new age," prosperity is just around the corner—the corner of the boxing ring in which the winning messiah stands. Such triumphs sell more tickets, and confer on the producers their own salvation through capitalism.

A few speeches in *Messiah in America* might be read as a wry, subtle critique of rivalries between Yiddish theatre producers alive in Nadir's time. Maurice Schwartz and Jacob Ben Ami initiated such a rivalry when their two companies competed around the same time (1918–19) Nadir wrote the story on which he later based his play. Ben Ami, who rehearsed his company in Coney Island at one point, could have inspired the play's Coney Island sideshow scenes. There were other famous rivalries among the creators of Yiddish theatre in New York (notably those between Jacob Adler and Boris Thomashefsky), and other directors and actors might have seen themselves in Nadir's characters when the play based on his story was performed first in 1929 and then in 1933.

Long before Zero Mostel portrayed a scheming theatrical producer in a film created by Mel Brooks, Nadir developed this earlier comic version of *The Producers*. Nadir's confidence men sell tickets to the arrival of the messiah, instead of producing a musical that celebrates Hitler's arrival as Fuhrer. While Mel Brooks did not derive his plot from Nadir, Brooks's sense of humor, influenced by the Borscht Belt's stand-up comedians and *tummlers* (Yiddish for entertainer or social director), may have benefited from the same cultural circles known to Nadir. In Brooks's 2001 musical stage version of *The Producers,* based on his own film, the leading character boasts he was a protégé of actor Boris Thomashefsky. Nadir was not a protégé of Thomashefsky; but he knew most of the accomplished Yiddish actors in New York, and their plays, and also may have known Borscht Belt entertainers in the vicinity of his summer hotel in upstate New York

For most of his professional life, Nadir was better known as an essay-ist and poet than as hotelier, playwright, or collaborative stage artist. Born Isaac Reiss in Narayov, Galicia, in 1885, he arrived in the United States at age 13, when his mother joined his father, who immigrated to New York earlier. By 1902 he was publishing articles for a Yiddish news-paper; he was editing the Yiddish humor journal, *Der Groyser Kundes* (*The Big Prankster*) by 1909 and then co-editing, with Jacob Adler, *Der Yidisher Gazlon* (*Jewish Bandit*), another Yiddish humor periodical, in 1910. Hav-ing found a place in the world of Yiddish satire, he also made his mark as a poet with *Vilde Rozyn* (*Wild Roses*), a volume of erotic verse in Yiddish that appeared in 1915. "Moishe Nadir" was one of several pseudonyms Reiss employed, as he followed the tradition of other Yiddish satirists—Sholem Aleichem and Mendele—who wrote under pseudonyms. "Nadir" translates as "here, take" or "take this," as in "Take this and choke on it." Perhaps the name was a warning to readers to brace themselves for his acid humor—or it simply invited readers to take and read his publica-tions, which they did. In the twenties and thirties, tens of thousands of leftists read his poems and satiric columns in *Frayhayt* (*Freedom*), the Communist Party-funded Yiddish newspaper that in 1929 became the morning paper, *Morgn Frayhayt,* and in other journals. The fiery polem-ics, the erotic and epic poems, and the theatrical capes and coats he sported like a dandy brought Nadir considerable public attention.

Nadir's provocative and satiric newspaper columns were more widely noticed than his achievements in the theatre, but he left his imprint there too, as playwright and critic. In addition to adapting short stories for Artef, and seeing his own plays performed by the same company in the 1930s, Nadir collaborated with the distinguished Yiddish director, Maurice Schwartz, who staged several of his plays, including *The Last Jew* in 1921. His three-act musical, *The Tragedy of Nothing,* was produced at the Irving Place Theatre in 1927. A number of his one-acts and longer plays were performed by Modicut and Artef before Nadir published them in a 1932 collection. Artef toured a play based on *Rivington Street*, a long poem published in 1932. He also contributed to the Federal Theatre Project's 1936–37 cabaret revue, *We Live and Laugh*, discussed later.

Few details about his productions can be found in histories of Yiddish theatre, although in her memoir actress Celia Adler briefly recalls some of the satiric sketches the "great humorist" Nadir wrote for Maurice Schwartz.[8] Schwartz collaborated with Nadir again after his negative newspaper reviews of plays led some theatre producers to ban the critic from their houses. Schwartz, an actor and master of disguise himself, helped Nadir create a new identity—complete with false beard—so he could get past theatre guards on the lookout for the feared reviewer. "And so my enemies will increase their 'guard.' . . . The cashier has all his eyes out," Nadir reported, "he is so flustered he gives back more change than he should. It's a frenzy of activity! But it doesn't help."[9] Like the first false messiah in his play, Nadir found his beard to be a distinct advantage in the Yiddish theatre world.

At the time that he wrote *Messiah in America*, Yiddish theatre was still quite alive and popular in New York, with over a half-million Yiddish-speaking Jews in the city supporting fourteen Yiddish theatres and ten Yiddish newspapers. Not all of these people attended Nadir's plays or Artef, of course; that could explain why, when recounting his need to don a disguise as a critic, Nadir also recalls that the theatre he criticized was robbing the public of its "remaining bit of intelligence . . . turning [spectators] into fools."[10]

Messiah in America displays no sympathy for fools. The misled public that worships false messiahs in the play exhibits a naive, all-accepting attitude toward impostor saviors. After the first messiah's arrival is announced with a flurry of tabloid newspaper headlines, a gullible public eagerly greets the old man and, with prompting from Menachem Yosef, pays homage with expensive gifts.

The Messiah of 1929

Audiences attending Nadir's own play were less naïve, and far more amused by the first false messiah's appearance, than the spectators portrayed within his play, if an account of its 1929 staging is any indication. Yiddish writer Lamed Shapiro saw Act One of *Messiah in America* performed in 1929, and recalled the audience around him laughing at the white-bearded messiah, "a Galician Jew and a wimp, [who] couldn't manage to stay on his feet and continually needed to be supported in someone's arms to keep from collapsing on the ground. . . . People laughed not just at America but at the messiah as well."[11] Shapiro watched a performance of Act One at the Civic Repertory Theatre on 14th Street in New York City; the excerpt from Nadir's play was part of an evening celebrating the 1929 publication of his book, *A Lamp in My Window*.

"The grotesqueries of Jewish America held the hall in an unending convulsion of laughter," Shapiro writes. Not entirely pleased by the event, he also confesses to feeling ashamed, "as though I were laughing at someone down and out," and he wonders if Nadir has "forgotten what the messianic hope, the messianic vision meant to him over there in Narayev [Galicia] during the years of his youth." In these last words Shapiro himself forgets that the character on stage is not a messiah, but an impostor, a greenhorn immigrant hired by a theatre producer to impersonate a savior. Nadir and his actor appropriately portray the false messiah as a man incapable of standing upright; Simkhe is not an upright man. The physical pratfalls, as well as the satiric dialogue, undermine the messiah's position, and prompt the laughter at him. Nadir sets up this physical comedy early in the play, when Jack describes his uncle as a sick man who can't perform heavy labor or stand on his feet for long. Stage directions in Act One call for the old man to faint. The crowd exclaims: "He fell, our messiah." This messiah's later boxing victory verges on the miraculous, even if he has a horseshoe hidden in his glove.

The first act's scenes of a faltering savior enhance Nadir's satire of the theatre world. Desperate to sell theatre tickets, Menachem Yosef hires the impostor for his beard—his messianic face—without auditioning him very carefully. That the old man can't stand up for long attests to bad casting by the producer as much as anything else. A messiah who can stand on his feet might be better received, and Menachem's rival, Zipkin, understands this; his younger, stronger false messiah can walk unsupported, ride a motorcycle, and dance. Zipkin knows better than Menachem how to cast the role of false messiah, which makes sense given his background. Most of the freaks—the abnormal characters—featured in his Coney Island show are frauds, like the young messiah. A Jewish actor portrays the sideshow Indian (the man who sold Manhattan). A man also portrays the bearded lady: the gender-bending He/She is not actually half man and half woman. Having hired other frauds, Zipkin has no trouble finding a sensational false messiah. "The grotes-queries of Jewish America" to which Lamed Shapiro referred find new company in the sideshow world of Coney Island.

The Messiah of Coney Island

While not exactly a "freak" like the figures in his play's Coney Island sideshow, Moishe Nadir also stood apart from the crowd. As a fervent supporter of Communist programs from 1922 to 1939, he separated himself from many Yiddish poets and artists through his politics, par-ticularly after 1929, when other Yiddish writers left the Communist newspaper *Frayhayt* to protest its defense of Arabs after a pogrom in Palestine. Paul Buhle suggests that Nadir has been ignored "because, 'Great Cynic' and nihilist turned Communist (until his break with the Party in 1939), he remains *treyf* [not kosher] to the Jewish establishment. Only recently has he been partially rehabilitated to one of those oddities worth a passing mention."[12] His Communist tendencies contributed to the posthumous neglect of Nadir's plays—to his position as an outcast if not a sideshow freak—even after he broke with the Party.

In a Coney Island sideshow, outcasts and freaks are applauded, or at least regarded with fear and awe, for their abnormality. The critic Leslie Fiedler once argued in his book *Freaks* that dwarves are the Jews of the sideshow world[13]; Nadir's vision of Coney Island unites Jews (the pro-ducers) and sideshow artists (curiously, no dwarves) in a world where they are popular. Their business is to be and sell "attractions."

Throughout *Messiah in America*, although business acquires gro-tesque, fraudulent, and comic shadings, the producers who deal in side-show attractions and false messiahs succeed. They know what their public wants: Nadir's own voice might be heard through Zipkin, when the producer advises Jim, the Bearded Lady:

All America is Coney Island, little fool. Fake, swindle, bluff— that's what America stands on. From ancient days people have wanted bread and circuses. Today they still want the same. . . . The god of bluff is the greatest god in the world, Jim. Greater than Jesus of Nazareth, greater than Edison or Ford . . . he must be worshipped with all your heart. If not, nothing happens, no chance of success.

Nadir hardly endorses such worship; the god of bluff becomes another target of his satire. P. T. Barnum's belief that suckers are born every minute becomes a major tenet of the faith, and one religious ritual takes the form of a boxing match between the two false messiahs. Those seeking the true messiah need tickets, not prayer or piety, to bear witness to the savior's arrival, secured through showmanship and successful competition. The outcasts of the world (the sideshow employees) join the paying spectators around the boxing ring, waiting for one of their own to be acclaimed.

Messiah in America incorporates several popular American entertainment forms that cast the audience as participants. When the play was staged in San Francisco in 2001, spectators began to cheer for their favorites in the boxing ring scene, as if they were sitting in a sports arena rather than a theatre.[14] Chants of "Zip, Zip, Zip" broke out after the sideshow manager was introduced in the ring. Nadir wrote both the boxing scene and sideshow dialogue in a manner that allows actors to prompt audience cheers and comments, as sideshow barkers and boxing arena announcers often have. Given the right delivery by an actor portraying Jack the Bluffer, an audience may well cheer and laugh when he escorts a producer to the center of the ring and declares: "On this side, weighing in with close to one million dollars in previous earnings, Mr. Menachem Yosef." Cheers could similarly follow Jack's introduction of "the equally rich and glorious Mr. Zipkin." The audience is cast as a character—the crowd—through these speeches. Similar casting occurs in the sideshow, when Charlie the Barker tells the audience they are "now standing before one of the great wonders of the century." If the audience accepts its role in these scenes, the theatre itself becomes a melting pot, where diverse identities merge into that of the carnivalesque and sporting crowd. In Nadir's carnivalesque world, we see components described by Russian critic Mikhail Bakhtin; in the sporting crowd, we see hints of Bertolt Brecht's favorite audience. Nadir's play resonates with the theories of Bakhtin and Brecht.[15] Perhaps it is not bluff, fakery, or swindle, but the inclusiveness of these scenes, the rousing popular theatre that turns spectators and outcasts onstage into equals—all witnesses to a world where anyone, even an old man who can barely walk around the ring, can become an American champion.

The process of assimilation through boxing is also a process of deracination. Yiddish and messianic identities yield to something more universal: an exchange of punches and the title of world champion. Even if the Old Messiah wins the fight while wearing Hasidic garb (long black coat, black hat, earlocks, long beard), the traditional image of a pious man gives way to that of another immigrant winning acceptance and acclaim as he takes a place in the line of fighting Irish, Jews, and African Americans who preceded him in the ring.

The grotesque scene of a white-bearded elderly messiah fighting a Coney Island sideshow's messiah in the ring also gives vivid physical form to Nadir's satire of what has been called the "the debased and mystified relations between men in capitalist society." Walter Benjamin observed that Marx "was the first to illuminate with criticism the debased and mystified relations between men in capitalist society, [and he] thereby became a teacher of satire; and he was not far from becoming a master of it."[16] Extending Marx's satiric attitude toward capitalism, Nadir humorously writes a description of the "firm economic base" that Zipkin and Menachem secure through their joint investment in fighting messiahs. Zipkin tells this his partner:

> You're a producer for theatre, I for circuses—fine. . . . You know what comes to mind? It comes to mind that we can arrange a prizefight, a boxing match between both messiahs, right at my circus. First of all for the publicity. Second we can make a dollar that way, because what sport won't pay fifteen dollars a ticket to see two messiahs fighting? Besides, right after the fight we get rid of the false messiah, the defeated one, and we keep the true messiah, the one that won. So we win two ways: first, we put our messiah monopoly on a firm economic base: one man instead of two. Second, we save half the money which the other messiah would have taken. Third, we cut out other competitors because they'll be afraid to take a beating.

As companies laid off their labor forces, and breadlines lengthened in the thirties, even messiahs were being thrown (or beaten) out of work at Artef. Still, one messiah needs to be kept alive, if the firm is to have any economic base at all.

The longing for a single, world champion messiah, which Menachem and Zipkin exploit, was acknowledged by Nadir and his associates too. If not the Messiah in person, at least social justice and human dignity associated with a messianic era were wanted by skeptics, including Moishe Nadir. Nadir's play is hardly an endorsement of messianic movements. Its scenes ridicule the fervor with which followers embrace false messiahs. Nadir and Artef were far from devout in their regard for some Jewish traditions; and the depiction of messiahs in the play focuses on the deceptions, misled hopes, and profiteering such legendary arrivals engender, not on the joy and faith with which the Jewish and Christian religion traditionally welcome saviors.

Even though Nadir ridiculed corporate greed and exploitation of traditional Jewish yearnings for a messiah, the theatre ensemble that staged the play in 1933 can be seen as part of a secular messianic movement. Artef's political philosophy favoring anti-capitalist, worker-centered Yiddish culture contained a modicum of messianism within it. The theatre collective's audiences, and some of its artists, participated in Communist Party and union activities, rallies, and marches that united those on stage and off. If the satiric play Nadir wrote, and others in the same tradition, did not bring on the Messiah or full employment during the Great Depression, at least this Yiddish theatre and the activists who bought tickets to it promised everyone a role in their movement for social change. That is, everyone who spoke Yiddish.

Nadir's Messiah and Benjamin's: A Speculative History

Imagine that everyone in the United States spoke Yiddish in 1933. With widespread understanding of the language, Nadir's satire of salvation through capitalism could have toured the country, spreading laughter and political awareness everywhere. *Messiah in America* and Artef's theatrical art would have become widely known as part of a larger messianic cultural and political project that sought to make social justice, equality, redistribution of wealth, and internationalism the America way. The play introduced a few impostors, false messiahs; but as deliverers of radical culture, the author and the Artef actors who performed the satire in 1933 were themselves "endowed with a *weak* Messianic power"—their coming had been expected by earlier advocates of change, as Walter Benjamin suggested during the same decade in another context.[17]

Throughout the Great Depression, these messianic Yiddish artists would continue to address the concerns of labor, the unemployed, exiles, and revolutionaries in America. All that was necessary for Artef to move the nation forward with its radical culture was for Americans to speak Yiddish and attend the theatre.

From the transformation of America into a Yiddish-speaking nation, with Artef as the country's most prominent theatre company, momentous changes might follow. Here is a scenario for cultural and political change in 1933. Bertolt Brecht visits the United States and sees several studio collaborations between Artef artistic director Benno Schneider and Moishe Nadir; immensely impressed, Brecht asks Schneider to stage the world premiere of his play, *Mother Courage,* in a Yiddish adaptation by Nadir. National acclaim for Brecht and Artef builds, as critics applaud Schneider's wildly inventive staging of Brecht's epic theatre, which has much in common with Nadir's satire in its mordant depiction of events. The chorus of praise ensures that by 1940 Artef's *Mother Courage* tours the United States and every unoccupied country in Europe. Brecht's friend, Walter Benjamin, intent on learning Hebrew and moving to Jerusalem, hears so much about Artef from Brecht that he learns Yiddish and moves to New York instead, where he lives until 2010 as a Professor of Marxist Midrash (Hebrew for "commentary") at Columbia University.

In his theses about the philosophy of history, Walter Benjamin observes that "the Jews were prohibited from investigating the future. The Torah and the prayers instruct them in remembrance, however." The theatre collective of Artef, already engaged in radical remembrance of traditions and history through such plays as its 1932 staging of Kushnirov's *Hirsch Leckert,* about Jewish workers in Russia resisting the Tsar, finds in Benjamin an aesthetician eminently suited to comment on its experiments. His book on Yiddish theatre inspires worldwide production of plays by Nadir in repertoire with classics by Sholem Aleichem, Mendele, and Artef's *Mother Courage* (known as *The Jewish Mother*). In the 1940s, the young Mel Brooks, Danny Kaye, and Judy Holliday meet Nadir and Schneider in a Borscht Belt resort, hear about their exciting satires, and discover within Artef's leftist Yiddish sense of humor the inspiration for new political comedy and songs. Along with Brooks's *The Producers, Messiah in America* opens for a long run on Broadway as an antic anti-capitalist musical.

The world also becomes a stage. Late in the forties, when Israel still is debating whether Yiddish or Hebrew should be its national language, the achievements of Nadir and Artef—heralded by Benjamin, his friend (and professor of Jewish mysticism) Gershom Scholem, and thirty-six anonymous holy men and women wandering the world—lead to a decision that the former center of Yiddish culture, Poland, not Israel, should be the Jewish homeland, resulting in preservation of Palestinian rights in the Mideast and rights of return to Eastern Europe for all Yiddish exiles. With Palestine autonomous, peace in the Mideast, and no need for American troops in the region, the $700 billion saved in Pentagon expenses (known as the "Iraq peace dividend") funds universal health care and full employment in a new, twenty-first-century American Works Progress Administration (WPA). Artef, now part of the WPA's New Federal Theatre Project, enjoys a summer home in Warsaw, with a regular season in New York, Paris, and Moscow each year. And Moishe Nadir posthumously is declared Poet Laureate of the United States in honor of his contributions to American theatre.

Yiddish theatre in America was not as influential or far reaching as my imaginary history would have it. The messiahs portrayed in Moishe Nadir's play were only actors. And yet the author and artists with whom he collaborated were messianic, if only for an hour or two at a time, as some of their plays showed audiences the promised land (America, not Jerusalem), a territory where Walter Benjamin's philosophy of history and Bertolt Brecht's political satire lived on the stage of their Yiddish American counterparts. It was a world where, as Benjamin wrote, "every second of time was the strait gate through which the messiah might enter."[18] Although no one knew what the messiah would look like, he or she could have been an artist at Artef. By now many of that era's messianic idylls about peace, justice, and internationalism have subsided, or been destroyed by Hitler, Stalin, and American anti-Communism; but some of the humor, the optimism, the social activism, and the daring survive, like ruins, in the texts of plays and in theatre history.

The remains of thirties Yiddish theatre in America might also be regarded as a dybbuk, a resistant spirit still at large. In Ansky's classic Yiddish play, *The Dybbuk*, we are told, "If someone dies before his time, his soul returns to the world to live out the span of his years, to finish the undone deeds, to feel the unfelt joys and sorrows."[19] In 1926 when Yosl Cutler collaborated with Zuni Maud on the first of several puppet plays parodying *The Dybbuk*, their work suggested that the theatre troupes staging Ansky's play in New York at that time kept the dybbuk at large in our consciousness. Yiddish theatre itself was a source of dybbuks, at least in Maud and Cutler's comic vision.[20] Will its undone deeds ever be finished?

A few of the events in this cultural history represent missed opportunities, points of near intersection where radical Yiddish theatre might have moved more fully into the mainstream of popular and international political theatre, and influenced writers, stage directors, actors, and ordinary citizens alike, with significant successes outside Yiddish theatre's usual locations on Second Avenue in New York City. When Brecht's play, *The Mother,* opened in New York in 1935, the playwright actually visited Artef, and he wrote briefly about one scene in a Yiddish play at Artef (*Haunch, Paunch, and Jowl*) that displeased him.[21] He knew Artef's artists, and they knew him to some extent, although they never collaborated. (Earlier, when Brecht's *Threepenny Opera* first opened in New York in April 1933, its producers advertised in the Yiddish newspaper, *Morgn Frayhayt,* and must have expected some Yiddish-speaking theatregoers to attend the English-language production.)

Interest in Yiddish theatre was also shown by Clifford Odets, whose *Waiting for Lefty* attracted considerable attention to the concerns of the labor movement in 1935 when the author and Sanford Meisner staged the play in New York. (Instead of waiting for the messiah to arrive, Odets'cab drivers wait for a labor organizer named Lefty, who does not arrive.) Odets chose to have his play *Awake and Sing* translated into Yiddish and staged by the Yiddish Unit of the Federal Theatre Project in 1937–38.

Yiddish theatre's reach extended to the Catskills resorts in New York where Danny Kaye (born David Daniel Kaminsky), Mel Brooks (born Melvin Kaminsky), and Judy Holliday (born Judy Tuvin) performed for Yiddish-speaking audiences—although they performed mostly in English in the 1930s and '40s—before they went to Hollywood. Not far from their resort locations, Moishe Nadir once ran a summer hotel in Lake Sheldrake, where puppeteer Yosl Cutler first met Nadir and his radical politics. The prospects that Brecht, Odets, Kaye, Brooks, and Holliday could have met Nadir, or joined Benno Schneider in collaborative creation, are not entirely imaginary; they knew a number of the same Yiddish artists by reputation if not personally. And they responded to some of the same economic and social crises, although hardly in a uniform manner.

In addition to *Messiah in America,* other innovative Yiddish satires staged in the 1930s have not yet been translated or published in English. Their resourceful responses to American crises remain unheard by many Americans, including theatre scholars and historians, which means the events described here are rarely mentioned in the annals of theatre history. In archives and rare book collections, Yiddish plays of the period survive as neglected documents of resistance to poverty, injustice, unemployment, and displacement and as fragments of a lost world where messiahs arrived on stage. (Years later, when an angel flew onto the stage in 1992, and a man named Prior Walter passed on to the other world in Tony Kushner's *Angels in America,* Yiddish briefly could be heard on stage again in a radical American play. But that is another story.[22])

Without question, the audience for messianic and satiric Yiddish theatre in the thirties was small, compared to the audience attending Second Avenue musicals, melodramas, and the Yiddish Art Theatre. Certainly the audience watching Artef's studio perform plays like *Messiah in America* was smaller than the one attending its main stage productions on Broadway, as will be seen. But those participating in the smaller stage events could be compared favorably to the watchman about whom Isaac Bashevis Singer spoke when asked if he ever expected to see the Messiah. "I have the same hopes as the people of Chelm [legendary city of fools]," Singer answered. "There, a man is employed to welcome the Messiah. It's not well paid, but it's a steady job."[23] Perhaps anyone writing about this theatre today also takes up the profession of the man from Chelm, as did some of the writers and actors associated with Artef.

Earlier messianic cultural activity can be found in the nineteenth-century satiric Yiddish novels of Mendele (Sholem Abramovitsch), whose writings are part of a modern tradition wherein, as critic Dan Miron observes, Jewish literature "assumed the prophetic role of a 'watchman of Israel.' It was meant to replace the Rabbis, the Talmudists, the Hasidic leaders, the mystics, and even the biblical prophet himself as a guide of the Jewish people in modern times."[24] Artef and Nadir's theatre drew more on the writings of Karl Marx and his followers, and on Mendele and Sholem Aleichem's comic Yiddish literature, and less on the Bible, for their messianic project, but they did not entirely neglect rabbis and Hasidic leaders, sometimes satirizing them in irreverent plays. Not simply waiting for a messiah to arrive, these artists imagined what his world would look like, and showed it on stage, an activity that did not necessarily require prophecy. The world of messiahs and wonder rabbis in Nadir's satire and the puppet plays of Maud and Cutler looks much like New York in the thirties, complete with Yiddish-speaking capitalists and Communists. In their own ways, these satirists followed the example of producer Menachem Yosef, who observes in *Messiah in America* that "since we all believe in the messiah, and since he is bound to come, why shouldn't he come a little sooner? And if he is going to come, why shouldn't he come direct to our firm?"

The Communist Messiah

When theatre collaborators at Artef responded to the economic and political crises of the 1930s, their new Messiah was Communism. The Messiah had to be created, not simply awaited—and created through a political and social movement, not simply through theatre. The radical politics explored by Yiddish theatres like Artef developed in concert with, and gave another voice to Yiddish political activism of the period. Historian Paul Buhle notes, "While the Communist trade unionists fought union leaders and management in the garment trade, a recreational and fraternal network blossomed. Yiddish enthusiasts threw their energy into the shules [schools], into new summer camps where children could have an intensive Yiddish Jewish education and enjoy a break from city life, into amateur and semi-professional theatrical activity."[25] Artef's theatre developed with the support of groups of workers whose members bought tickets to benefit performances. In fact, Artef staged the May 17, 1933, New York performance of Nadir's play, *Messiah in America,* as a benefit for the propaganda work of the Yiddish Bureau in the Central Committee of the Communist Party.[26]

It could be argued that the Messiah of Communism welcomed by Yiddish-speaking Americans was as false as the messiahs in Nadir's play. Although traditional East European messianism is the main form of salvation parodied by *Messiah in America,* Zipkin at one point suggests that the new, would-be savior takes his orders from Moscow. "I'm not saying he is, God forbid," admits the sideshow master, "but it could happen. Isn't he an internationalist? He redeems all peoples and nations? . . . That means his ideology is thoroughly Bolshevik." Nadir wrote Zipkin's lines with tongue in cheek, to mock smear tactics used against American radicals. When the sideshow owner and his assistant Charlie discuss whether the Old Messiah might be a greenhorn red, secretly working for the Comintern, they practice a variation of red squad tactics used against other New York immigrants in the first decades of the century. Their short-lived plan to defame an old man supposed to be the Messiah, and too innocent to engage in any political scheme, renders the political persecution desperate, incompetent, and comic.

Nadir's false messiahs are hardly spokespersons for Moscow or Bolshevism, as they work for American businessmen, whose capitalist speculation in messiahs he satirizes. In doing so, the playwright enlists theology in the service of historical materialism, a practice Walter Benjamin advocated in his 1940 theses on history.[27] (The Yiddish American artist Nadir engaged in this practice without any prompting from the German critic; but Benjamin might have been the perfect critic for Nadir's plays, had he seen them.) As the false messiahs in the satire turn into commodities, Nadir's satire looks askance at commodity fetishism, which is also a kind of worship.

The play's comic dialogue about the Communist Messiah also could be read as a nonmusical variation on the Yiddish song, "What Will Happen When the Messiah Comes?" ("*Vos Vet Zayn Az Meshiakh Vet Kumen?*"), which according to Eleanor and Joseph Mlotek, was sung with Soviet references in the 1920s. The answer to the traditional song's question, "Who will teach the Torah?" was "*Lenin rabeynu,*" or "Lenin our teacher"; the answer to "What will we eat?" was "*Broytkartlekh,*" bread ration cards.[28] The song also echoes Jewish references to Moses, known as "*Moshe Rabeynu.*" Nadir might have been familiar with another Yiddish Messiah song written by Jacob Jacobs: "The Messiah Comes, They Say the Messiah Is a Bolshevik" ("*Meshiaskh Kimt, Men Zogt Meshiakh Iz a Bolshevik*") was recorded in 1922. Historian Henry Sapoznik notes that the song's "story of the Messiah's long-awaited arrival and his inability to get past Ellis Island" because of his Bolshevism was "the oddest song" among many responding to the Soviet revolution.[29] Perhaps Nadir heard Jacobs sing the comic number in a Yiddish vaudeville show, and its humor inspired his own scene about a Bolshevik Messiah. In any case, Nadir's false messiah is only briefly suspected of Communist tendencies; producers Zipkin and Menachem Yosef decide such attributions would not be profitable, and instead decide on a capitalistic merger of their holdings. (Today their outrageous bottom-line decision might be appreciated for its humor even in the former Soviet Union, where free market practices have replaced Communist ideology.)

As will be seen, Nadir himself was too immersed in American Yiddish culture to follow the Soviet line or a "Bolshevik" messiah without reservation. But he and other Yiddish theatre artists at Artef acknowledged the Moscow State Yiddish Theatre (Goset) as an exemplar of stage art in an age of revolution. The Soviet state-sponsored Yiddish theatre Goset proved that secular messianic theatre could thrive—at least for a few decades, before Stalinism ended it. Artef staged the plays of some of the same authors as did Goset, and in that sense made its New York theatre part of an internationalist movement. The Yiddish language, too, moved from Eastern Europe to many other locations where Jews immigrated. While the audience for Yiddish theatre in the United States may have been limited, the prospective number of spectators around the world was larger. The puppeteers Zuni Maud and Yosl Cutler of Modicut performed for that larger Yiddish audience when they left New York to tour the Soviet Union, Poland, France, and England in the thirties. Nadir met some of his comrades abroad too. At home, in New York, he and others at Artef also moved into larger circles, collaborating with the Federal Theatre Project for a time, after the Communist Party's 1935 call for broader cultural and political alliances in a Popular Front against fascism. And though Sholem Aleichem did not live to see the Popular Front, new interpretations of his comic plays and stories by Goset and Artef won considerable praise for these Yiddish theatres, and made Aleichem, posthumously, a contemporary of Soviet and American radicals in the thirties.

Critic Naomi Seidman observed that from its inception Yiddish literature was not only "created for a collective . . . it also created, imagined, and sustained this collective as a feature of its textual world."[30] The collective of Yiddish literature included women and ordinary people—who spoke and read the language—at a time literatures in other languages were often inaccessible to them. The same inclusive vision can be found in radical Yiddish theatre. Artef's collective had a small physical presence within the theatre among those who created and witnessed the stage plays, but there was a much larger public present in the plays themselves. Oppressed, displaced people around the world were given a voice by actors who spoke for them. In this sense, many of the theatre's constituents lived on stage, as literary and theatrical inventions; but Nadir's satire in *Messiah in America* suggests, in a mocking paean to bluff, that public leaders on the other side—the side of self-serving power and greed—also depended on fictions to preserve their privilege, without acknowledging that their world, too, was a theatrical construction as false as the play's messiahs. The messianic impulses of Nadir and Artef led them to create in theatre a world that would accommodate their vision of history and their community, when the world outside would not. Working-class struggles for social change could be seen on stage when, in David Lifson's words, "Artef reproduced the strikes in the needle trades in *Roar of the Machines*, and the farmers' food riots in *Drought*, and the bonus march of the veterans in *The Third Parade*."[31] Other Artef productions portrayed conflicts between employees and employers through adaptations of folklore and humorous fiction by writers like Sholem Aleichem.

Outside of Artef, in other Yiddish theatres of the thirties, one could find other depictions of union solidarity, strikes, and pleas for social justice and anti-militarism. Modicut's innovative political satire included a rent strike celebrated by Yiddish-speaking puppets and a Hitler puppet that bared its fangs. The popular Second Avenue comedian Menasha Skulnik led a union of kosher chicken cutters through a strike to victory, in the 1932–33 musical comedy, *Getzel Becomes a Bridegroom.* While hardly known for radical political action, Skulnik in the role of Getzel was part of the larger theatre movement through which Yiddish culture responded to crises of the period. The comic actor Leo Fuchs crooned in Yiddish about economic and marital catastrophe. He used only one English word, "trouble," in a popular song with that title performed during the Great Depression; his comic song, and the remarkable dance that accompanied it, wrested grotesque humor and jubilation from the struggle to survive. Yiddish culture's capacity to endure and cheer its audiences in dark times, and to ridicule wealth and abusive authority, also surfaced in the Federal Theatre Project Yiddish Unit's cabaret revue of 1936–37, *We Live and Laugh,* and its well-received productions of the Sinclair Lewis play, *It Can't Happen Here,* and David Pinski's *The Tailor Becomes a Storekeeper.* Artef was not alone in the development of satiric Yiddish theatre.

Emma Goldman's Yiddish

The radical satire created by Nadir, Artef, and some Federal Theatre artists also resonated with the early Yiddish political activism of Emma Goldman, not only in its affinities with anarchist, Communist, and union support of working-class culture but also through the great benefits language conferred on it. New York City police once were unable to prosecute Emma Goldman for her speeches, because, as an officer reported, "she spoke to this group of Jewish women on the Lower East Side, and I'm sorry I couldn't take down what she said because she spoke in Yiddish."[32] Yiddish speech conferred protection from police surveillance on Artef's radical theatre artists as it did on Goldman. Artef may not have needed the protection, as Yiddish theatre in general was less threatening to American officials, and less frequently obstructed by them, than fiery political speeches. (For example, police closed Sholem Asch's *God of Vengeance* in 1923 when the play, with its lesbian love scene, opened in English at the Apollo Theatre on West 42nd Street. A jury convicted the producer and lead actors of presenting an immoral drama, which ran, incidentally, for 133 performances before it closed. No legal problems arose earlier when it was staged in Yiddish.[33])

Artef, by creating political and satiric theatre in Yiddish, was speaking mostly to the initiated—those who already knew what Goldman and others termed "the jargon." The creators of theatre at Artef were committed to working-class history and culture by virtue of the fact that the actors themselves were workers, and rehearsed after a day's labor in the garment industry or another profession outside the theatre. Initially they trained in classes at the *Frayhayt* Dramatic Studio directed by Jacob Mestel. The training program, started in 1924, was followed by formation of the Arbeter Teater Farband (Worker's Theatrical Alliance), or Artef, which offered full-scale productions. Before studio graduates entered Artef they took classes in Yiddish, as well as lessons in diction, declamation, movement, history, and literature. They undoubtedly heard some political theory from teachers like critic and historian Nathaniel Buchwald, but Artef actors also learned the vocabulary of the labor movement and met activists within it on their day jobs.

Artef's Yiddish-language performances were visited more frequently by English-speaking audiences after the ensemble's Russian anti-conscription play, *Recruits,* and Sholem Aleichem's comedy about a lottery-winning tailor, *200,000,* received favorable recognition in the English-language press. These successes attracted Broadway and Hollywood celebrities to Artef, and for a brief period, the theatre advertised names of well-known actors appearing in its audience, rather than those on stage. As for the less famous working-class spectators, in 1937 Emanuel Eisenberg wrote as follows:

> Plain ordinary decent folk couldn't even get a look-in [at Artef's plays] for a time; they were trampled down by actors and directors and producers and even writers who were coming to find out how the miracle of an ensemble company had been worked. Actors had been practically ordered to attend by the producers whose works contained them. This is probably one of very few instances on record where sheer watching was supposed—or hoped—to impart the spectator with an equal gift.[34]

"Sheer watching" was necessary because many visitors did not understand the Yiddish they heard. (And "sheer watching" did not provide sufficient education in ensemble work for the guest artists witnessing

An Artef Presentation

"200,000"

●

Sholom Aleichem's
immortal story
of a tailor
who won a
Lottery

●

AMONG THE RAPTUROUS ADMIRERS OF THIS PLAY:

FANNIE BRICE	BEN HECHT	WORTHINGTON MINER	LILLIAN TAIZ
ROSE CAYLOR	LILLIAN HELLMAN	CLIFFORD ODETS	PAULA TRUEMAN
FLORENCE ELDRIDGE	SAM JAFFE	ANN PENNINGTON	WILLIAM WYLER
JED HARRIS	ARTHUR KOBER	IRWIN SHAW	ERNST TOLLER
MOSS HART	FREDERIC MARCH	HERMAN SHUMLIN	

Figure 1.2

Artef's 1936 advertisement for Sholem Aleichem's *200,000*. *Courtesy of the archives of the YIVO Institute for Jewish Research, New York.*

Artef's creations; no English-language ensembles won renown as successors.[35]) Artef's English-language audience members may have missed some of the textual humor and political nuances in their "sheer watching" of the Yiddish plays. It is questionable whether the ensemble would have been greeted with the same enthusiasm if its English-speaking visitors had fully understood the words in Artef's anti-capitalist and anti-militarist scripts.

On the other hand, the political speeches of Emma Goldman had considerable impact in public after she became proficient in English. She was arrested and deported for her speeches against war and American militarism, which government authorities understood. Perhaps as long as Goldman spoke Yiddish in the United States, she was safe from prosecution. Artef and Nadir, by choosing to continue their radical speeches in Yiddish long after Goldman was deported to Russia in 1919, encountered little persecution from American officials. (Goldman briefly figures in Nadir's *Rivington Street*, performed by Artef in 1932, and discussed in Chapter 2.)

Politically conscious artists who quarreled in Yiddish over the abuse of power and excesses of wealth benefited in another regard from the language that lends itself to quarrels. Here is how the humorous lexicographer, Michael Wex, describes Yiddish:

> Disharmony lies at the heart of Yiddish. Or, to put it more simply, this is a language that likes to argue with everybody about everything. . . . Yiddish begins by putting itself into an adversarial relationship with the entire physical world. As long as the Messiah is still missing and the Temple remains unbuilt, the whole world is in a sort of metaphysical *goles* [exile] from which it, too, needs to be redeemed.[36]

Disharmony within the language and an adversarial relationship with the world that lacks a Messiah, however, do not always lead to leftist views critical of wealth and power. American Yiddish plays often show less concern for political organizations and unions than for family, with personal crises requiring adjustments to assimilation, social mobility, and the abandonment of Old World practices such as arranged marriage and orthodox religion. Despite breaking with past cultural and religious practices, Jewish life goes on in these plays; the new, younger generation finds its own way, its own romance and new professions, without radical politics or satire of messianism. While conducive to quarrels, the Yiddish language was not necessarily the source of them. In the world of Yiddish theatre, notable differences arose between proponents of *kunst* or "art" theatre and the so-called *shund* (or literary trash) theatre creators. Some artists wanted their theatre to avoid the popular *shund,* which attracted and entertained working-class Yiddish families, and instead sought to raise their audience so it would appreciate a level of artistry comparable to Ibsen's. Nadir humorously imagined the impact of the demand for "higher" art on ordinary theatregoers in his monologue for "The Average Theater Goer." The title speaker complains that "when a play really does please me because there is dancing and singing in it and it's lively, [the Yiddish critics] come along and say that it doesn't even begin to please me, that it is trash and that it revolts me. In plain words, according to them, plays which please me do not please me because they really please me very much indeed."[37] Nadir's own plays employed popular forms of culture, from boxing to puppetry, for topical satire. That *shund* could sympathetically portray radical activists and the Yiddish labor movement will be seen later.

The division between American advocates of *shund* and higher art can be traced back at least as far as the late nineteenth-century efforts of Boris Thomashefsky to create a Yiddish theatre company in New York. In 1893, Thomashefsky met resistance from German-American Jews who feared that his American premiere of Goldfaden's comedy, *The Witch,* would bring dishonor and degradation to the Jewish community.[38] Other debates between proponents of "art" and *shund* followed, and Nadir entered the dispute from time to time.

The appeal of *shund* through Yiddish musical comedy, which began with Goldfaden in Romania in 1876, has lasted as long as Yiddish theatre itself. (As late as 2005, a Yiddish musical revue titled *On Second Avenue* won praise from the press in New York.) But a curious reconciliation of differing sides in the *shund-kunst* debate was effected through radical theatre presentations of writing by the great Yiddish humorist Sholem Aleichem in the twenties and thirties. When Artef and Goset produced versions of his stories and plays about impoverished, oppressed Jews, the works were staged with innovative and sophisticated acting, which joined high levels of artistry and concerns with class and wealth in popular comedy. For this achievement, Sholem Aleichem deserves praise as a major contributor to radical Yiddish theatre—although his plays achieved less of this acclaim during his own lifetime than after it. Through Artef and Goset, his writing provided occasions for remarkable new, left-wing stage productions and popular Yiddish stage satire to which Nadir and his associates contributed. The productions also made radical Yiddish theatre part of an international movement; Aleichem's language and humor could be understood (despite variations in dialect) by friends, comrades, and relatives from New York to Moscow, Warsaw to Bucharest—cities that all had Yiddish theatres in the first half of the twentieth century. (Nadir, for example, wrote about Goset's Moscow staging of a Sholem Aleichem play.)

Ruinous Laughter, Anger, and Joy

During his association with Artef, Moishe Nadir created stage adaptations of classic Yiddish texts by Sholem Aleichem and Mendele, as well as a few plays of his own that the company produced. Most of these productions featured Artef's students, who comprised the company's studio, rather than the more accomplished Artef actors in the main ensemble; perhaps Artef was reluctant to give Nadir's tendentious satire full, main-stage productions. A Yiddish-language newspaper announcement for the May 27, 1933, performance of Nadir's *Messiah in America* at the East New York Worker's Club, 608 Cleveland Street, New York, promised that "the whole actor's collective of Artef will participate in the program."[39] But the limited-run presentation received less publicity and less press attention than Artef's main season of plays. Artistic director Benno Schneider staged many of the studio projects written by Nadir, including the 1933 presentation of *Messiah in America*; but he was praised for larger Artef productions such as *200,000* and *Recruits,* which reached Broadway stages, rather than anything he directed for the East New York Worker's Club, or other tour sites. That discrepancy may be one reason Nadir himself expressed reservations about some of Schneider's directing. After Schneider staged the play *Jim Kooperkop* (not written by Nadir) for the main company in the 1930–31 season of Artef, Nadir asked this question in print:

> Should we present plays which the director likes because they enable him to demonstrate his skills; should we stage dazzling productions in order to outshine the bourgeois theatre; or should we stage militant, hostile, *revolutionary* [plays]—not in the sense of their art form, but rather in the sense that they portray the spirit of our struggles, of our ruinous laughter, of our anger and joy?[40]

Nadir created the second kind of play—militant, hostile, revolutionary— and questioned whether Schneider cared for it. The "spirit" of his struggles, his laughter, anger, and joy still can be found in his neglected plays, and those of his colleagues.

In Schneider's defense, it should be said that while capable of staging "dazzling productions" on Broadway, and in large theatre houses, he also did direct smaller scale, more portable productions, which may have more fully served Artef's goal of reaching workers. *Messiah in America* and chamber pieces, like Chaver Paver's *Motl Peysi the Cantor's Son* (1934) and *Nit Gefidelt* (*Not Fiddled,* 1935) based on Sholem Aleichem stories, would not "outshine the bourgeois theatre," but their tours to workers' clubs and community centers initiated a decentralized, alternative theatre. Benno Schneider moved from his early work with Vachtangov at the Habima in Russia, to New York collaborations with Artef, which sometimes opened in Broadway houses; but his stage work also traveled to the East New York Worker's Club and other forgotten locations, where Schneider, Nadir, and other Artef collaborators created new proletarian theatre, and enlarged the audience for it.

Perhaps this is one reason Nadir collaborated with Schneider and Artef on studio productions several times between 1929 and 1933. The satirist and poet became involved with Artef's studio early in its formation. As Edna Nahshon notes, in the late 1920s, Artef adapted a plan for "small-scale studio presentations for which no large budgets were needed, and which, in their modesty, would not attempt to represent the ultimate model for proletarian theatre art.... It was also agreed that poet Moishe Nadir would play a major role in carrying out these plans."[41] By the end of the 1929–30 season, the studio ensemble had performed Nadir's adaptation, *Benjamin Quixote*, based on Mendele's satiric novel, *The Travels of Benjamin III*, and directed by Schneider. Another studio evening in the same season was based on Nadir's own tendentious poetry, titled *Hand Over the World, Bourgeois*. Nadir continued to provide plays for Artef studio productions through the 1930s. He shared the studio space with Sholem Aleichem and Mendele (through his own adaptations), which kept him in excellent company. His *Pain in the Neck* was on a double bill with Paver's *Not Fiddled*, presented at an Artef educational meeting as late as 1939.[42]

Studio plays by Artef continued throughout the thirties, and Nathaniel Buchwald offered them special praise in 1935 when he noted that while Artef won attention on Broadway, the company had been

> producing not only "regular shows" at regular playhouses, and at modest admissions, but has made good theatre available to workers in their own neighborhoods, performing sometimes upon bare platforms, sometimes upon improvised stages and always to admiring audiences.... It is not generally known that the Artef has to its credit a score of short plays and skits of the *mobile* type and that neighborhood bookings of Artef groups and individual concert performers have been more numerous than its performances of full-length plays.[43]

Not only *Messiah in America* but also Nadir's epic poem, *Rivington Street*, discussed in the next chapter, entered this mobile repertoire. The playwright may have shared Buchwald's enthusiasm for the traveling plays, since his best theatre texts were among them.

Buchwald also had some concerns about the mobile theatre's soundness as an artistic forum. He noted Artef's "deplorable tendency, of late, to neglect the work of the *mobile* type and the danger of its attaining a state of 'splendid isolation' and tearing itself loose organizationally from its mass basis." In retrospect, his anxiety about neglect and isolation of the work appears to have been warranted; aside from news releases printed to announce workers' club stops for the plays, and a list of the studio plays that Artef itself printed in its tenth-year anniversary book in 1937, few records of the mobile theatre's activities survive.

While not calling for Nadir's plays to be staged by the main company, Buchwald was critical of that company's failure to stage new American "proletarian" plays more often. David Lifson in his history of Yiddish American theatre writes that "Buchwald attested the fact, that there was a conflict between Artef and the proletarian writers who complained that Artef had abandoned the Jewish writers' work."[44] Nadir and other writers of new and experimental plays were not exactly abandoned by Artef, but their work with students in the studio was indeed neglected by critics and historians.

In addition to the opportunity to tour plays, there were other advantages to studio work, including removal from box office pressures and an openness to more experimental forms by the young actors and their audience. (Two of these Artef actors, Jules Dassin and David Opatoshu, later received considerable attention for their film work.) In a list of Yiddish theatre's accomplishments, Lifson notes that the "studio groups among the drama clubs and the *Freiheit* and Artef studios provided the inspiration for the New York Civic Repertory's 'First Studio' and the Theatre Guild's Studio which became the Group Theatre." Inspiring the Group Theatre, which began in the early 1930s, is no small achievement.[45]

Even if largely unnoticed by press critics, the activities of Artef's studio and its mobile theatre gave Moishe Nadir incentive to write some of his plays. His adaptations of Sholem Aleichem and Mendele were completed for studio production. Other plays, such as *Messiah in America,* if not specifically written for Artef, were eminently suited for it. Nadir first published *Messiah in America* in the *Frayhayt* in 1928, and said it was adapted from a story he wrote in 1919. The play appeared in print some years after Nadir helped create the Arbeter Teater Farband (Artef) in December 1925, at a meeting where he was one of the featured speakers, along with Nathaniel Buchwald and Jacob Mestel, other Artef founders.[46]

Artef's first play was produced in 1927. It is possible Nadir would have written and published *Messiah in America* if Artef did not exist; but the collective's creation could have prompted his play's creation, and Artef's internal debates on revolutionary theatre may even be reflected, indirectly, in some of the play's self-conscious dialogue about theatre and messianism.

In an essay on Yiddish poetry, Irving Howe and Eliezer Greenberg once noted that Yiddish culture was destroyed "through the brutalities of Nazism and Stalinism, and also the gentleness of American assimilation."[47] The assimilation portrayed by Nadir, with one messiah a world champion and one messiah dead at the end of the boxing match, is not so gentle. But the play also offers a comic portrait of survival. Messianism lives on, however fraudulent, how impious its promoters. The Old Messiah is a survivor, like Yiddish culture itself. At one point during the boxing match, Zipkin argues that anger, not culture, enabled the Jews to survive as a race, and has "given them so to speak a historical knockout." But Nadir gives messianic Yiddish culture in America a new life through his humor and social criticism. His play portrays the assimilation and death of a few Yiddish-speaking Americans. Many more prospective Yiddish spectators have been lost since he wrote *Messiah in America*. But like the Old Messiah, the culture goes on, and theatrical satire like Nadir's remains one of its enduring treasures. If there has not yet been a revival of interest in Nadir in recent years, or a rush to translate his work, at least renewed American interest in other Yiddish theatre has begun with the staging of Tony Kushner's adaptation of Ansky's *The Dybbuk*, Robert Brustein's adaptation of I. B. Singer's *Shlemiel the First*, and new productions in English of Asch's *God of Vengeance*. Michael Chabon's 2007 noir detective novel, *The Yiddish Policemen's Union*, offers a new tale of Yiddish messianism gone awry. *Messiah in America*, and Nadir's other satires, also might interest a current-day audience, especially if the words are translated into English.

A Gallery of Rogues

Nadir's unflattering depiction of greed and deception was originally performed for Yiddish-speaking audiences; but its social criticism is no more directed at Jews alone than Ben Jonson's *Volpone* is a satire of

Italians simply because his characters live in Venice. In both cases (and that of Leopold Bloom and Max Bialystock in Mel Brooks's stage version of *The Producers*), the satire transcends its ethnic, geographic, and religious references, and its original language. Without question Nadir's satire depicts American Jews who speak Yiddish, but that is not their outstanding feature. Their otherness—their life among immigrants, sideshow freaks, rival messiahs, and exceptionally talented artists—might include Jewishness, but it is hardly limited to that identity. Earlier works like Melville's novel, *The Confidence Man,* and Twain's portrait of unscrupulous Shakespearean actors in *Huckleberry Finn* provide Nadir's confidence men with illustrious non-Jewish American predecessors. Jews should be honored to have their own representatives in the gallery of rogues sketched by Jonson, Melville, Twain, and, more recently, Nadir and Brooks.

The skepticism toward messianic leaders and their promoters that Nadir expresses in his satire represents one of his lasting contributions to leftist Yiddish culture. However enamored Nadir himself might have been with Soviet politics and Communism, his humorous rejection of misguided religious fervor, and of those who profit from such fervor, transcends the specific situation in his play, and evokes comic wariness of other messiahs, too, in an age of personality cults and ideological police states. In the title essay of his book *Confession,* Nadir describes how he became an associate of Communists when he was invited to write for their newspaper, *Frayhayt,* and how the cult of Lenin worship led to the cult of Stalin worship. He writes with humor and some self-deprecation about the party line he accepted for much of his career as a writer.[48] Nadir recants his worship of the "God" of Soviet Communism in this 1940 essay, which was published posthumously. His later disillusionment with a savior (and redemptive history) was anticipated by his 1919 short story, *Messiah in America,* and the play based on it. For years, Nadir "tried as best he could to accept and assimilate Communist ideology," notes Harvey Fink, "but he experienced many moments of open and hidden opposition to the inflexible laws governing 'proletarian art.' Neither did he have an easy time swallowing the general Communist line."[49] Nadir's collaborators in Artef did not always follow a Communist Party line either; as David Lifson observes, "It was no secret from the start that Artef was of the Communist movement. . . . But artistically it attempted independence of expression. . . .

The matter of productions deviating from ideological precepts was to lead to sharp conflicts."[50] Nadir's mockery of messiahs (and of those who red-bait a messiah) gives theatrical voice to his own heterodoxy and Artef's.

Satire like Nadir's clears the ground, as it questions orthodox behavior and seeks to end dependency on false hopes—to end the suffering and martyrdom that messianic followers endure, and sometimes perpetrate. He is not entirely negative. A call for freedom of conscience can be found within his satire too. In "The Chosen," an ironic response to an *Evening Mail* newspaper editorial, he described the Jewish people as "the feverish conscience of the world, and the world hates its conscience—naturally. We have no crowns but our heads; no scepters but our arms; no fatherland but our souls. . . . An exotic, incomprehensible people, we Jews."[51]

Whether or not this admission describes all Jews, it fits Nadir himself, with his "feverish conscience" and his internationalism bound to no particular country. His conclusion that "conscience" and lack of fealty make Jews an "exotic, incomprehensible people" suggests that the playwright is an equal-opportunity offender—he gently mocks himself, as well as others.

Nadir's wariness of messiahs and their followers also surfaced in a 1915 Christmas satire he published in *Der Groyser Kundes* (*The Big Prankster*). As Aaron Rubenstein observes, Nadir purportedly conducted an interview with the famous Jew, Jesus Christ. Conversing with the savior in Yiddish, Nadir expressed concern that Jews still suffer, although he hardly expected Jesus to help them at Christmas, when the savior had to "hover around the gentile houses."[52] In *Messiah in America,* Jewish messiahs again deliver little relief to Jews. Not limiting his satire to one religious leader, Nadir can be regarded as an ecumenical iconoclast.

His anti-religious, anti-messianic satire also can be seen as part of a larger Yiddish theatre tradition that the writer Joseph Roth summed up after he watched the Moscow State Yiddish Theatre (Goset) perform in Berlin. Roth said, "The theatre remains Jewish even when it attacks Jewish traditions. Attacking tradition is an old Jewish tradition."[53] It is unfortunate that in some circles, Nadir has been remembered (or despised) far more for his association with Communists than for the comic writing and ironic distance with which he departed from messianism in his iconoclastic theatre.

The Future of Yiddish Theatre:
A Prophecy

If Nadir's Old Messiah wandered back onto the stage today, he might pass for one of the men whose absence humorist Harry Golden lamented a half-century ago, when he predicted the future of Jewish culture in America. By the year 2000, said prophet Golden, American Jews "will comb the highways and byways looking for some elderly gent with a beard—an immigrant from the old country—whom they can sit up on a platform and 'enjoy' as the representative of their past."[54] Golden said that a survivor from the old Yiddish ways, if he has a very heavy accent, will be so rare that as a public speaker he can command fees of five thousand dollars for a single lecture. The price would probably be much higher now, due to inflation in the value of cultural heritage. In the twenty-first century we have few survivors of Yiddish theatre who still talk about the old days. But today and tomorrow, I predict, some people will want to hear about the old culture, its actors, its satire, and melodramas, because they are nearly gone, or threatened with disappearance. Which is ironic, because Yiddish theatre was threatened with extinction, and had to fight for its survival, almost from its beginning in the United States. An 1899 history of Yiddish literature published in the United States expressed doubts that Yiddish theatre would last another ten years in America; it lasted much longer. In fact, you can still see Yiddish plays performed in New York, as well as in Montreal, Bucharest, and Israel.[55]

Not only has the art survived, in a reduced form, but Yiddish theatre—like Yiddish culture itself—was aware of the need to survive, and shared that urgent sense with its audience, for more than a century. Many Yiddish plays, comedies and tragedies, can be seen in retrospect as expressions of a determination to go on, to continue one's family, one's religious beliefs, one's traditions, in a new world such as America where the old ways are questioned and need to change or face extinction. Jewish commitment to survival sometimes requires a fight for justice, or a strike for fair pay, particularly in the 1930s, but not only then. From its beginnings in the nineteenth century, when Yiddish theatre thrived in Eastern Europe among Ashkenazi Jews, and when they immigrated to the United States to escape persecution and seek better living conditions, the traveling players and writers carried with them not only their own language but also a shared determination to find a better life, greater economic opportunity, and justice—a determination inseparable from the Yiddish culture that developed in New York and other urban centers of the United States.

Walter Benjamin never wrote about Yiddish theatre's past or its future, but his philosophy of history inadvertently provides an approach to the subject. As noted earlier, Benjamin observed that "the Jews were prohibited from investigating the future. The Torah and the prayers instruct them in remembrance, however." We should be wary of investigating the future of Yiddish theatre too; if it has one, it is not terribly promising. On the other hand, it once was promising; remembrance of Yiddish theatre and its past is an activity in which scholars and historians have engaged for decades. Then too, as Benjamin noted in his theses on history, there can be no resistance or revolt without memory of the past. He saw the "struggling, oppressed class" "nourished by the image of enslaved ancestors rather than that of liberated grandchildren."[56] (The freeing of Jews from slavery in Egypt still is invoked every year at Passover as an act of liberation to remember and renew.) Yiddish theatre itself might be regarded as an act of remembrance, as many play productions amount to remembrances and celebrations of past Jewish creativity and culture. Yiddish theatre's acts of remembrance might continue in new plays, as well as revivals and studies of older works that celebrate survival and the need for radical change in time of crisis.

American theatre of the thirties provides wonderful examples of this genre. But Yiddish theatre also responded to crises when it began as an ensemble form in 1876, the year Avrom Goldfaden started to stage Yiddish musical comedies in Romania. Before that time, Jews rarely acted in theatrical roles, except in Purim festivals, and at weddings, where the entertainers known as *badchanim* would tell stories, joke, sing, and dance. One of the first comedies Goldfaden wrote concerned the military draft, which he himself faced and evaded at the time he was writing *The Recruits.* Theatre at that moment was not only entertainment, but a humorous form of protest against militarism and conscription. When Yiddish theatre was banned in Russia, Goldfaden and other Yiddish theatre artists moved to America. Its American origins were born, in part, out of flight from persecution and anti-militarism; given that beginning, it is not surprising the theatre continued to raise its voice against injustice and violence, even in musical comedies.

Far from being nostalgic for the old country and not especially pleased by the prospects for profit, assimilation, and success in the new country either, Moishe Nadir was not the only Yiddish writer to see

America through wide-open and wary eyes. The cultural and political sensibility that took shape in his Yiddish satire, his enduring humor, and that of his associates deserves to be heard again. That *Messiah in America* has received few stagings and little critical attention does not mean it is a neglected masterpiece, or a promising commercial property. Its satire of business, theatre, and religion lacks the sentimentality and songs of some more popular Yiddish plays. Its criticism of American popular culture, including Broadway attractions and religious extravaganzas promising salvation, probably would not have attracted a Second Avenue audience in the thirties. Still, while the messiahs in the play may have been false prophets, Nadir himself offered a poetic vision of America that turned out to be farsighted. We still live in a time when promoters sell the public salvation, although today's messiahs may promise redemption through wars to end terror, or new tax cuts, or perfect automobiles. Forms of the false advertising, financial acquisition, ideological chicanery, and sideshow sensationalism that he mocked continue to thrive in the arts, politics, and religion; it is not too late for Nadir's Messiah to return to the stage.

His other satiric plays and poems deserve reconsideration as well. *Rivington Street*, also staged by Artef, responded to the Great Depression by recalling the promise America once held for Jewish immigrants on New York's Lower East Side. The epic poem, considered in Chapter 2, still holds within it some of the promise that Nadir and other Yiddish writers wanted to see fulfilled in the thirties.

2

Nadir's *Rivington Street*

The Lower East Side Arises

> *What's it they sing in the Yiddish theatre?*
> *Oy, po-ver-ty,*
> *How I love you from a distance.*
> *Oy, po-ver-ty,*
> *Remind me please of better times.*
> —Nadir in *Rivington Street*[1]

In an essay titled "The Lower East Side: A Place of Forgetting," anthropologist Jonathan Boyarin argued that "on the Lower East Side, in Brooklyn, in the suburbs, or elsewhere, forgetting—of text, folklore, meaning-invested geography—is a central fact of Jewish life in our times."[2] Boyarin's 1992 essay remains persuasive; not only American Jews, but the American nation as a whole seems to suffer from collective amnesia these days, and forgets much of its past, particularly the history of urban communities now dispersed or gentrified. The situation was quite different sixty years earlier, when Moishe Nadir and his theatre colleagues at Artef publicly started to remember local history, Yiddish folklore, and the meaning-invested geography of the Lower East Side. Remembering became a public act, a theatrical act, and a political act with the 1932–34 stage performance of Nadir's extraordinary poem, *Rivington Street*. Not only the names of streets on the Lower East Side but also the names of neighborhood residents, writers, activists, merchants, buildings, newspapers, synagogues, dances, theatre, and other amusements were recited aloud in what could have been a memorial service; but rather than mourn the past, the performance organized survivors of the Depression. As a stage play, the work literally brought people together in the same space, to hear a performer of *Rivington Street* move from recollection to a call for an assembly like their own, only larger, to rise up and march: "people ... close to one another in the thousands, thousands, thousands." An actor, not a messiah, arrives to inspire the crowd; but on stage Nadir's speeches envision residents of the Lower East Side joining together, and becoming their own messiah, as they prepare to save themselves and their history in a time of crisis.

First performed on March 20, 1932, as part of the Artef theatre company's sixth anniversary celebration, *Rivington Street* remembered the culture and politics of Yiddish-speaking immigrants on the Lower East Side by presenting decades of their history in spoken form.[3] Of course, Nadir's text still can be performed; by reading through it again, actors might even reverse, briefly and modestly, that "central fact of Jewish life in our times"—the loss of memory and culture—through recollections of the vibrant places and times, and the spirit of survival that Moishe Nadir located in his writing.

Losses of culture and memory are not independent of economic and social change, and Nadir takes these additional factors into account in his poem when he refers to the flight of Jews from poverty on the Lower East Side to wealthier communities. The entire nation faced threats to its living conditions in the decade Artef staged the poem, of course; situations faced by Yiddish-speaking residents on the Lower East Side in the thirties can be seen, in retrospect, as a microcosm of the larger population's struggle for self-preservation and improvement in the midst of widespread financial hardship and displacement. Artef's actors could hardly solve national economic problems through their theatre; but *Rivington Street* recalled to their public the momentum of progress and radical change, and pleasures of the past, at a time when these had been disrupted. As the line in the song "Oy poverty" said, Yiddish theatre could remind an audience of better times—past and future prospects; so Nadir and the actors did with the recital of *Rivington Street*. The author does not announce in this play that the Messiah approaches, but a secular messianism drives his vision of the Lower East Side arising, as the narrative moves from recollection of past pleasures toward a future delivered from poverty and economic insecurity.

The 1932 premiere featured Hershel Gendl, an Artef actor who had earlier participated in his ensemble's stagings of Aleichem's *Aristocrats* and Avrom Veviorka's *Diamonds*. Gendl's experience with the satiric writing of these two authors would have prepared him well for the verbal humor and radical politics within *Rivington Street*. Performing the poem,

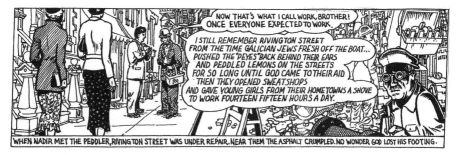

Figure 2.1

Rivington Street comic strip illustrated by Spain Rodriguez; poetry translated by Harvey Fink. *Courtesy of the artist and* Jewish Currents.

Gendl portrayed an old street peddler living on the Lower East Side. Nadir briefly compares his basket-carrying peddler to the famous Yiddish stage character, Hotsmakh, a merchant in Goldfaden's play, *The Witch*. By 1932, if Hotsmakh had lived longer and immigrated to America, he probably would have been down and out, like Nadir's Lower East Side fruit seller. No Hotsmakh-like rescue of a distressed young woman occurs in Nadir's poem; but before the Rivington Street peddler exits, he contemplates an enormous change, insisting that "things have to start moving" for millions of unemployed citizens. In his dream of social movement, the American peddler may be more daring, and a more inclusive advocate for the distressed, than the vendor in Goldfaden's comedy.

Like Goldfaden's play, Nadir's dramatic poem offers a genial portrait of the peddler's world, at least some of the time. Neither author's world is free of threats; but *Rivington Street* introduces many humorous, pleasant memories, along with an awareness of recent economic catastrophe. The epic opens with a proletarian Yiddish writer—Nadir himself—encountering the bearded, Yiddish-speaking peddler early in the morning. The first encounter is comic in conceit, though not flippant, as the two men stand near a site of construction. With a steam shovel digging, acetylene torch blazing, and the street torn apart, the writer wonders aloud whether they stand near Rivington Street. He is understandably disoriented; machinery ripping up the street has made the scene unrecognizable. The fruit peddler responds to a question about the location as if it is a question about his own knowledge: "Does he know Rivington Street?"

And know it he does, not only the location where he and the poet stand but also its social history, which he describes in great detail. A simple question about the location evokes from the old man an intricate, anecdote-filled history of the neighborhood. His long answer to a short question gives the poem a subtly humorous dramatic structure. Hearing more than he asked for, the proletarian writer is told about the lives and deaths of the immigrant community, where Jews arrived from Eastern Europe, learned new language, preserved some Old World customs and beliefs, and surrendered others, as they adjusted to America's new economic and social systems. While a number of the immigrants moved on to wealthier neighborhoods and high-paying professions, many, like the peddler, found themselves with almost nothing, or far less than they had dreamed of securing, when the stock market crashed in 1929. The peddler was a cloak maker for thirty-four years before he lost his job and took to the streets. He witnessed decades of change on the Lower East Side, and the proletarian writer hears of them, much as the audience in a theatre would, listening to the actor Gendl in 1932.

The Wandering Jew's Mobile Theatre

The act of speaking aloud to an audience is built into the poem, which makes it particularly suitable for public performance. Set in public space (on the street), the peddler's story requires only one actor and no set. (The poet also speaks during the poem; presumably Gendl played both roles. Notices for the theatrical event credit only him as performer.) On May 21, 1932, *Rivington Street* was read in Carnegie Hall, during a "Moishe Nadir Evening." The actor Gendl was still presenting the work on April 6, 1933, as part of an Artef program at the Mecklin Square Theatre, on Boston Road and 169th Street in New York. The play was also performed in February 1934 at Chicago's Eighth Street Theatre; this date indicates the poem was kept in the Artef repertoire for several years.[4] The poem was not read aloud in Madison Square Garden, as far as can be ascertained; but the peddler's statement that "we are . . . a whole Madison Square Garden" might have elicited smiles from smaller audiences, as they listened to his overestimation of the crowd size.

As a touring production, *Rivington Street* constituted one of the theatre works "available," as Nathaniel Buchwald wrote in 1935, "to workers in their own neighborhoods, performing sometimes upon bare platforms, sometimes upon improvised stages and always to admiring audiences." This accomplishment by Artef has been forgotten over time, but even in 1935, Buchwald noted that "in the revolutionary theatre field it is not generally known that Artef has to its credit a score of short plays and skits of the mobile type and that neighborhood bookings of Artef groups and individual concert performers have been more numerous than its performance of full-length plays."[5]

Like the writer who asks about Rivington Street, an audience hearing Nadir's poem in 1932 or 1933 probably would have recognized some of its own experiences, and the life of its own community, in the peddler's recollections. Not to think of themselves must have been hard for spectators, their friends, and relatives, when the fruit seller recalled Lower East Side street life:

> *I still remember*
> *The street, don't cha know . . .*
> *I still remember the East Side*
> *When life here was*
> *So dull*
> *When my auntie Mekhle*
> *Would look out her window*
> *On Grand Street*
> *And if she noticed*
> *A Jewish funeral procession*
> *She would grab*
> *The black shawl*
> *Put it on her head*
> *And run down to cry . . .*
>
> *If I know where Rivington Street is!*
> *I still remember Rivington Street*
> *When Adolph Mandel had a bank there*
> *And how the poor guy*
> *Made a mess of it*
> *Just like your Bank of the United States.*
> *I still remember Rivington Street*
> *When Yamulovski*
> *And Max Cobra*
> *Had Jewish banks on East Broadway*
> *And also, please pardon the expression, shit their pants.*

> *I still remember Rivington Street*
> *When Governor Street Park was called*
> *Room Bedroom Park,*
> *And Ben Hador was playing*
> *In the Windsor Theatre*
> *And girls wore little caps*
> *And blue worsted bloomers*
> *And rode on bicycles,*
> *Or on tandems with their boyfriends,*
> *That's when they sang:*
> *"A Bicycle Built for Two" . . .*
>
> *I still remember Rivington Street*
> *From the time people danced*
> *The Hesitation*
> *And the Maxixe*
> *And the Cakewalk,*
> *And the Padespan*
> *And the Fox Trot*
> *And the Turkey Trot*
> *And the Merry Widow Waltz.*

The litany of specific names and places continues; and if listeners do not recognize them, their sense of loss is an appropriate response too, because the poem is ultimately about loss and change—loss not only through the passage of time but also through changes in economic and social conditions, including the tearing down and rebuilding of streets, and the end of banks and incomes that accompanied the Great Depression. Flashes of humor break through the litany, as should be expected from a satirist like Nadir. Even the recollection of a death becomes a source of humor, when the peddler remembers his bored aunt enjoying the street life of a funeral procession.

The opening stanzas of the poem introduce two irreverent forecasts of change that become clearer and more significant as the poem progresses. There is a change in religious outlook, which the peddler offers with his startling first words:

> *God's unlucky;*
> *whatever he tries lately doesn't work out.*

God's unlucky
And we're unlucky too,
And the world is shaking.
And God's lost his footing,
And banks are crashing

These lines referring to the crash of the nation's economic system suggest there is no longer a divinity capable of protecting His creation; humankind is on its own. The description of construction crews digging up the ground near Rivington Street, literally shaking the earth with steam shovels that "disembowel the earth's intestines," hints that the future of the earth and even God's condition now rest in human hands. The crew's wrecking of the street represents progress of a curious sort—it may lead to improved transportation in the future; but the imagery also suggests that humankind and its steam shovels are making the ground give way under God's feet. The disturbances brought about by human industry are not always commendable, as the poem hints here, and indicates more fully later in references to war and unemployment.

Describing the past wonders of Rivington Street—the culture of its residents, fragments of songs, dances, conversations, and dreams—Nadir engages in cultural anthropology through his poetry. He too digs below the surface, retrieving artifacts (or descriptions of them) and lost practices, as his narrator, the fruit peddler, traces local history through his memories.

The fact that Nadir's poem is written in Yiddish means the colloquial language of the period still can be heard (by those who know Yiddish). He includes many American-language phrases too, indicators of assimilation—"potato Yiddish" that mixes Old and New World vocabularies into the language of a transitional period. Song lyrics like "Everybody's doing it, / Doing what? / the turkey trot" are transliterated into Yiddish and Hebrew typeface in the printed text of Nadir's poem; when read aloud, they convey very American language.

Nadir's multilingual poem restores some of the Lower East Side's past to readers and listeners. The author says at the very start of the poem that he had been walking in the direction of the cemetery "to pay his last respects to his young desolate years" when he met the peddler; in a sense, the poem is a memorial service, as well as a celebration, for the once vibrant, pre-Depression neighborhood in which Yiddish immigrants lived.

Figure 2.2

Rivington Street comic strip excerpt illustrated by Spain Rodriguez. *Courtesy of the artist and* Jewish Currents.

Recollections begin with an earlier, more innocent period of life on the Lower East Side, and the poem's structure moves forward in time to the latest and most disturbing developments. Initially, even political issues recalled by the peddler seem quaint; the "old political issues," as he calls them, include "5 cent carfare," the "full dinner pail," and the president who "kept us out of war." The disasters that took place early in the century receive passing reference with mentions of "the Beilis trial, the Triangle fire, the Titanic, the earthquake in Messina and in San Francisco." Labor strikes such as the 1910 strike by cloak makers receive more attention, but the remarks on these struggles are also genial, early in the remembering. The relatively brief references to these events and to more pleasant ones (memory of "the time when actress Bertha Kalish was the Jewish Dusa when nobody knew who Dusa herself was . . .") offer a faint impression of the past. The peddler introduces more detailed and personal recollections, revolving around less famous people and events, as he goes on. He even casually introduces us to his own name, dropped among a series of lesser known facts in his local history:

> *I still remember how crazy Abeh*
> *With his flaming eyes*
> *Came running to me during the war,*
> *And grabbed me firmly by the wrist of my hand*
> *And with tears in his eyes he pleaded:*

"Here is 15 dollars, Mr. Gelboym,
now please won't you stop the war."

Perhaps Gelboym the peddler had some standing in the community during World War I—at least enough of a presence that crazy Abeh thought he could end the war. We don't know if he was a pacifist, but we learn more about the peddler's own life from other incidental passages. He remarks at one point that "the anarchist picnics in Liberty Park / and in Olmer Park / . . . were picnics not so much for us / as for the mosquitoes . . ."—this suggests he had some anarchist tendencies as well as mosquito bites. The peddler also probably was active in the cloak makers' union since he heard "Max Pine from the cloak workers . . . talk a mile a minute" in his past, and mentions he was a cloak maker for 34 years.

The peddler reconfirms his working-class identity when he asks his listener, "Who do you think we are?" and answers he is not a well-paid poet or social critic like Bialik, "who for celebrating a pogrom demands 15 cents a word, / and for shouting 'help' charges a dollar and a quarter." And he notes he has no exclusive control over words of complaint; he is not like "a Mr. Leivick, who on the little word 'oy' has a copyright in Washington." "I'm too small / for such big thoughts / which assault me often," the peddler admits, and he is fortunate that the poet Nadir is present to hear him and frame his monologue in a narrative that gives the thoughts resonance in a larger context.

His vivid details about life in Europe suggest that the peddler lived there and took a ship to America. Toward the middle of his monologue, with some longing and regret he remembers the world that immigrants left behind:

And a sweeter word
Than "Europe" did not exist
Among Rivington Street Jews.

Ah, Europe, Europe . . .

If only I had the luck to
Go to Europe . . .

Go, and you'll come right back.
You'll hanker after pitcher beer and bananas . . .

After traveling through memories of Europe, the peddler brings his thoughts back to the Lower East Side and its cultural and political ferment. Activists and innovators, including Emma Goldman, her lover Ben Reitman, actor Boris Thomashefsky, and Sholem Aleichem, receive recognition from him. The prosperity achieved by some immigrant Jews is duly noted, with attention given to the period when "Americanization" "broke out," and the rich uptown Jews came downtown to teach the Rivington Streeters "how to blow our noses, refined, / applying our little fingers / first to one nostril, then to the other / giving two refined blows."

Rich Jews are acknowledged as outsiders, almost foreigners, who moved

> *Out into wide-open America,*
> *To uptown,*
> *To the rich Yahudim,*
> *To Fifth Avenue*
> *To Riverside Drive,*
> *To Morningside, to the Palisades . . .*
> *Atlantic City, Lakewood, Asbury Park . . .*
> *Miami, Palm Beach . . .*

The wealthy and the well known receive their due, but then the peddler returns his attention to the down and out, and to immigrants whose future no longer looks so promising because the Great Depression continues to deny them a better life. Wondering if his listener is tiring of the guided tour, the peddler asks:

> *What do you think, mister, I talk too much?*
> *But the thing is that I don't talk alone.*
> *My troubles are talking*

The fruit peddler has within him voices, speeches, the "talking" and the "troubles" of the entire endangered community. (More recently, the great Italian satirist Dario Fo developed a comparable repertoire of one-man theatre presentations in which he portrays a variety of characters and what he calls a "chorality" of voices to present politically important developments from a popular and leftist perspective.[6])

From the Street to the Stage

The peddler often repeats the lines and statements he first heard in public settings—union meeting halls, dance halls, street corners, building stoops, and theatres. By situating his story outdoors on Rivington Street, and recording expressions heard in public settings, as recalled by the peddler, Nadir literally brings street life and its language into his poem, and onto the stage when the verse is performed. Here, as the Russian critic Mikhail Bakhtin said of a character in Rabelais' *Pantagruel* and of his popular street language: "The man who is speaking is one with the crowds. . . . This is an absolutely gay and fearless talk, free and frank, which echoes in the festive square beyond all verbal prohibitions, limitations, and conventions."[7] Bakhtin refers here to speeches of a barker in the marketplace, a character not so different from a fruit peddler crying his wares on Rivington Street. Nadir's character knows that

> *Like on Rivington Street*
> *There's a fair going on inside me,*
> *Thousand of voices are yelling,*
> *And I don't know which one to follow.*

If the peddler is lost, without direction, it may be due to the exhaustion of his own resources. He can't pay his rent, and some of his free and frank speech may be due to the fact that the peddler has nothing left to lose:

> *All I know is there's*
> *a terrible crisis out here,*
> *And I haven't paid the rent,*
> *D'ya hear,*
> *In over three months*
> *And that any day now they'll be*
> *Putting me out on the street*
> *Me and my bag and baggage*
> *What do you think, mister . . .*
> *Ya think capitalists will somehow*
> *Squirm out of the crisis, or not?*

Figure 2.3

Rivington Street comic strip excerpt illustrated by Spain Rodriguez; poetry translated by Harvey Fink. *Courtesy of the artist and* Jewish Currents.

The peddler is almost ready to be recruited by the Communist Party that Nadir himself supported; he blames capitalism for his troubles and for the Depression. He becomes fearful when a policeman passes nearby, and clearly does not see representatives of the law as his friends. But the poem is not simply agitational propaganda. Too much verse is devoted to the delights and gossip of Rivington Street's everyday life. The monologue includes a call for a movement against capitalism, but that comes only after the peddler has reconstructed in memory the promises of prosperity and opportunity that the Lower East Side once represented, and captured in speech rhythms the momentum of burgeoning community life. The poem's lines first and foremost preserve Yiddish culture's colorful language and personalities, even if the accomplishments of past life have given way to evictions, unemployment, and poverty.

While we hear about the peddler's dire situation, and the nation's, the old man continues to hold his basket of nuts, figs, carobs, and tangerines. He is not yet starving. Nor is he selling these goods when he meets the poet; but later, after Nadir has listened to him for quite a while, the old man asks his listener:

> *Maybe you want some halvah, mister?*
> *Roasted almonds maybe? Some figs? . . .*
> *No? Then no.*
> *Maybe a few nice little carobs? (a bit wormy)*

This late pitch for a sale further jogs the seller's memory, and he goes on to discuss the current crisis. He is after something larger than a few pennies for fruit. The peddler struggles to preserve his own identity, and insofar as he lives by selling wares on the street, it is inseparable from the past and future, the old order and new disorder of Rivington Street itself:

> *Listen, sometimes it seems to me*
> *That I myself am the old Rivington Street,*
> *That for now doesn't want to be spruced up.*
> *Filled with cobwebs of superstitions,*
> *And with the mold of tradition,*
> *And with inferiority complexes. . . .*
>
> *With one hand I pull to the future,*
> *With the other I clutch at the past!*
> *And I'm scared to let go,*
> *'Cause maybe the future's a chasm*
> *And yesterday's a high mountain peak.*
>
> *Like Rivington Street I'm excavated,*
> *I'm torn up, ruined and depressed.*

The peddler's long monologue can be compared to the torn-up street too; the fragments of memories, shards of other people's speeches and his own ideas, constitute a stream of consciousness that at times seems pulled in many directions, as he acknowledges. At the same time, there is another character present, the poet, who is silent for most of the time. But Nadir not only listens—like the theatre audience; he also writes the poetry we hear, gives it shape, and passes on the life of the street to new audiences.

The peddler anticipates this growing audience when he uses the plural "we" toward the conclusion of the poem:

> Once good times rolled in America!
> A schooner of beer—five gratser—free lunch.
> A stuffed spleen dinner with stewed fruit
> And with sasparilla cost just thirteen cents.
> And if, now and then, some crisis came up,
> Then that was also more bones than meat.
> How can you compare it to today's crisis?
> These days everything's so enormous, enormous!
> Buildings 104 stories tall!
> Theatres full of twenty thousand people at once!
> Wars, earthquakes, choleras, bankruptcies,
> Unemployment, mass production, piece work,
> All doled out with a generous hand.
> In the next war, folks figure soldiers will be paid by the piece,
> A dollar ninety for a dozen enemies ,
> Two dozen—three dollars fifty.
> How much unemployment do we have these days?
> Twelve million? Sixteen million?
> The figures, God knows, are rising like yeast.

As he invokes these large numbers and crises, the peddler leaves behind local events of the past, and addresses the current situation as if he is speaking on behalf of all the aggrieved. In his stage presentation, the actor portraying the peddler at this point could identify himself as part of the crowd, and also could acknowledge his own profession, in lines that invoke the Yiddish theatre as a point of reference for his own feelings:

> And Wall Street keeps crashing
> And stocks falling
> And falling and falling.
> The only thing that's on the rise
> Is poverty.

What is it they sing in the Yiddish theatre?
"Oy, po-ver-ty,
how I love you from a distance.
Oy, po-ver-ty,
Remind me please of better times."

Approaching the end of his *spiel* as the sun begins to rise, the peddler (like a ghost or dybbuk who has to vanish at daybreak) knows he has no sale, no great commercial prospects on the street, for all his oratorical gifts:

So, won't you buy something, mister?
The sun's almost up, and I've wasted
The whole night on nothing...
What d'ya say? Some nice little almonds? ...
Cigarettes?
A string of dried figs?
How about a nice little apple?

There is another use for his voice besides salesmanship, and the peddler comes close to saying so before leaving the poet. He offers a fascinating political confession to his listener. After optimistically predicting that things will start "moving in America, if not today then tomorrow. / They'll have to start moving / 16 million people won't just lie down, not me and not you," the peddler denies he is a Communist.

an outright
communist I'm not,
even so, I scrape by ... just like everyone else.
But take it from me
Come the revolution,

They won't be let down.

What've I got to lose here? What?

Rags? Hunger? Poverty?
My misery? My basket?
34 years I've worked at cloaks
And worked my way up to be a peddler.

> *What kind of peddler am I to them?*
> *What I really am is a worker. . . .*
> *At one time I had talent.*
> *I could've been a poet or a watchmaker.*
> *But now all I am is*
> *A sick Jew with a basket.*
> *Mayor Walker and the bankers*
> *The bosses and coppers,*
> *They can all go to hell.*

He is not exactly Marx and Engels declaring that workers have nothing to lose except their chains; but the peddler knows he too has little to lose through a revolution. Before he departs, the old man expresses the hope that millions of the unemployed will "start moving" in their own interests. The ancient graybeard passes the spark of insurrection on to the poet he addresses, and Nadir himself continues to describe the movement of people the peddler started to imagine. He sees those who suffer from poverty, unemployment, and hunger joining together in a march with "a will glowing brightly." The peddler never gets to the point of a revolution here, even in his speech, but Nadir takes up the cause where the old man leaves off.

Unlike Nadir's satiric play, *Messiah in America*, first published in 1928, this poem written in the depths of America's economic crisis offers no humorous portrait of false messiahs, no fatuous salvation. Instead of a messiah, we meet a man on the street, an aged peddler with a thorough understanding of local living conditions, and a sense of the need for change. Neither God nor Communism is jubilantly upheld as savior by the peddler. Nadir's closing images in the poem suggest that, to change social conditions, an assembly of men and women on the street has to act on its own behalf.

The peddler's recital creates one such assembly, or at least it is an act of assemblage, a poetic method of bringing together many individuals on Rivington Street. Both the peddler and the poet who records the older man's words are recollecting actual names, events, places, many of which could be found in newspapers of the period. Oral history and poetry become one, in a form of theatre that does not display the "defiance of history" Irving Howe once attributed to Yiddish literature. Howe's elegiac conclusion to his observations on Yiddish writers was that "[c]ollapsing the distinctions of history, Yiddish literature bridged the gap between eternity and time. The prophet Elijah stepped into its pages with the assurance he must have felt in crossing the plains of Palestine; he jostled greenhorns on the Lower East Side, Yemenites in Israel, rabbinical students in Vilna. The central premise of Jewish survival is a defiance of history; the cost, beyond measure."[8] Rather than defy history, Nadir's theatrical poem revives voices from the Lower East Side's streets, remembers them, and through the spoken word keeps alive local Yiddish history, including its political consciousness. Unlike a newspaper or history book, recitation of the peddler's words in front of a live audience brings together the living and the dead, the Artef audience and the Lower East Side's immigrant population, much as the narrative of the poem does in its concluding lines.

Alone in the early morning fog, looking at the street and its surroundings, the writer envisions a "flame" of street demonstrations far different from the acetylene torch flames mentioned in the poem's opening, where construction workers weld metal on Rivington Street. His last words bring the imagery full circle, as the flame rising from the heart of local factories, stores, offices, attics, and pushcarts is predicted to spread worldwide.

Fire in the Theatre

Audiences hearing the poem's recitation in 1932 and 1933 might well have read additional meaning into these lines, as the world outside the theatre was starting to see marches of protest against hunger, unemployment, and war. A *Morgn Frayhayt* headline for January 4, 1933, reported that seven hundred workers marched to prevent the eviction of eight families on Charlotte Street in the Bronx. The same day's paper included news of rent strikes, labor strikes, and an anti-war protest. The *Frayhayt* political cartoon drawn that day by William Gropper, Nadir's friend, showed Soviet industry moving at full blast, while Americans stood in front of a closed factory.[9] (Not every New York paper devoted as much favorable attention to labor activism and Soviet progress in the thirties, but the *Morgn Frayhayt* was a paper read by Nadir and much of Artef's audience, and it represented their interests.) Nadir's closing vision in *Rivington Street,* his imagery of a spreading flame of resistance, had a counterpart in political assemblies of the thirties, which were another form of street life, with far more participants than the two men who meet in the poem. *Rivington Street* offers not a celebration of such marches as much as a prelude. Marx and Engels' call for workers of the world to unite takes a new, poetic shape as Nadir foresees the dead, the exploited, and their successors on the Lower East Side rising up.

> *And I, the stranger*
> *On his way to visit the grave*
> *Of the years of his youth*
> *The desolate years*
> *Where he spit out his lungs*
> *In a Sheriff Street sweatshop at Mr. Borgenich's,*
> *Could see through the frosty fog*
> *Over Rivington Street*
> *Corpses rise up from their graves . . .*
> *And armies of living slaves*
> *Awakened by the flaming tongues of wrath,*
> *Their voices like torn bells,*
> *And the fire of acetylene-torches*
> *That cauterize the wounded insides of the earth;*
> *And a bridge—a walking bridge of people,*
> *People, people.*
> *Broad shouldered, hard and wounded,*
> *Close, close, close;*
> *One next to the other, in the*
> *Thousands, thousands, thousands.*
> *And a will glowing brightly,*
> *And famished eyes glowing*
> *Like hard crusts of bread*
> *Glowing bright in new steel bridges;*
> *And all striding there . . . there . . . there . . .*
> *Hunger striding, dressed to the neck in people!*
> *Vengeance striding, dressed in hunger and death!*
> *A flame rises from your heart, O Ritt Street,*
> *And Pitt Street*
> *And Willett*
> *And Sheriff and Columbia*
> *And Cannon and Stanton*
> *And Rivington and Broom*
> *And Hester . . .*

A flame rises up from my prematurely dead youth.
(O, East Side! O, East Side of mine!)
A flame rises from your Howe factory,
And from you needle shops
And fur shops . . .
A flame that will unite
With all the flames throughout the world;
That will rise
Over the citadels of poverty,
Over the fortresses of work,
Over the catacombs of dead religions,
And like a great sheet of fire will fill
With the red storm-wind
And cover the pus-filled specters
Of poverty, of need, and of blood,
And will flame
The length and breadth of the world
And flutter
And flutter
And flutter.

The future foreseen by Nadir in his conclusion looks almost biblical in its vision of the "fire next time." But human resistance, not divine force, lights this fire against oppression and keeps it burning. Nadir could not have known Walter Benjamin's theses on the philosophy of history (unpublished during both of their lifetimes), but he confirms some of the theses through his writing of *Rivington Street*. He chooses, in Benjamin's words, "to articulate the past historically . . . [which means] to seize hold of a memory when it flashes up at a moment of danger. . . . Only that historian will have the gift of fanning the spark of hope in the past who is firmly convinced that even the dead will not be safe from the enemy if he wins."[10] He articulates the past historically, and also theatrically, in this poem that fans the spark of hope into a flame.

3

Prayer Boxes as Precious as Diamonds

How Soviet Yiddish Satire Fared in America

When Moishe Olgin reviewed the New York premiere of the Soviet satire *Diamonds* in 1930, he wrote that Avrom Veviorka's play was "perhaps needed more in America than in the Soviet Union. There they have the Red Army to fight the remaining speculators."[1] In America, the struggle against speculators and capitalism would have to be conducted by other means, such as satiric theatre, until a revolutionary Red Army arrived.

By staging *Diamonds* in its original language of Yiddish, Artef's New York theatre ensemble did not significantly reduce profiteering and speculation in the United States; but the production brought part of the Russian revolution—its new satiric Yiddish theatre, and its secular messianism—to America. Audiences and theatre artists in both countries benefited from the Soviet government's support of the Moscow State Yiddish Theatre (known under the acronym Goset), which first staged *Diamonds*. Goset gave artists in Moscow a chance to produce Yiddish classics and contemporary plays. Artef staged some of the same plays in New York after their Moscow premieres. The Yiddish theatre creators at Artef must have felt that if they were not directly participating in the Soviet revolution, at least they were enlarging the audience for revolutionary Soviet culture in New York. If they also reduced market speculation through their satire, so much the better.

Veviorka's *Diamonds* premiered at Goset in the fall of 1926, four years before the Artef production. Critics received the work more favorably in New York than in Moscow. Historian Jeffrey Veidlinger, in his thorough study of Goset, reports that the play, known as *137 Children's Homes* in 1926, was the Moscow Yiddish theatre company's "biggest failure, both critically and financially. . . . Reviewers, such as Mikhail Zagorskii, no longer felt that shtetl [small town] life should be portrayed at all, even for educational purposes—it was simply too horrible for a comedy."[2] By contrast, in New York, Yiddish theatre critic Nathaniel Buchwald praised the selection of the play, and wrote that "*Diamonds* ought to become the hit of the Artef. It is a successful play, a play with recognizable live characters. . . . You fall in love with it at first sight."[3] Moishe Nadir also liked the jaunty and explosive material of the comedy.[4] Olgin's view that the play was needed more in New York than Moscow was borne out: at least he, Nadir, and Buchwald enjoyed the satire of Soviet corruption more than the Soviet critics did. Perhaps the American Yiddish trio's distance from Russia, and from conventional Judaism, let them see more humor than the Russians in Veviorka's barbs at Jews who had not welcomed the Soviet revolution.

Diamonds comically depicts a corrupt and changing Russian society with scenes about the buying and selling of phylacteries (*tefillin*), leather-boxed amulets Jews wear during morning prayers. A search for one special pair of *tefillin* filled with diamonds drives the lead character, Nicholaivich Shindel, through a number of humorous scenes, and reveals different attitudes toward traditional prayer implements in the new Russia. Some men use *tefillin* to pray; others, to smuggle diamonds.

All of the characters in the play are Jews, and almost all of them engage in a comedy of errors and deception. The few who support the revolution, and those tradesmen and women who criticize it, or seek to profit privately and maintain their small businesses after the revolution, behave in self-serving manners. Though not anti-Semitic or against revolution, the play portrays Jews who are far from heroic. They are not even charming as scoundrels, for the most part, although Shindel is more or less mistaken for a messiah by some of the provincial townsfolk. The comedy surfaces in their excesses of messianic fervor and greed, and in Comrade Shindel's imposture. The comrade claims to be on a mission to support 137 children's homes, and acts in the name of the proletariat and the government in Moscow. By reciting official names and jargon to his provincial hosts, Shindel covers up his diamond-smuggling operation, gives his crime an air of official sanction, and inadvertently suggests that his language (filled with tributes to "the proletariat" and government agencies including Cheka, the secret police) may be used by scoundrels as well as supporters of the revolution.

The use of revolutionary jargon by scoundrels, no longer surprising in our era, might have sounded a little jarring to Moscow theatregoers in 1926, and to New York Yiddish enthusiasts of revolution in 1930. Soviet loyalists in the audience probably agreed with Comrade Shindel's reply to Levine, a Cheka investigator who claims to have seen him before, when his profession and his nose were different. Shindel says, "You have a fine sense of humor . . . only this is no time for jokes. . . . A proletarian needs to know when to joke."[5]

Moscow's Yiddish theatre critics evidently felt that 1926 was not the time for Veviorka to joke. Their response did not deter Artef. The New York ensemble's selection of a satire concerned with the status of Yiddish-speaking Jews living under Soviet rule was consistent with the collective's interest in Yiddish culture, social change, and Communism. If some of the Jews in the play were counter-revolutionary, or more concerned with personal profit than the needs of society as a whole, the same could be said of characters in satires written by Moishe Nadir, Chaver Paver, and other Artef playwrights living in New York.

The smugglers in *Diamonds* are arrested before the play ends. The ending implies that no illegal trade will be permitted under Soviet law. But the play also acknowledges the existence of corruption and a black-market economy within the Soviet system. Jews whose shops have been closed by government restrictions hope that Comrade Shindel will rescue them by rescinding orders that nationalized and closed their small, local businesses. The theatres that staged *Diamonds* were, in their own ways, offering satiric discourse on Soviet economic policy. Lenin's "New Economic Policy" allowed for some private businesses to continue during the early twenties; Veviorka's play reflects that change, by showing the shopkeepers rejoicing when they hear Moscow will permit their businesses to reopen. The shopkeepers attribute their reprieve to Shindel's influence in Moscow, and wrongly commend the false messiah who appears to bring salvation. (He promises to exert his influence in Moscow in return for "contributions" to children's homes, a *quid pro quo* that ostensibly benefits orphans, not the fund collector.) Then Shindel is arrested as a smuggler. He has his own private business, you might say, and the state closes it. The Jews in the new society depicted by Veviorka are thus denied their savior. Curiously, their savior is not a religious man; quite the contrary, he buys old *tefillin* as part of what he calls an anti-religious campaign, and Soviet Jews sell the leather prayer boxes because they need money. Threats to their livelihood as shopkeepers, not to their religious practices, alarm the Jews portrayed here. That their provincial synagogue may be turned into a children's home disturbs almost no one.

Artef and Goset cannot be accused of staging an unequivocally pro-Soviet play, which may be one reason Soviets wrote unfavorably about the production in Moscow. The entire play "is not revolutionary and owes nothing to the revolution," wrote one Moscow critic."[6] Veviorka's play shows *shtetl* (small town) Jews misled by a man who claims to represent the government. The impostor is stopped by Cheka's secret police agents; it could even be said that the law and order forces of the revolution end criminal activity with Shindel's arrest. But initially, the Jews who welcome Shindel as a Jewish official from Moscow see him as a man embodying the revolution; his commands and entreaties are greeted as if Moscow had ordered them. The townspeople turn out to be his victims, and he preys on their needs for help. "Prey" rather than "prayer" is the operative word, as Shindel and his assistant Schwarzer prove to be unscrupulous; the confidence men pretend to bring aid and comfort to children in orphanages and to shopkeepers in need of permission to sell wares. The fact that the provincial Jews need economic relief, and receive none, hardly flatters the Soviet government. Before the play ends, welcome orders from Moscow permit the shop keepers to reopen their businesses; but the same government, or its local representatives, had earlier closed the shops. The Soviet regime is no more of a messiah than Comrade Shindel.

When the gems hidden in the *tefillin* and the valuable *tefillin* are misplaced early in the play, a farcical search follows. Shindel and his assistant Schwarzer begin to buy old *tefillin* from the local populace, in the hope that they will find their missing diamonds in one of the amulets. It turns out that Schwarzer has kept the diamonds all the time; Shindel's buying of the amulets was thus unnecessary. There is no honor here, even among Soviet proletarian thieves.

No character in *Diamonds* turns out to be wholly innocent, or wholly removed from excessive behavior that lends itself to comic acting. Shindel's arrival encourages the provincial city's Jews to express their complaints and seek remedy through statements as exaggerated as his own.

When the visiting impostor begins buying sets of *tefillin,* one citizen asks to be paid two million, but he quickly settles for two hundred. The comic exchange doesn't end there. Shindel prepares to pay the Jew two hundred, and asks if the seller has change. He is told, "If I had change, I wouldn't sell my father-in-law's *tefillin.*" Shindel borrows the sum needed from Frau Segal, a woman so enamored of him she pays for the *tefillin* he buys without knowing he is trying to recover smuggled diamonds. She expects the man will marry her, and makes his business (except the illegal part) hers.

In New York, if not in Moscow, the audience for the play may have shared some of the same qualities shown by characters in *Diamonds.* That is to say, they too welcomed a man from Moscow, namely, the playwright Veviorka, and expected cheerful news from him. The author was no false messiah like Shindel. But Artef's importation of Soviet theatre to New York, as part of the messianic project discussed earlier, placed its audiences in a position comparable to that of the Jews who welcome Shindel, contribute to his fund for children's homes, and sell him phylacteries. In New York, as in the play, there were Jews who wanted to hear a Yiddish-speaking man from Moscow, to share with him the sensations of revolutionary triumph and promise. There was a difference between the two populations; the Jews in New York, at Artef's theatre, knew Shindel was an impostor, and laughed at his adventures. The Jews in the play saw little or no humor in their situation. Still, the play attracted interest in New York, as Shindel did in his story, because Moscow's revolutionary regime was the point of origin.

Zayde's Zayde

The Moscow production also initially might have attracted Artef's interest because the lead role of Comrade Shindel was played by the great Russian Yiddish actor Solomon Mikhoels, who later became the artistic director of Goset. In 1925, a year before *Diamonds* opened, Mikhoels had portrayed Menachem Mendel in *Jewish Luck,* a Soviet film based on Sholem Aleichem's writing. His superb performance in the film suggests the high caliber of comic acting he could have brought to the role of Shindel. Russian critics complained that Shindel's imposture was apparent from the start, that there was no development, no dynamic to the story, all of which could have been the case.[7] But Mikhoels in *Jewish Luck* demonstrates he was capable of the nonrealistic, lyrical style of performance *Diamonds* invites, as its characters repeat lines and phrases in a kind of orchestrated refrain with comic variation. It is difficult to take *tefillin* seriously when they are given an ancestry like this one, heard more than once in the play:

> I give you the holy *tefillin* of my holy *zayde* [grandfather]. I received them from my *zayde*. My *zayde* received them from his *zayde* and his *zayde* got them from his great *zayde* and his great *zayde* got them from his great great *zayde* and so on higher, higher, and still higher—a huge chain of *zaydes* all the way back to Ezrah the Scribe.[8]

Even if accurate, which is doubtful, the lineage of the *tefillin* described here goes on too long, to the point of absurdity, which is just the point. The recital of these lines, spoken to increase the sales value of the amulet, undermines the speaker's credibility; he wants to break the chain of family inheritance that he claims confers value on his *tefillin*. Similarly, Shindel will at different times in the play repeat statements about his support of the proletariat and his ability to call Lenin's office on the phone; with repetition such statements become less credible, and more humorous, as they become the doubletalk of confidence artists.

Perhaps appreciation of the vaudeville-like doubletalk within the play contributed to the favorable reception of *Diamonds* in New York. The satire was one of a number of plays that moved (without the original cast or director) from Moscow to Manhattan's Artef. Another reason for its favorable reception—the pro-Soviet fervor of Artef's members—can be read between the lines of a "Worker's Theatre" report issued in 1933. On May 9th of that year, "an Artef Congress with 110 delegates from 75 organizations heard reports . . . [which] established the fact that the chief shortcomings of the Artef were, first, that the Artef failed in developing a repertory depicting the life of the American worker, second, that the Artef did not take part in the struggle of the workers through its strong propaganda weapon—the theatre."[9]

While Artef was said to be neglecting American proletarian life, it did its part in depicting the life of Soviet workers, and sharing Soviet theatre with Americans. The same 1933 report notes that Comrade M. Katz, who had just returned from the Soviet Union, was given an ovation in New York. He "spoke of the tremendous role that theatre plays in the Soviet Union, and which Artef should play here as a proletarian theatre."

There was no comparable revolution in the United States to create the political conditions through which the Soviet state subsidized the Yiddish theatre of Goset. But this did not deter Artef's stage combat against capitalist speculators, which continued not only through other Soviet Yiddish plays but also through American works like Nadir's *Messiah in America*. Nadir's play received only a small studio production by Artef in 1933, as noted in Chapter 1, while Veviorka's Soviet satire was given a full-scale production, complete with attention from leading American Yiddish theatre critics. Artef's revolutionary fervor favored Russian authors over Nadir's homemade satire of messianic capitalism. *Messiah in America*, first published in 1928 (two years before Veviorka's play was staged by Artef), can be seen as an American counterpart to *Diamonds*. Both satires feature false messiahs who are Jews. Both authors wrote for Yiddish-speaking audiences sympathetic to Communism and wary of traditional religious beliefs.

The Yiddish Gogol

The comparison should not be pursued too far. While Veviorka's play, written in 1925, shares some thematic concerns with Nadir's work, it is consciously modeled after Gogol's classic nineteenth-century satire, *The Inspector General*, which also portrays a Russian population rife with complaints and corruption. The man who asks to be called Comrade Shindel, and claims to be a Soviet government official from Moscow, on a mission to find supplies for 137 children's homes, is less innocent than the impoverished wanderer mistaken for a government inspector in Gogol's play. But in Gogol's play and Veviorka's, the man supposedly representing the government sees the local population grant him authority and influence because of his alleged connections to those in power. In both plays, the confidence man gains confidence in himself, to the extent that he woos both a mother and her daughter at his own peril; the man promises both women that life with him in the capital will be better than life in the provinces. The daughter whom Shindel courts in *Diamonds* eventually reports his questionable behavior to the Cheka.

There are differences between the two plays. Gogol's government impostor is thrust into his false position when townspeople mistake him for an important figure from St. Petersburg. Veviorka's impostor, Shindel, takes on the misleading role of a Moscow government official by choice, as soon as he enters, to cover up his diamond smuggling. He exploits the fact that Jews in a small town are new to the ways of the revolution. When Shindel informs the provincial shtetl's residents that he is on a mission to secure supplies for children's homes, where orphans need food and other assistance, he reminds them that Lenin said that children are the future. Shindel quotes Lenin as if the statement had been addressed to him personally. In fact, it is doubtful Lenin ever knew Shindel, and much more doubtful he would approve of a Soviet man smuggling diamonds across the border by encasing them in *tefillin*. But the local residents have *tefillin* they will gladly sell, because they are short on cash, and the fact that the buyer is a friend of Lenin doesn't stop them from asking for two million per amulet.

Before he is arrested, Comrade Shindel persuades many Jews in the provincial *shtetl* to conduct business with him; in doing so, he brings them into his fold—as dupes in the new, post-revolutionary world. The scenario suggests that the new Russia has within it some of the same old human failings: greed, deception, corruption, and ignorance (some of the same vices Gogol satirized in Tsarist Russia). Presumably the revolution will proceed to eradicate these failings, as it goes on after the curtain falls; but the fact that Gogol's plot has been revived, and relocated in post-Tsarist, post-Leninist Russia, implies that the names of government officials change faster than human behavior.

Nicholaivich Shindel succeeds with his masquerade for a time because he is a Yiddish-speaking Jew among other Yiddish-speaking Jews. Written in Yiddish, the entire play was performed in that language in Moscow and New York. Once during the play, when Comrade Shindel invokes the name of Lenin, he is told "Lenin is a goy" by a Jew who hints Lenin is less reliable than a fellow Jew like Shindel. It turns out Shindel is less reliable, or no more reliable, than Comrade Lenin. But Jews in the provincial town seem prepared to follow a Yiddish-speaking Jew more readily than they will follow another official; if their religion and language lead them to follow Shindel, they also lead the followers astray. The Jews erroneously favor charitable works on the basis of religious affiliation. Asked whether the children's homes he supports house Jews—as if the homes would not otherwise deserve support—Shindel, revolutionary confidence man that is he, replies that the children are not only Jews but also proletarians, which in this comic situation makes them doubly deserving of support.

Initially suspicious of Shindel's motives to visit the provinces, Levine finds himself thrown off track by the story about securing supplies for children's homes. The visitor's repetition of this story becomes a running gag early in Act One, part of the playwright's flair for comic dialogue. After Shindel tells some locals, "I need to provide supplies for 137 children's homes in Samarker province. And nothing more," his assistant Schwarzer is asked if Comrade Shindel has a wife or children. Schwarzer replies, "He has 137 children's homes in Samarker province, and nothing more." He doesn't have 137 homes or a wife. But his devotion to children's homes "and nothing more" does not deter the bachelor from courting several women.

Love and *Tefillin*

Frau Segal's daughter, Fridka, turns out to have a friend in the Cheka. Her flirtation with Shindel helps her find out his secrets and expose them. But Fridka's relationship with the buyer of leather amulets becomes curiously erotic in the third act. She asks him why pious men kiss their *tefillin,* asks if he loves the prayers printed inside them, and then says she wants a pair of the amulets. Fridka knows Shindel is attracted to her, and humorously turns the prayer amulets into objects of affection, at a time when the impostor would rather be kissing her. Fridka's mother enters just as Shindel is about to hug the daughter, and he tells the startled Frau (to whom he earlier hinted at a marriage proposal) that his interest in Fridka is only fatherly. He also unwittingly takes Schwarzer's *tefillin* that have diamonds in them, and gives the box to Fridka without opening it. After she surrenders the *tefillin* to her friend Levine, the Cheka has sufficient evidence to arrest the smuggler.

Shindel is not a terribly romantic man. Frau Segal finds the invitation to accompany him to Moscow attractive, and tries to become friendlier with him. She asks the impostor his first name. He responds that it is Nicholaivich, "only I prefer that you call me Comrade Shindel." Only his mother ever called him by his first name. He places the title of Comrade above all others, as a dedicated Communist, and a decidedly businesslike suitor.

For most of the play, the prayer amulets are not objects of affection, but prospective sources of wealth. They acquire new value, not for religious reasons, but because the smuggler needs the diamond-filled set that Schwarzer claims to have lost. Most of the townspeople don't care whether Shindel buys old *tefillin* because he is a pious Jew or because he is a government official conducting an anti-religious campaign, and paying for cessation of prayer box usage. One misguided *shtetl* resident asserts that in Moscow they have no *tefillin* like his, implying that such leather goods are rare and would be welcome in the center of the Soviet revolution. Other Jews who offer to sell their *tefillin* need the money for food. The revolution has not served them well economically. Sale of their religious artifacts may help them survive, at least briefly; but their own shops remain closed, and prayers for prosperity have not brought it, with or without *tefillin*. Gershon, the most devout Jew in the play, remains so pessimistic about the future of Judaism that he surrenders the synagogue key to Levine, and asks him to turn the holy place into a children's home.

Tefillin are regarded as sacred objects, or promotives of prayer, mainly by Gershon. Schwarzer, Shindel's assistant, pretends to be a religious fanatic who needs *tefillin*. "I still can't be without *tefillin*," he tells Schindel, in a running gag that explains how the *tefillin* belonged to his grandfather's grandfather, a whole litany of grandfathers; but his words are only a diversion, a pretended piety concealing Schwarzer's interest in smuggled diamonds.

Schwarzer abandons his claim to ownership when interrogated by Levine in the last scene of the play. Sensing the Cheka will arrest him, Schwarzer changes his usual statement, and says that the *tefillin* are owned by the proletariat. His unwittingly funny answer parodies the rhetoric Shindel uses throughout the play when arguing that private ownership no longer exists in the Soviet Union. Not quite satisfied with that answer, Levine asks who was praying with the *tefillin*. Schwarzer, not sure whether the proletariat prays, doesn't know what he should say and then blames Shindel for the smuggling operation. To Shindel, his accomplice laments, "You have ruined me. I pleaded with you, don't touch any *tefillin*!" Somewhere between the Old World, where it is blasphemous to use a religious object for smuggling, and a new state, in which the proletariat doesn't pray, two Soviet Jews named Schwarzer and Shindel have nowhere left to go except prison.

Levine articulates the most learned reference to the prayer traditionally inscribed and stored inside *tefillin*, when he enters with uniformed Cheka officers who arrest the smugglers. In wordplay on the Yiddish term for "diamonds"—*brillianten*—Levine refers to a scribe who wrote brilliant, diamond-like *parshas* (scripture portions) for *tefillin*, and then he opens the contraband *tefillin* to reveal the diamonds inside. The prayer box, if not the prayer inside, turns out to be as precious as diamonds.

Since its 1930 production at Artef, *Diamonds* has not been translated into English. It remains a Yiddish play written for and about Soviet Yiddish Jews. The text survives as a revealing historical record of Yiddish theatre. Its depiction of Jews responding to the Soviet revolution has taken on new meaning since the Soviet Union disbanded and more than a million Russian Jews have left their birthplace for Israel, where they are more likely to speak Russian or Hebrew than Yiddish. The revolutionary rhetoric and mission of service that Shindel invoked now sound hollow, as they should when spoken by an impostor; but they have the additional hollow sound that follows a failed revolution. The revolution failed to give state control to the proletariat—much as the *tefillin* were supposed to belong to the proletariat. Veviorka's play anticipated fissures within the Soviet system that official rhetoric like Shendl's covered up for decades. Shindel was a false messiah, a Soviet Yiddish version of Gogol's inspector general; but today we can see that the revolution itself was a kind of false messiah. The role this false messiah plays in *Diamonds* makes the work a tragicomedy about a messianic revolution that, like the play, had a limited run in Russia.

Over the course of its next eight seasons (1931–40), Artef continued to present Soviet plays, as well as other Yiddish plays that Goset had earlier staged in Moscow. These included another work by Veviorka, *The Steppe on Fire* (staged by Artef in 1933, never staged by Goset); Maxim Gorky's *Yegor Bulichev* (1934); Lipe Resnick's *Recruits* (1934, a Soviet-era adaptation based on an older play by Israel Axenfeld); Gorky's *Dostigayev* (1935); *Benjamin Quixote* (adapted by Nadir from Mendele's Yiddish novel, *Travels of Benjamin III,* and staged by Artef's studio in 1930 and 1935, after Goset staged a different adaptation in 1927); and Moishe Kulbak's *The Outlaw* (1937, staged by Goset a year earlier under the title *Boytre the Bandit*).[10] The Gorky plays were not originally written in Yiddish and not all of these plays were staged by Goset, but their production in New York further engaged Artef's actors with the Soviet revolution and its theatre repertoire.

During the same decade in which Artef enthusiastically imported Soviet plays to New York, stage artists in Moscow contended with harsh state control of their theatre. A number of Yiddish and Soviet plays did not conform to the Stalinist regime's demand for socialist realism. The same year (1930) in which Artef staged *Diamonds,* Moscow critics and officials severely criticized Vladimir Mayakovsky's *Bathhouse,* a satire of Soviet bureacracy directed by Vsevolod Meyerhold. After the play's denunciation (and a failed love affair), the playwright committed suicide. Meyerhold's experimental departures from socialist realism endured a decade of criticism, which ended in his arrest and execution in 1940. Goset lasted longer under the Soviet government's watch, in part because of the canny, resourceful leadership exerted by its artistic director, Solomon Mikhoels. Soon after he assumed that position, "Mikhoels quickly learned that to revive the Yiddish theatre, he had best follow the state's criteria," according to Veidlinger.[11] Mikhoels survived a number of purges under Stalin, but critics started to question his "alleged formalism" in 1936, and later accused him of supporting Zionism.[12] Mikhoels was murdered under suspicious circumstances that were officially called an accident early in 1948, after leading Goset through dozens of productions from 1929 on.

The charge of "formalism" could cover a multitude of artistic offenses, but it is tempting to think of this accusation as an unintentional compliment to Goset and its actors. Some of their best performances moved away from realism toward a more comic and grotesque style. As Norris Houghton observed, after visiting the Moscow State Yiddish Theatre in the mid-thirties, "A peculiar form of the grotesque seems to attract the Jewish actor, who plays in a highly stylized and oddly musical monotone."[13] This approach to acting was particularly suitable for a satire like *Diamonds,* with its gallery of rogues and vaudevillian doubletalk.

From Artef to the Federal Theatre Project

Under Benno Schneider's direction, Artef also was able to perform *Diamonds* in a nonrealistic, grotesque style of comedy. In New York the artists could engage in such artistry without the pressures to conform to socialist realism faced by Soviet artists. An absence of state subsidy for Artef freed the company from state demands, although there were other pressures. The greatest opposition that Artef encountered in the thirties arose within the New York Yiddish community, furious at Yiddish American Communists (and their standard bearers in Artef) after Stalin and Hitler signed the nonaggression pact of 1939. The theatre company's survival depended on box office attractions, benefit nights, and a supportive Yiddish-speaking public, all of which declined late in the thirties. In the same decade, the left-wing American Yiddish writers' association Proletpen also expressed disappointment that so few of its members' plays—in contrast to Soviet creations and Yiddish classics—entered the Artef repertoire.

Some of the artists seeking an alternative to Artef performed new American plays in Yiddish for the Federal Theatre Project. Its Yiddish Unit, which began in 1935, enjoyed a federal subsidy that subjected participants to government pressures, rather than those from the box office; but for a few years, the Federal Theatre Project offered Moishe Nadir, Chaver Paver, choreographer Lillian Shapiro, and other Artef collaborators and peers the opportunity to stage new radical and satiric writing in Yiddish, with government support. They had their own American Goset.

4

The Federal Theatre Project in Yiddish

"The Society of the Sorely Perplexed" Takes the Stage

The Soviet government may have been the first national body to subsidize innovative Yiddish theatre, but it was not the only one. During the Great Depression, the Congress of the United States also financed Yiddish stage artists. Between 1935 and 1939, the Federal Theatre Project introduced Yiddish classics and new plays in New York, Chicago, Los Angeles, and Boston.

The vaudeville revue *We Live and Laugh,* which opened in 1936, and produced a new edition in 1937, brought Artef veterans together with other Yiddish artists in New York, under the auspices of the government-sponsored theatre program. One among many adventurous performances launched by the Federal Theatre Project, the vaudeville revue included Moishe Nadir as a writer. It is not difficult to imagine the Yiddish satirist announcing, "Finally the United States government is falling into line with the Kremlin, at least as far as the Yiddish theatre is concerned: we now have a state-sponsored experimental ensemble. All we need is our Shliome Mikhoels [the Soviet Yiddish actor]!"

The Federal Theatre Project's Yiddish Unit in New York did not last as long as the Moscow State Yiddish Theatre or Artef; but productions such as *We Live and Laugh,* and a popular Yiddish version of Clifford Odets's *Awake and Sing,* added to the repertoire of left-leaning drama that the longer-lasting companies initiated. Its projects also were freed from the financial pressures Artef faced. Salaries were paid as part of a congressionally funded employment relief program; weekly checks for the artists were not dependent on ticket sales. This permitted innovations, including the support of a large Yiddish vaudeville troupe in 1936.

While England had music halls, and France and Russia had cabarets, vaudeville's circuit of variety entertainment, with an array of comic sketches and novelty songs, thrived across the United States early in the twentieth century. The American-language vaudeville houses gave a start to the Marx Brothers, Burns and Allen, Fanny Brice, and many others who later moved on to radio, film, and television. The Yiddish vaudeville circuit featured stage performers like Leo Fuchs and Yetta Zwerling who later were seen more widely in plays and films.

Some jokes about immigrants in vaudeville sketches denigrated ethnic minorities, and Yiddish vaudeville was no exception. However, the vaudeville revue titled *We Live and Laugh* proved to be more politically progressive, more literary, and less dependent on old standbys than others. Well received by critics in the Yiddish press and English-language papers, the show ran for ten months, until March 1937. The trade journal *Variety* wrote that the production gave "the Yiddish theatre its first taste of revue on a big scale."[1] The *New York Times* announced, "The Federal Theatre Project added another bright feather to its cap last night when one of its units, the Yiddish Intimate Theatre, presented its first revue."[2] Nathaniel Buchwald, an affiliate of Artef, wrote in the *Morgn Frayhayt* that the revue was "entertaining in the best sense of the word ... in good taste and colorful, competent staging ... in the vein and style of the [New York cabaret] Chauve-Souris." A. Mukdoiny stated in the *Jewish Morning Journal* that the revue "stands culturally and artistically on a very high level ... the best that one can desire."[3] Some of the revue's most inventive sketches—Nadir's "Prisoner 1936" and actor Jacob Bergreen's "Stars," with its "Society of the Sorely Perplexed"—stand as exemplary models of topical Yiddish satire that, with modest revisions, would still entertain audiences today.

We Live and Laugh opened a half-year before the more ambitious Yiddish Unit production of Sinclair Lewis's *It Can't Happen Here* in Manhattan. The revue's success can be seen in retrospect as the harbinger of other popular Federal Theatre Project stage productions written in or translated into Yiddish. Hallie Flanagan, artistic director of the Federal

Theatre, attended the Yiddish Unit's New York opening of *It Can't Happen Here* on October 27, 1936. The play opened across the country in seventeen cities that night, and Flanagan had time to see only two of the versions on the first evening. She watched Act One performed in English at the Adelphi Theatre in New York City, and Act Two in Yiddish at the Biltmore Theatre. According to her, the Yiddish performance displayed "continental volubility and gesticulation . . . in contrast to the quiet playing at the Adelphi [and] included several scenes, notably the concentration camp scene, omitted at the Adelphi, and on the whole I thought it a better show."[4]

Both the Biltmore productions of Lewis's anti-fascist play and the vaudeville revue, *We Live and Laugh,* subsequently were cited as proof of the Yiddish Unit's ability to create new, popular theatre. In a government report on "The Yiddish Theatre of the Federal Theatre Project" written in 1937, Leo Schmeltsman observed, "The success of plays like *It Can't Happen Here* and *We Live and Laugh* built prestige for the Yiddish Theatre Project."[5]

In the same report, Schmeltsman suggests that the Federal Theatre Project infelicitously began its Yiddish division, as the "directors of the Yiddish Theatre Project exhumed long-forgotten relics and antics of the primitive Yiddish repertoire and produced them with deplorably bad taste." His short history of the unit's evolution recounts how complaints about early productions led to a survey:

> Directors and actors of the project, Yiddish editors and dramatic critics, and executives of the Hebrew Actors' Union were interviewed. Subsequent to this survey recommendations essential to the improvement of the Yiddish Theatre Project were submitted to Federal Theatre authorities. . . . The first step in raising the level of Yiddish productions began with an excellent translation of *It Can't Happen Here* by Benson Inge and Benjamin Ressler.

Benson Inge, Almost a Messiah

The success of *It Can't Happen Here* and other Yiddish productions within the Federal Theatre Project can be traced to the opportunities and risk-taking that Hallie Flanagan and her staff afforded American artists. But some credit should go to one man in particular, Benson Inge, who deserves to be celebrated for his advancement of socially progressive theatre in a time of crisis. Almost forgotten today, Inge co-translated *It Can't Happen Here* into Yiddish with Benjamin Ressler, ensured that other plays about fascism and anti-Semitism reached Yiddish-speaking audiences, and planned for a renaissance of American Yiddish drama in the thirties. His government-funded encouragement of socially aware Yiddish plays deserves more recognition, if not emulation, by those who want to renew the endangered genre of Yiddish theatre, and sustain other minority cultures. The Federal Theatre Project's Translations Department, which Inge supervised, selected for translation and production in their original language not only Yiddish texts but also plays in Italian, Russian, German, Spanish, and French. Inge and his staff helped keep multiple cultures alive on the American stage, and ensured that theatre would reach more than just the dominant culture's audience. He also co-edited a Federal Theatre magazine on foreign theatre news, which meant American artists could follow what was going on in the rest of the theatre world.

Previously a drama critic for the *New York World Telegram*, Benson Inge became supervisor of the Translations Department in 1937, after it merged with the Anglo-Jewish Play Department of the Federal Theatre Project's National Service Bureau. Although plays in many languages passed across his desk, Yiddish texts clearly were a special interest of his. Through Inge's own translation, through his letters to writers and producers, and through publication of an Anglo-Jewish play bibliography and visionary statements, he encouraged the staging of left-leaning Yiddish plays inside the Federal Theatre Project, and placed the government's theatre arts program in the service of some of the country's most innovative non-English–language authors.

While he was not quite the Messiah of Yiddish theatre, Benson Inge offered new prospects to Yiddish writers and actors at a time when many of them faced unemployment and neglect. (The Yiddish Unit of the Federal Theatre Project, which at one time had a staff of twenty-five, also deserves recognition here for support of new stage productions. Inge did not act alone.) An unsigned statement from Inge's department—quite possibly written by him—promotes a very bold approach to Yiddish theatre late in the thirties. Renouncing older Yiddish theatre in favor of new plays, the document's author is far from modest as he states,

There is a general impression that the Yiddish Theatre, as it flourished in America since 1900 has a literary (classic) tradition all its own. This is not entirely so. There is and always has been much folklore and substance for Yiddish material but a limited theatre supply. Goldfadden, Gordin and even Hirshbein or Pinski are passé today, and few of their creations could be successfully restored. Except for Maurice Schwartz and the Artef Group there is little hope for development in the commercial field. It is therefore left to the Federal Theatre to bring about a renaissance. And the Anglo-Jewish Play Department is dedicated to this task. It was entirely natural for the erstwhile divisions of the Federal Theatre, growing out of seeming chaos, to carry along, during its early tides, much of the driftwood and debris of past generations. The Jewish units, perhaps more than the other branches, followed the lanes of least resistance. A recent checkup discloses only too clearly the disorganization and emergency-pressed productions which flourished at the time. Whether it was *King Lear* or *The Eternal Wanderer* or *The Forgotten Child* or *The Sacrifice of Isaac*. Never anything purporting to bring the standards of the Yiddish Theatre into realms coveted by Schwartz or the Artef companies. The Federal Theatre is, currently, in the fortunate position of entering the struggle begun by individual entrepreneurs—and forging ahead into a leading position. There never has been the question of a lack of audiences—Yiddish playgoers, assimilated or not, are the most avid playgoers in the world. It is only because of this insatiable desire that the catchpenny producers have managed to survive until now, hashing and rehashing ancient scripts, inasmuch as they never incurred investments for original work. With the establishment of the Anglo-Jewish Play Department in the National Play Bureau (working in conjunction with the Play Policy Board) it will now, for the first time, be possible to help improve the standards desired by the largest number of Yiddish patrons. The Jewish presentation of *It Can't Happen Here* proved conclusively the manner in which universal material may be altered, translated or adapted to suit Jewish needs. This has encouraged the Anglo-Jewish Play department to make intensive research into universal literature—either in play or novel form, for consideration by the various Jewish units.It is the aim of this department to discourage, wherever possible, the productions of archaic pieces, plays which have had their hey-day in Jewish Theatre history . . . [this department] would like to be in close and constant touch with the various units, these at present being in New York, Boston, Chicago, and Los Angeles for an interchange of ideas on production schedules. It will not in any way attempt to be bureaucratic or dictatorial, but shall try to ease the burdens of experimental, progressive groups.[6]

The confidence and exuberance of this manifesto, with its call for a renaissance and its plan to please "the most avid playgoers" in the world, match the tenor of other Play Bureau and National Service Bureau documents signed by Benson Inge. (The National Service Bureau was part of the Federal Theatre Project, and housed Inge's translation program after the Anglo-Jewish Play Department merged with the Translations Department.) While the proposal raises expectations that were never fully met, the reasoning behind it reflects a moment of optimism others may have shared with Inge early in their tenure with the Federal Theatre Project.

Benson Inge saw these ideas take hold in New York, with his Sinclair Lewis translation and the cabaret revue, *We Live and Laugh,* but for him that was only the beginning. He wanted to see new Yiddish plays staged in English as well as in their original language, and wrote letters to producers and writers to initiate numerous additional projects. Inge's correspondence, preserved among the National Archives' Federal Theatre Project papers, reveals that he asked Moishe Nadir for a Yiddish translation of O'Neill's *The Hairy Ape,* and "any other plays, your own or translated, pertaining to the Jewish scene," which Nadir cared to submit. (Artef's studio staged the O'Neill translation as *John the Stoker* in 1934–35 before Inge approached Nadir.) Inge asked H. Leivick for English and Yiddish copies of the play *Chains,* which Artef produced in 1937. He asked Peretz Hirschbein for an English version of *The Prophet Elijah,* and said he might seek an English translation as well. He considered securing a Yiddish translation of Elmer Rice's *Street Scene,* and an adaptation of Sholem Asch's novel, *Three Cities.* He commissioned a Yiddish translation of George Kelly's popular play, *The Show Off.* As soon as Inge received the Yiddish translation of Clifford Odets' *Awake and Sing* in June 1937, he sent copies to the Federal Theatre Yiddish units in Boston, Los Angeles, and Chicago. (The Yiddish version of the Odets play was performed with success from December 1938 to April 1939 by the New York unit, and by the Los Angeles unit for ten days in April 1938.) Leon Kobrin agreed to Inge's request for an English translation of *Yankel Boyla.* Seeking a Yiddish translation of Sherriff's *Journey's End,* Inge asked a publisher in Poland for a copy in 1938. (A Yiddish copy of the play can be found among the scripts of the Federal Theatre Project now preserved in the National Archives.) He approved and secured a Yiddish translation of Mike Gold's play, *Money*. In one of his most productive exchanges of letters, Inge began by asking David Pinski for a copy of Ansky's *Night and Day,* on which Pinski collaborated, and ended by securing a new play, the staging of which remains one of the most striking achievements of the Yiddish units in the Federal Theatre. (That play, *The Tailor Becomes a Storekeeper,* is considered at length in Chapter 6.)

Not all of Inge's letters led to productions; but the correspondence testifies to practical measures taken for presentation of new plays in Yiddish, and older Yiddish plays in English, which would create a repertoire of innovative drama accessible to a large American audience. What historian Gray Brechin noted about the public works programs initiated during Franklin Roosevelt's tenure in the White House might also be said of Inge's programs: they "enlarged the public domain, providing [Americans] with a multitude of spaces [and occasions] in which to come together both as citizens and a national community," and, it should be added, as a theatregoing community.[7]

Inge's endeavor met obstacles at the Boston Yiddish theatre unit in 1937. In a letter addressed to Jon B. Mack, State Director of the Federal Theatre Project in Massachusetts, Inge said he "fail[ed] to understand why [Boston Yiddish unit director Morris Schorr] would choose such ancient material as *The Stranger* or *The Idiot*. I do not mind reviving plays of this nature as 'museum pieces' but I certainly am not in favor of their presentation as against selections of a more progressive, purposeful and literary standard."[8] He sent Schorr a copy of the "Yiddish translation of *Haunch, Paunch and Jowl* which was produced by the Artef Theatre, last season," and asked for Schorr's opinion of it. Inge earlier had proposed a compromise to Schorr; he was willing to have Schorr present a play of his own choice, "providing you also include in your program one or more of the plays which we have recommended: *We Live and Laugh* is an excellent example of a revue which ran for a long time in New York, and *Prof. Mamlock* is another worthwhile script. This last one may be presented in English or in Yiddish, which we would translate for you."

Another script he recommended was Odets' *Awake and Sing,* the Yiddish translation of which he mailed to Schorr on June 18, 1937, with a cover letter stating that the play's translation by the Yiddish poet Z. Weinper had been "ordered . . . by the playwright himself."[9] The play, with its

Figure 4.1

Audience in line to see *We Live and Laugh*, New York, 1936. *Courtesy of the National Archives.*

portrait of New York tenement life in the Depression, and its insistence that "We don't want life printed on dollar bills," already had won acclaim with the Group Theatre's American language production in 1935. When the Yiddish translation was staged, Odets may have enjoyed hearing the recital of phrases that he originally inserted in the English-language version, then deleted in response to criticism from his Group Theatre associates Lee Strasberg and Harold Clurman. Odets "pared [some of the play's] ethnic specificity and some 'gross Jewish humor' . . . [and] eliminated or translated many of the Yiddish expressions that peppered *Blues*," scholar Ellen Schiff writes of *I Got the Blues*, Odets' early draft of the manuscript. Schiff reports that Odets put aside "many Yiddish colloquialisms, such as 'noo,' 'ich vays nich,' 'voo den?'. . . Still, Yiddish syntax and cadences are frequent melodies in *Awake and Sing!*"[10] Those cadences must have been more audible in the Yiddish rendition of the play, which ran from December 1938 to April 1939 in New York.[11]

In a 2006 American-language production of *Awake and Sing* at Arena Stage in Washington, D.C., director Zelda Fichandler decided to "restore some of the Yiddish expressions found in an early draft of the play," according to drama critic Misha Berson. Fichandler said, "If Odets were alive today, with Yiddish having entered and affected the English language, he would agree with that choice and find it in tune with the lyric

Figure 4.2

Awake and Sing poster, Yiddish Unit of the Federal Theatre Project, New York, 1938. *Courtesy of the National Archives.*

uplifting of Jewish speech, boiling over and explosive, that characterizes his writing."[12] Like it or not, a century after his birth in 1906, Odets was remembered as a playwright with a Yiddish vocabulary. But Odets was known much earlier for his Yiddish-influenced theatre by those who attended the Federal Theatre Project's New York presentation of *Awake and Sing* in 1938.

The play by Odets and selections from the Artef repertoire that Inge recommended constituted some of the modern, "progressive, purposeful" Yiddish theatre he wanted Federal Theatre Project directors to stage. One of his recommendations—but only one—appears to have been heeded by Schorr in Massachusetts. The register of plays staged by the Federal Theatre Project in Massachusetts after the 1937 correspondence lists the "ancient" *Two Kuni-Lemels* by Goldfaden and *200,000* by Sholem Aleichem, and also Friedrich Wolf's *Professor Mamlock,* staged in Yiddish at Peabody, Massacusetts, in February 1938. Inge's office deserves some credit for this showing of Wolf's anti-Nazi play, as well as its longer English-language run at the Daly Theatre in New York.[13]

With his staff Inge also edited and wrote the foreword to an annotated bibliography titled *Anglo-Jewish Plays: In English and Yiddish.* Published by the National Service Bureau of the Federal Theatre Project in 1938, and sold for twenty-five cents a copy, the volume listed twenty-five play titles, their cast sizes, and genres and summarized their plots in English and Yiddish. Now out of print and difficult to find except in archives, the booklet merits republication in an enlarged edition. Inge succinctly explains the importance of the small volume in his foreword: "With this record of material from the Jewish and Anglo-Jewish field— the first of its kind attempted anywhere—the Translations Department of the National Service Bureau hopes to revive and perpetuate that creative spirit which distinguished the Jewish artist."[14] The foreword also describes the kinds of plays discussed, and the reasons for their inclusion, in words that sum up Inge's criteria for selection and support of Yiddish plays:

> Several of the titles, as in the case of *The Dybbuk,* and *Two Hundred Thousand,* are examples of Yiddish stagecraft that will always live. They grow brighter with each revival. . . . Then there are those plays which have not yet seen the footlights, notably *Frankfort Chronicle, Magnolia Street,* and *Generations.* These point the way to a brighter and more progressive day in Yiddish Theatre cul-

ture. Finally there are titles which, undertaken by this department to fill a real need for new material, have been translated from successful plays in English and other languages. Such are *Awake and Sing, Israel in the Kitchen, Professor Mamlock, The Show-Off,* and *Assignment for Tomorrow.*

Most of the plays Inge lists, with the exception of Yiddish classics by Aleichem and Ansky, were still new and topical at the time he chose to include them in his annotated bibliography. The scripts examine anti-Semitism, sweatshops, the labor movement, unemployment, war casualties, and Russia before and after its revolution. Some of the authors—Hirschbein, Leivick, Feuchtwanger, and Odets—already had achieved recognition, but their plays, and those of lesser known authors on the list, remained exceptional in their imaginative exploration of the period's most pressing social, cultural, and religious issues. These plays were not likely to be staged by commercial producers of Yiddish theatre on Second Avenue; but the Federal Theatre Project, had it continued beyond 1939, might have introduced such works to the sizable Yiddish-speaking audience in New York and other American cities, and pointed the way "to a brighter and more progressive day in Yiddish theatre culture."

The promise within Inge's plan to enlarge the audience for progressive Yiddish theatre also can be read between the lines of a January 12, 1937, memo from Cyrilla Linder, a regional research supervisor of the National Service Bureau. The memo informed Bureau director Francis Bosworth that more English translations of Yiddish plays were needed in Los Angeles: "Such plays might perhaps attract an audience of increased size through the interest of the younger element of Yiddish speaking people in this community which now numbers approximately 100,000."[15] According to Dale Wasserman, who worked for the Los Angeles Yiddish Group, a unit of the Federal Theatre Project under the direction of Adolf Freeman, when the company "did manage to attract younger audiences, it was usually by staging Yiddish plays in English. The company would present the same piece in English and then in Yiddish on alternate evenings. When the English version was played, the audiences became correspondingly younger."[16] Plays produced by the Los Angeles company included *Professor Mamlock, It Can't Happen Here, The Treasure,* and *Awake and Sing.*

In New York, where Inge and his staff had their offices, the Yiddish Unit of the Federal Theatre also produced a number of remarkable new

Yiddish plays, which are discussed here in detail. The Translations Department director's progressive plans were slowly taking effect before Congress denied funds to all programs within the Federal Theatre Project in 1939. Benson Inge's correspondence, and the manuscripts of plays he collected, stand as a record of messianic efforts to transform Yiddish American theatre through translation and new play production.

Contact between the progressive artists from Artef and the Federal Theatre Project's Yiddish Unit continued after the Federal Theatre Project ended. As Nahshon notes, Lem Ward directed writer Chaver Paver's play, *Clinton Street,* for Artef after he "met Chaver Paver at the Federal Theatre, where he directed the latter's Yiddish version of Odets' *Awake and Sing.*" Then "Artef took over" their plan to stage Paver's own play when the Federal Theatre "closed down before these plans materialized."[17]

Moishe Nadir was another one of the Artef artists who collaborated in New York with the Yiddish Unit of the Federal Theatre. *We Live and Laugh* included a poem and two sketches by him. Artef choreographer Lillian Shapiro and composer Maurice Rauch worked on the revue too. Artef was still performing and rehearsing its own large cast plays during this period, but some of its actors, including Harry Bender, Luba Eisenberg, Sol Eisikoff, Joseph Shrogin, and Lydia Slava, appeared in the vaudeville revue. Roles given to these actors in the 1936 revue were not necessarily large ones. Harry Bender played half of the horse in "The Wonder Horse," a townsperson in "Village Wedding," and one of the Jews in the "Underworld" minyan, for example. He had a more prominent role as Dr. Greenhill in the Yiddish production of *It Can't Happen Here.* Historian David Lifson reports that "during the last few years of the 1930's, many Artef actors obtained steady jobs with the Federal Theatre Project. These actors were not permitted to work for both the government and for Artef."[18] "This broke up the ensemble," Jacob Mestel's wife told Lifson.[19]

At a time when jobs were scarce and unemployment was rampant, the prospect of a steady job on the government's payroll may have lured some Yiddish actors—including those at Artef—away from less reliable job prospects in their own company; but they also may have seen the opening of the Yiddish Unit of the Federal Theatre Project as a chance to enlarge their base of support, and reach more of the American public through progressive plays and new translations, which was Benson Inge's vision. Inge clearly knew Artef's repertoire, shared its commitment to leftist theatre, and endeavored to continue something like its work through the Federal Theatre Project.

Hallie Flanagan's vision of theatre also influenced Artef, or attracted its interest, insofar as Artef adapted and staged her play, *Drought*, in 1931, several years before she was hired to direct the Federal Theatre. Flanagan was not pleased with changes in her script made by Artef director Benno Schneider, but this did not deter her from supporting Yiddish theatre and Inge's Artef-influenced vision.[20]

To Chelm and Back

In its four-year life, the Federal Theatre Project never had time to develop a new ensemble of Yiddish actors as cohesive as the one Artef trained during the twenties and thirties. But some Artef actors might have been attracted by the promise of the ensemble recruited for *We Live and Laugh*. A plan for the vaudeville revue was announced early in the Federal Theatre Project's formation, in a November 1935 bulletin titled "Federal Theatre," published by the New York office of the program:

> More than 50 of the 75 persons needed for the Yiddish Vaudeville theatre have been employed, Zvee Schooler, assisted by Judah Bleich and Wolf Barzell, directing. First on the production schedule is "Chelm," a musical playlet by Mani Leib, score by George Touller. Next is "Miners," a mass recitation by Morris Rosenfeld and David Edelstad. Other material will be drawn from the works of David Pinsky, Isaac Goldstone and Sholom Aleichem.[21]

The same bulletin announced other Federal Theatre Yiddish projects, including a staging by the famous Boris Thomashefsky of Osip Dimov's *The Eternal Wanderer,* and Philip Gross's direction of Peretz Hirschbein's *The Idle Inn.* These two plays were the kind that would later lead Benson Inge to protest against ancient "museum pieces," and he probably had these two particular productions in mind when he used the phrase. But *We Live and Laugh* was a different matter. Its innovative plan took hold, and the revue opened to acclaim six months after the "Yiddish Vaudeville" project was announced.

Most of the original text of *We Live and Laugh,* along with programs listing the cast, and production photographs, have been preserved in the

National Archives. The subjects of the 1936 revue's ten scenes vary considerably. Their titles reveal at least some of their content: "Village Wedding," "Cantor's Audition," "Seamstresses," "Underworld," "Prisoner 1936," "The Wonder Horse," "Miners," "Provincial Theatre," "Six Brothers," and "America, America."[22] Some scenes depict Old World traditions, and some show decidedly new American situations encountered by Yiddish speakers.

The Old World of Eastern Europe is vividly recalled through narration in "The Village Wedding." With few individual characters given lines of dialogue, this scenario for pantomime and dance describes *shtetl* life before, during, and after a wedding. We hear, for example, these lines:

> *A girl lies in bed . . . [and wonders]*
> *Everyone has a wedding.*
> *When will I?*
> *How will he look?*
> *From where will he come?*
> *Perhaps he won't come?*
> *Years go by . . .*
> *A student strolls with a girl.*

Description of a wedding follows, complete with wedding jester, betrothed couple, and relatives.

The Old World and its legends are reconceived more imaginatively by poet Mani Leib in his verse play, "The Wonder Horse," which the Federal Theatre Project's in-house bulletin of 1935 originally described as "a musical playlet" titled "Chelm." The title may have changed, but the play still refers to Chelm, the Polish town toward which a poor farmer sets off with his horse. One photograph of the playlet shows the horse formed by two actors in a horse suit, an amusing, nonrealistic representation that would have added some visual humor to the action. The poor man hopes to secure riches in Chelm, a locale usually regarded in Yiddish folktales as a city of fools. Hungry and tired, man and horse fall asleep by the roadside. They wake when another Jew points out three gold coins on the ground, near the horse's tail. As soon as the rich men of Chelm hear about this miracle, they bid for the horse, buy it from the poor traveler (now rich), and await the dropping of more gold from under the horse's tail as the scene ends. The outcome of Leib's scatological satire of greed is not hard to predict: horse manure, not gold, will

Figure 4.3

"The Wonder Horse" with Litvak (Isidore Meltzer) on the horse (Jack Gold-man and Harry Bender) and unidentified actor in *We Live and Laugh,* New York, 1936. *Courtesy of the National Archives.*

fall into the hands of the men from Chelm, who live up to their folkloric reputation as fools. The brief but timely parable brings Chelm's history of folly up to date. During the Great Depression, money turns into excrement everywhere. Dreams of riches transform Yiddish Americans into fools too and amuse the theatregoing public.

Although originally announced as a musical, the Leib script does not indicate whether any of the verses were sung, and the printed program names no composer for the scene. If it had songs, the mini-musical could have been titled "Geltdiggers [Money Diggers] of 1936."

In the short sketch titled "Underworld," American gangsters who speak a mixture of Yiddish and American mobster slang kidnap a man. The victim protests he is just a poor Jew—which is precisely why the gangsters need him, as it turns out. They want a tenth man for their prayer minyan. Crime is not incompatible with religious observance; it just introduces new, more compelling methods of making a minyan.

Meyer Lansky and Bugsy Siegel elsewhere would prove Jews can be as thuggish and criminal as any American. Here the comedy simply suggests that good Jews need not forget to pray, just because they are gangsters. The portrait is not flattering to Jews, as it implies that they may not be assimilated, they may not have abandoned their religion, but they are still capable of crimes like kidnapping. (Nadir's sketch in the revue's first edition also portrays a Jewish criminal, as described later.)

The revue provided several graphic scenes of exploited labor. In "Seamstresses," based on writing by the great Yiddish author Peretz, a chorus of women laments endless sewing, which becomes especially trying when they have to complete a wedding dress on a tight deadline. The words and imagery suggest they sit still and sew forever, with little rest and increasing weariness, while others outside have time to celebrate a wedding.

A comic encounter between Old World practices and new ones surfaces in "Cantor's Audition," which the program credits to Sholem Secunda, the composer best known for the popular Yiddish song, "Bei Mir Bist Du Shon." A variation of this sketch with humorous musical numbers by Secunda had been performed in the 1931 short comic film, *Cantor on Trial*, directed by Sidney Goldin and featuring Cantor Leibale Waldman. The dialogue for the film was written by Isidor Lillian, who received no credit as author in the playbill for *We Live and Laugh*. There are differences in dialogue, but the overall scenario and some lines in the film were revived for *We Live and Laugh*. (Since Secunda was involved in both projects, he may have secured the proper permissions, or perhaps he wrote enough of each script to feel he could take sole credit for the stage version.)

The sketch opens with members of a synagogue and their president playing cards, when they are informed that a large number of cantors wait outside, ready to audition for the position of synagogue cantor. The audition committee halts its card game, after arguing whether a candidate with Galitzianer or Litvak background would be preferable. (The rivalry between groups from these two Eastern European regions was still alive and amusing to many Yiddish immigrants at the time.)

The first auditioner tells a long joke about horses (one a Litvak, one a Galitzianer, one a Romanian) and mares, then sings a rather old-fashioned song in Hebrew with many "oy veys" and other Old World sounds. This old-style cantor, and the second candidate, who comes from Vienna, are rejected in favor of a "modern," handsome, assimilated countryman who says he will accept the job only if his singing can be postponed on days when he has to play an important ballgame. This winning candidate sings a religious hymn fused with strains of modern American music, including refrains of "tup, tup, turu." (In the earlier film version of the sketch, Cantor Leibale Waldman sings a very funny Yiddish jazz variation on "Yes Sir, She's My Baby," and members of the audition committee stand up and dance to the tune. Waldman portrays all three of the cantors who audition in the film. The stage version might have ended with a similar comic showstopper, but stage directions leave out details the film provides.)

Throughout this sketch and a few of the others in the program, characters speak a mix of Yiddish and English, which attests to their acculturation and their willingness to give up Eastern European practices. In one of Moishe Nadir's revue sketches (discussed next) and this one by Secunda, the musical humor and the multilingual dialogue underscore the comedy of identity transformation among Jews, as Old World language and behavior give way to some American fashions. When one of the audition committee members remarks that the old-fashioned candidate and his looks won't "sell tickets" to the ladies of the congregation, and the handsome man is hired, the act anticipates part of the future of American Judaism, where religious services have been altered to appeal to youth and an assimilated generation.

Nadir's "Prisoner 1936"

Moishe Nadir provides a mordant perspective on American murder and justice in his sketch, "Prisoner 1936." A judge bored by the usual cases welcomes diversion in a New York courtroom where he and his clerk, Mike, speak both Yiddish and English. When Mike calls in "Prisoner 1936," the judge responds, "Sounds like a winning number. [*To clerk*] Play the last three digits for me and let me know the results tomorrow."

The judge perks up when he hears the case of Prisoner 1936. The accused cannot speak, the judge is told; but the mute man can play music. His Honor sees a chance for amusement in the courtroom and reminds Mike, "You once told me you wanted to be an actor and you know all the songs in the world. Here's my plan: I'll tell you what to ask the prisoner. Ask him. He will then answer on the fiddle, and you interpret what he played for me." The prisoner accused of murder offers his

Figure 4.4

Moishe Nadir's "Prisoner 1936" with Judge (Sam Lowenwirth), his clerk (Israel Mandell), and prisoner (Morrie Siegel). Yiddish Unit of the Federal Theatre Project, New York, 1936. *Courtesy of the National Archives.*

story musically, with a medley of songs played on a fiddle in response to the interrogation. (In a photograph of the 1936 production, the instrument held by the prisoner looks more like a mandolin than a fiddle; perhaps the judge knows the law, but he has much to learn about music.)

Asked his name, the prisoner plays "Yosl." Asked the city of his origin, he plays the popular, sentimental lyric, "Belz, Mayn Shtetle Belz." The judge comments, "It seems everybody in the United States comes from mayn shtetle Belz." The musical jokes draw on popular Yiddish and English songs. Told the defendant met a young lady, the judge asks him:

JUDGE: What was her name?
CLERK (*in Yiddish*): Ir nomen?
PRISONER (*on fiddle*): Dina.

The clerk prepares to interpret this song title, but the judge already knows it:

JUDGE: Dina, I know. Then what happened.
CLERK (*in Yiddish*): Vos hot pasirt?
PRISONER (*plays song*): Meydl, meydl, meydl, Ikh hab dir azoy lib
   . . .
CLERK: Vell, he made love to Dina.

The clerk skips over the repetitive references ("Girl, girl, girl") in the Yiddish song lyric, and offers a racier English summary of the love affair. The movement back and forth between Yiddish and colloquial English adds humor to the scene, with amusing curtness in the translation. The prisoner plays "Here Comes the Bride" to explain that he married Dina, and the clerk informs the judge, "She hooked him." (Nadir's choice of American slang comes through in transliterated Yiddish.) When the accused performs a Chopin funeral march to admit he killed his wife's lover, the clerk interprets this wordless music by saying, "Your honor, he took him for a ride," meaning he killed him. Although the killing is never admitted verbally, as the interrogation proceeds from one tune to another, back and forth between Old World and New World music and words, it becomes clear that the accused bludgeoned his wife's lover with a blackjack. Grim as the crime may be, it is difficult not to laugh at some of the courtroom proceedings, and that may be just the reaction Nadir seeks from his audience.

Once the musical confession is complete, the judge orders his prisoner to stand. Here and elsewhere in the sketch, Nadir employs the vaudevillian form in which a straight man (the clerk) feeds the comic (the judge) a line suitable for humorous repartee:

JUDGE: Well, the artist is guilty. I must find him guilty.
CLERK: But your honor, it's his first offense.
JUDGE: Why didn't you say so earlier? Tell him to rise. . . . Prisoner
    1936. The law doesn't know whether you are [the musician]
    Misha Elman, a Rubinov, or a Rumshinsky. On your fiddle
    you have given us to understand that you killed a person. But
    that is no evidence you acted with intent to kill. . . . Jealousy
    can drive a person to murder in a minute. In America it is called
    a brainstorm. But in Belz it's called *meshugas*—craziness.

The judge then pardons the accused on the grounds that the jealousy that drove him to murder was "meshugas," and "the court takes into consideration that you are mute and unable to speak." He is set free with the provision that he "should never kill again. . . . Because here in the United States you could still get into trouble if you love like that." The immigrant's past life in Eastern Europe and his muteness become extenuating circumstances. Dispensation of justice here verges on farce, which may be Moishe Nadir's point. But the scene is more than a farce, and that is why Nadir does not end it with the acquittal.

The judge instructs his clerk to ask the exonerated man if he understands the verdict. Asked this question in Yiddish, the prisoner shakes his head "yes," smiles, moves toward the exit, stops, holds up his hand, and says in Yiddish: "God and his judgment are just." In other words, he was a fraud, and won acquittal from murder charges by feigning muteness. The curtain falls on a scene of justice undone, at the same time God and his judgment are praised. Neither justice nor God's judgment is what they should be, or what they seem to be on first hearing in this 1936 scene. The world may have amusing songs and gifted artists, but that does not prevent murder or fraud, and may even abet them. Although the artist is acquitted, neither he nor the judge is exonerated by Nadir.

Early in the sketch, when the judge hears his clerk Mike singing, he asks whether the man is turning the court into a cabaret. That sums up much of the sketch, as Nadir's vision of American justice under God (years before the phrase "under God" was added to the Pledge of Allegiance) offers bitter humor and mockery of the judicial process, which becomes a source of entertainment, with antics more suitable for a vaudeville revue than a court of law. The situation has only worsened since Nadir wrote the sketch, as mass media devise infotainment from reports on wars, murders, and other violent acts. Some murder suspects now receive celebrity billing during and after their trials, which may become the subject of special films or television broadcasts. Nadir's satiric response to crass American spectacle takes different form in *Messiah in America,* where entertainment entrepreneurs deceive the public by presenting false messiahs. No representatives of divine judgment, but rather worldly New York justice, subject to the whims of a bored magistrate, becomes a diversion in "Prisoner 1936."

After Nadir's sketch, a more plaintive critique of America concluded the first half of the 1936 revue. A large group of actors performed Alfred Kreymborg's "mass recital," *America, America!* The choral poem, printed in English in 1934 in *How Do You Do Sir? and Other Short Plays,* asks where the prosperity of America has gone. The verse drama, spoken by workers, derelicts, and two rich kids named Jack and Jill, opens with an orator addressing a crowd in Manhattan's Union Square:

> *What have you done with all your gold,*
> *America, America?*
> *What have you bought and calmly sold*
> *Of human flesh and misery?*
> *What has it cost the growing poor*
> *To earn their cornered liberty?*

The rhymed lines describe hardship, daily struggle, and breadlines experienced by those whose "home has become a jail / where the wolves of poverty / wall them in and lose the key." The text then introduces Jack and Jill, who have "nothing in the world to worry about" because "Daddy's got a bank and the bank will pay." The final, third section describes the impoverished home life of Jim and Jane. Jane counsels her unemployed husband: "Be patient, Honey, don't get the blues— / Hundreds an' thousands are in our shoes." And he angrily replies: "Who owns the earth an' what have we got? / What right have they to make us rot?" These simple rhymes lack the wit of Nadir's writing, as well as the Jewish cultural orientation of his texts. Kreymborg's imagery is more generic, less culturally specific than that of other scenes in the revue, but his choral poem shares the discontent expressed throughout *We Live and Laugh.*

The Federal Theatre Project cast list for the Yiddish performance of Kreymborg's poem names the actors who portrayed the orator, Jack, Jill, Jane, and Jim and lists twenty-four other Yiddish actors who portrayed "The People." This sizable group of stage artists was given directions to recite the choral refrain, "America, America," "in growing unison, and from the loudest to the lowest pitch." In the closing lines of their recital, after repeating questions about hunger and poverty, the final pronunciation of "America" was to be "sounded in a threatening tone by the orator and crowd in a long and pregnant pianissimo." The very name of the country resonated with the discontent of "The People" as the first act of the revue ended.

After intermission, the audience would hear another chorus in "Coal Miners." This group of speakers discounts the dignity and worth of miners. Representing the mine owner's point of view, the chorus doesn't care about the workers' lives, and suggests the miners might as well be shot or hanged if they are rebellious, because they are practically dead already from their labors.

Different threats to life are portrayed more humorously in the 1936 revue's last two sketches, which pay tribute to artists; one concerns provincial theatre actors, the other, six brothers in a musical band. Both sketches show artists as survivors. The brothers with different instruments sing about hardship, about declining numbers in their band, and then fall to the ground, faint or near death, one by one; at the end they ask people in the tenements for whom they perform to give a little money and keep their street band alive.

The scene with the provincial theatre troupe centers on a deathbed visit by a doctor, nurses, the dying man's daughters, and other relatives; but the prompter (a character in the play) dominates the scene, as he tells everyone what to say, whether or not they like his instructions or can hear him. Finally the actor on the deathbed rebels, informs the audience he can memorize his own lines, and pushes the prompter offstage. His brief declaration of independence ("Dear audience, I can memorize my role. I've studied my role for six weeks") sums up a spirit of perseverance shown in both sketches, where the Yiddish actors and musicians dramatize their own artistic commitment to overcome obstacles and go on performing, which is ultimately one purpose of the revue.

While some of We Live and Laugh's sketches humorously portray difficult living conditions, most of them celebrate Yiddish-speaking Jews who want to work. The fact that the Federal Theatre Project provided employment for Jewish and Yiddish-speaking artists during the Depression becomes a subtext for scenes that show Jews accepting jobs as seamstresses, minyan-maker, modern cantor, and courtroom musician in the United States. The characters, like the actors performing the scenes, work during the Great Depression, thanks to the producing organization—the United States of America—which brings them on stage every night. To paraphrase Nadir's judge, the producer has taken into consideration that these Yiddish actors need to work, and given the extenuating circumstances, he created a Yiddish theatre for them. Their jobs are to portray characters with jobs, jobs they dislike, jobs that bore them, new jobs. Even the poor farmer who owns the Wonder Horse leaves his farm, and becomes a salesman.

When the *New York Times* reviewer praised the show in 1936, he wrote that "a large company, which naturally does not include very many well-known names, gave a spirited account of itself, to the delight of a capacity audience."[23] He neglected to explain why the company "naturally" did not include many well-known names. The answer lay in the fact that the revue was neither a commercial venture nor a star vehicle, as were some of the era's most popular Yiddish productions, when they featured members of the Adler family or Menasha Skulnik or Molly Picon. The Federal Theatre Project's Yiddish theatre program hired those in need of relief work, not stars, and created unglamorous productions, often concerned with unemployed or exploited individuals. The names of the actors were not well known, for the most part, and they were not given special billing; but through their collaboration with a variety of writers and directors, in a setting removed from box office pressures, their revue implemented Benson Inge's proposal to create Yiddish theatre "of a more progressive, purposeful and literary standard."

We Live and Laugh Again in 1937

Some of the Yiddish Unit's most adventurous topical satire appeared in the second, 1937 edition of *We Live and Laugh,* translated into English for the Federal Theatre Project by Julius Schmerler and Isidore Edelman. Like the first edition, the 1937 script remains unpublished, and is filed away in archives. Neglect of the material after its premiere seems to have been anticipated by one comic scene in the revue, a mock symposium that asks panelists how the Yiddish theatre can survive. The creators of the revue knew at the time that their theatre was imperiled, and joked about its doubtful future in the sketch titled "Stars." Other revue numbers found perils elsewhere: in a local barber shop, local newspapers, fascism, and war.

The only writer who contributed to both editions of the revue was Moishe Nadir. His sketch about cigar store statues had been published in 1932, and his pro-labor, anti-war poem in the program was previously performed at Artef's studio during the 1932–33 season; but in 1937, his verse protesting militarism and empire was by no means out of date. In "Troops on the March," Nadir describes preparations for war, troop movements, and casualties. He calls for a change in battle plan, for soldiers to become revolutionaries and to join with their comrades: the unemployed, workers on strike, and peasants. Although not specifically concerned with Jewish or Yiddish culture here, Nadir includes some anti-religious lines, which begin as follows:

> *Wherefore?*
> *What for?*
> *Whom for?*
> *For Caesar's glory.*
> *For God's glory.*
> *For glory glory hallelujah.*
> *Knows the priest that the old God is himself a butcher*
> *Who his own son did murder,*
> *And that murdered son*
> *Had with his blood redeemed us*
> *So we could on and on our life blood shed.*
>
> *I against myself.*
> *You against yourself.*
> *Friend against friend.*
> *Brother pierces brother.*
> *Worker against worker . . .*[24]

The contention that modern violence and militarism are abetted by Christ and his butcher father would not have endeared Nadir to some Christians. However, progressive Yiddish spectators may not have been scandalized, but cheered by his call for revolution.

Nadir's poem and other sections of the 1937 *We Live and Laugh* revue were far from neutral in their social and cultural criticism. The best sketches opposed one controversial stance against another in topical satire.

"In a Barber Shop" features two Yiddish-speaking barbers who violently debate about Jewish homelands. While one of the two shaves a customer, he praises the Soviet region of Biro-Birjan (sic) as a refuge for Jews. The other barber prefers Palestine. A Yiddish variation on an old circus clown routine titled "The Barber," the act places customers in peril. As the tonsorial artists become more excited, the partially shaven faces of their customers become more endangered.

WELVIL: Do you still maintain that Biro-Birjan is better than Palestine?

MENDIL: I wouldn't even compare the two countries . . .

WELVIL: What do you say to the terrific cold in Biro-Birjan?

MENDIL: And what about the unbearable heat in your Palestine? . . . See for yourself how big and rich Biro-Birjan is. Let me show you! Here is the Amur, full of fish of various kinds, also Schmalz-herring and Caviar. (*Points to place on customer's face.*) How do you like this little rivulet? (*Slashes the customer.*)

SECOND CUSTOMER: For God's sake! You are making chopped meat out of my face. Take that razor away.

MENDIL (*to customer*): Ha! Another reactionary? You don't like Biro-Birjan?

SECOND CUSTOMER: Who says I don't like it? I am in favor of whatever you like; but why is my face to blame . . .

The second customer knows enough not to argue politics with the man shaving him. Before the discussion is over, however, he and another customer suffer razor cuts, and run from the shop. The last words, shouted by men with bleeding, lather-covered faces, are "Help! Biro-Birjan. Help! Palestine." Instead of providing Jews with security, the prospective homelands incite violent conflict in the barber shop. The violence here might not look so funny on stage, unless highly stylized and removed from realistic effects. The sketch is a fantasy, after all, as were many plans for a peaceful Jewish homeland. At the same time, the writing addresses issues that were current and controversial in 1937, particularly since the Soviets had declared Birobidzhan an autonomous Jewish region in 1934 and Yiddish American Communists campaigned to support its settlement by Jews.

"Ladies' Auxiliary" by Max Hirsch portrays a group of Jewish house-wives who want to raise money for Jews living in Europe and for a cemetery—an unnerving combination. Professing large humanitarian goals, the women gossip among themselves about personal matters, particularly a new member's "diamond ring" bought in Woolworth's. The auxiliary club members want to avoid errors made by men, and resolve to "show the men that we are not only their equals, but even their superiors in every field of endeavor. To the Fascists, who are trying to put us back into the kitchen, we say . . . we, the women of today are not afraid of anything." One woman's husband then places a rubber mouse on the floor, and those assembled shout and flee in a gratuitous conclusion to the scene. The author comes close to putting the women back in the kitchen, as his closing joke sends the auxiliary into retreat. Comic possibilities that the women raise through their resolve to resist fascism, and follow the example of the Spanish People's Front in their own lives, remain largely unexplored in the scene's superficial, sexist ending.

"A Bit of Radio," by Isaac Gladstone, anticipates mass media's current tendency to overload programs with commercials. Songs and other diversions interrupt radio program advertisements for a funeral home, an orphanage, and kosher sausage; the parodies of commercials, especially their endorsement of a funeral home and an orphanage, cast a pall over the entertainment.

In "The Wooden Couple," a surreal sketch by Moishe Nadir, a Native American woman carved in wood, and a wooden statue of a spear carrier converse at night outside a cigar store. (The spear carrier might be Moses, or at least an Egyptian, given his recollection of palm trees and caravans. The original Yiddish text for this play, printed in 1932 as part of Nadir's collected plays, indicates the spear holder is a Turk, and also says the sketch features Turkish and Indian music and dance; none of this is explicitly stated in the Federal Theatre script.) In any case, the wooden characters know they are different from many other Americans.

HE: We are foreigners in a strange country and don't understand the customs.

SHE: I am not a foreigner. My ancestors were here first, but the Whites robbed them of their land.

United by their disaffection for urban American life, the couple undresses and prepares to dance in the moonlight. The arrival of a man who tries to light a match on one statue disrupts their passionate meeting. The wooden, carved characters laugh, and their human visitor flees. Native American and ancient Jew or Turk, or wooden facsimiles of them, stand together as odd, comic representatives of displaced peoples in America.

The cigar store scene offers a gentle, almost pastoral reflection on vanishing cultures. A few other comic sketches in the revue bring a greater sense of urgency to their topics; quite timely in 1937, the acts remain exemplary models of Yiddish satire from the period. The once-topical references now function more as historical documentation of an earlier time; but the self-serving and opportunistic positions taken by Yiddish-speaking Americans, and mocked in these scenes, still come across as self-serving and opportunistic.

In "News Dealer," the title character praises three different Yiddish newspapers: one Communist (the *Frayhayt*), one Socialist (the *Forward*), and one "intellectual" tabloid (the *Day*). Each time a customer arrives, Bennie the news dealer praises that customer's choice, and denigrates the other papers. A consummate salesman, he follows to an extreme the sales rule that the customer is always right—and assumes that the customer's newspaper is always right, at least until it is purchased.

Discussing the different papers with his customers, the news dealer delivers some biting assessments of the era's Yiddish dailies. One need not have read the papers in 1937 to sense how Bennie plays them against one another, tarnishing the reputation of each paper in turn. Asked if he has the Communist paper, the *Frayhayt*, Bennie responds as follows:

> BENNIE: If I have a Freiheit? Some question! You are a comrade, a communist, right? Well—don't your recognize me? Don't you see me on the picket lines? On the May Day demonstrations? If I have a Freiheit? And if not for the Freiheit would I be standing here to see these yellow rags, a curse upon them? It is for the sake of the Freiheit that I am here. And when someone comes to buy a yellow rag, I begin my agitation against this rotten yellow press, a curse upon it. But, comrade, we won't suffer long. The whole rotten capitalist world will crumble. Arise, ye pris . . .
> FREIHEIT READER: Goodbye!!!
> BENNIE: Goodbye. See you on the picket line.

Bennie may drive his customer away; the stage directions don't indicate why the reader leaves. The seller certainly goes too far in assessing the profile of readers, as he offers clichés and stereotypes about them; but his enthusiasm is strong. He praises a paper as if there could be no other choice, no doubt; and the temporary, improvised quality of his fervor makes the speech humorous. Here you have a man on whom you cannot rely, as Brecht once said about himself. But the news business thrives on constant change and novelty, and Bennie can change as fast as the daily news, or faster—three times with three customers. Presumably the readers are less inconstant than the news dealer. Asked if he has the *Forward*, Bennie replies,

> If I have a *Forward*? Some question. I, my friend, am a comrade from the very first days I came into this country of Columbus. And I read the *Forward* as regularly as a pious Jew says his morning prayers. What then shall one of ours, a progressive, read? The red communist sheet? Or the so-called Intellectual *Day* that feverishly zigzags from right to left? . . . [T]ake the news section [of the *Forward*]! Here is a piece of news on the last page: "Child born of strange mother." Small chance those red trouble makers will feature a news item that way. Then take our writers, Shalom Asch, Singer, or even Tunkeler, that rascal. These writers of ours have style. The language is simple, plain as plain can be. Yes sir! *The Forward* is the only newspaper of value.

A news dealer more versatile than the zigzagging *Day*, Bennie maneuvers across the whole spectrum of Yiddish politics and culture. It is tempting to call him a consummate actor; but then he meets a professional actor, and it turns out Bennie is no match for a man of the theatre. The stage actor asks to see three different Yiddish papers, and catches the news dealer off guard. Bennie can't understand such openness to diverse viewpoints on the part of a customer. This customer's allegiance is not so different from that of the news seller's—based on business principles rather than political or editorial views. The customer looks at all three papers, then declines to buy them, and explains, "I am a Jewish actor. I only buy Jewish newspapers when they contain my picture. Good-bye!"

"Whither Jewish Theatre?"
A Symposium

The self-serving behavior of actors resurfaces later in the revue, in an outstanding sketch titled "Stars." Written by Federal Theatre Project actor Jacob Bergreen, the playlet takes the form of a symposium on the Yiddish theatre. It features impersonators of four famous Yiddish actors, none of whom participated in the Federal Theatre Project (unless this representation of them by other actors counts as an appearance).

The forty-year old bespectacled chairman of the panel begins by announcing the following:

> My esteemed audience, Ladies and Gentlemen! We of the Society of the Sorely Perplexed have arranged a symposium on the Jewish Theatre, with celebrated stars participating. The Stars are late as usual, but they will come straight from their respective theatres. You will recognize them all. They will discuss the vital question: Whither Jewish Theatre? (*Looks at his watch*) We, the Perplexed were never in such desperate straits as at present.

The panel features four famous Yiddish stage performers, or rather, parodies of them: Maurice Schwartz, Aaron Lebedev, Menasha Skulnik, and Jennie Goldstein. Given pseudonyms in the sketch, possibly to avoid lawsuits, all four actors were still alive and known to Yiddish theatre audiences in 1937.

The four all exhibit high self-esteem (or simply egotism) during the sketch. Other sources suggest the portraiture was accurate. In his history of Yiddish theatre, David Lifson observed that Maurice Schwartz "considered himself a greater actor than [David] Kessler, [Jacob] Adler, and [Boris] Thomashefsky all rolled into one."[25] Actress Celia Adler said Schwartz "was far from being the great actor he considered himself."[26] Tenacious in his struggle to keep the Yiddish Art Theatre alive, Maurice Schwartz performed with his own company for decades, and outlived the parody of him created in the 1937 revue. Menasha Skulnik, whose impersonator prides himself on his reputation as a king of comedy, also survived the jibes of 1937 quite well, and went on to greater recognition in English-language radio and television.

While the famous Yiddish actors could withstand these parodies of them, their roles in theatre history require at least some small reconsideration, in response to the critique in the Federal Theatre Project's sketch. Famous they were. Audiences supported them on Second Avenue for years, and many theatregoers regarded them as "stars." Their fame was not much of a foundation for the future of Yiddish theatre, however, and the satire holds that against them. Asked to define or predict their art's future, the best they can do is cite their own achievements, their own standing. Instead of supporting a future generation of artists, and in that sense taking a step forward, instead of sharing their limelight with new Yiddish theatre artists, the stars simply take a bow.

The character parodying Schwartz sums up the star system's hold on progress in his self-serving speech:

> What have I not done? I have made productions, I have drama-tized novels, I have composed skits and songs. I have even dra-matized articles, but now vulgarity has crept into my theatre—soon they'll make a burlesque out of it, all in the name of Art. What I, however, really would like to find out, is why we have in the Jewish theatres more stars than in the sky. Everyone aspires to stardom. My actors demand star's wages. Every youngster is a star and a potential rival. Even President Roosevelt has become my competitor by donating several theatres to Art. In conclusion let me tell you that everything would be perfect if actors would only refrain from demanding wages. No wages and no stars. One star must remain—I, Boris Weis.

His humorous complaints are accurate. Roosevelt created rivals for the star system by supporting the Federal Theatre Project's Yiddish Unit, which made a burlesque out of Schwartz's star profile. At the same time that the star system, more than any other theatrical component, kept commercial Yiddish theatre in business for years, it also limited Yiddish theatre's future. As a rule, Yiddish-speaking audiences turned out to see famous actors, not unknown new plays or new actors, political plays, or ensembles. The Federal Theatre Project's Yiddish Unit, Modicut, and Artef's mobile theatre unit proved to be exceptions to the rule.

Fanny, the one actress on the panel, responds to Weis that "the Jew-ish public demands a female star." She doesn't dispute that one star in particular or another one is needed. Later her character, based on the Yiddish performer Jennie Goldstein, recalls the sentimental, melodra-matic tendencies of her past, and tells the audience she will return to show business and make them "feel at home again like years ago. You'll be once more at liberty to faint and cry to your heart's content." The future she promises Yiddish theatre is a return to the melodramatic acting and comforts of its past.

The character based on musical comedian Aaron Lebedev exhibits a similarly unadventurous attitude toward the future. He informs the panel chairman and audience, "You must give the people what they like. Offer them light musical comedies and lively, catchy songs like: 'I Like

She.' Heavy literature should be ruled out." In other words, he advocates continuation of the past's popular Yiddish entertainments, the *shund* and musicals in which he thrived, the antithesis of the Federal Theatre Project's best offerings. With this character, once more the answer to the question, "Whither Yiddish Theatre?" is "Back to the Past." ("Step back," these actors more or less advise newcomers.) Light musicals remained popular in 1937, and it is no accident that the opening stage directions for the sketch request that "while the curtain rises, the music plays various Jewish musical hits." The "musical hits" of Yiddish theatre were undeniably among its greatest attractions, along with plays featuring comedians like Menasha Skulnik.

When he arrived on stage, Skulnik used to ask the audience (in Yiddish): "Do you recognize me?" Not taking any chances, he would answer, "It's me, Mensha Skulnik." In "Stars," the Skulnik impersonator follows the original's example, and enters asking: "And do you recognize me? I am Shlemiel Gutkin." Almost the same as the original, except that the actor's name changes in this parody. In a memoir, the composer Sholem Secunda recalls that his collaborator "Skulnik was satisfied as long as he had his own place on stage, his funny little hat on top of his head—his badge of distinction—his own little hesitant walk, and his own brand of speech and humor, that was enough for the audience to be convulsed with peals of laughter."[27] "His own" is the operative phrase. Whether or not Skulnik was quite as self-centered as the "great comedian" named Shlemiel in the revue, he was a star attraction, and in the sketch he lets the audience know it.

Gutkin's perception that Jewish audiences want him to "render my songs my own comic way" contains humor in its self-praise and persuasive analysis. Audiences loved Skulnik's idiosyncratic, nasal style of speech and song. By the time this sketch surfaced in 1937, however, Skulnik's style was no longer inimitable, or so the sketch implies. Each of the four stars parodied here became familiar enough to Yiddish audiences that their essence could be captured and humorously criticized in a short comic sketch.

As if his own self-promotion is not enough to reduce the competition, Shlemiel Gutkin admits he has forgotten the names of the other actors on stage: "I remember only one name—my own—Shlemiel Gutkin." He also has enough memory to boast, "If the jokes are old, at least I deserve credit for remembering them."

Toward the end of the mock panel discussion, an audience member interrupts the proceedings and asks for more political and socially conscious theatre. The representative from the left, to which theatres like the Group Theatre, the Theatre Union, and Artef had given voice in the thirties, proposes an alternative to the theatre of stars. Although no more free of clichés than some earlier statements by the panelists, his words at least introduce another point of view.

> A MAN FROM THE AUDIENCE: Mr. Chairman, I too have something to say.
> CHAIRMAN: Who are you?
> A MAN: I am one of the masses. May I? (*Chairman nods.*) I have listened carefully to the artists, but they haven't told us a thing about the Theatre. All they have done is to praise themselves. Bravo! (*The artists bow.*) This is no place to advertise oneself. Not one of them suggested how to save the Jewish theatre from destruction. What we need is a revolutionary theatre that would portray truthfully the present-day fight for existence. We need plays with a social background.
> ONE OF THE AUDIENCE: Give him a social underground.
> A MAN FROM THE AUDIENCE (*continuing*): Give us anti-war plays, plays against Fascism, pictures of working-class life, strikes, Capitalism in its true form. Forget your smelly jokes, your vulgarity, and you will raise the prestige of the Jewish Theatre!

The play ends with the famous actors asking the only question about the future of Yiddish theatre that matters to them:

> ALL STARS (*go to the ramp, arms outstretched*): Will we make a living? Will we make a living?

Curtain lowers.

The man from the audience speaks on behalf of actors within the 1937 revue, as he asks for theatre to address pressing issues of the day. In retrospect, it might be argued that he was mistaken; revolutionary theatre and the anti-war plays presented by Artef and the Federal Theatre Project did not save Yiddish theatre from its decline, its near burial (the "social underground" of a funeral recommended by another spectator) in later years. The jokes and "vulgarity" of popular theatre featuring stars did not destroy Yiddish theatre, either. Larger social and cultural changes, including the assimilation of Jews in America, and the murder of millions of Yiddish-speakers in Europe, led to that decline, which no theatre could have averted or saved. The man in the audience who wants to "save the Jewish theatre from destruction" reintroduces the messianic impulse earlier observed in the programs of Artef and Goset. The speaker calls for a Messiah, or a group of messianic actors and writers, to save Yiddish theatre, not the world; here too, the Messiah has yet to arrive.[28]

Perhaps Yiddish theatre in America might have advanced further, and offered more new plays and translations in English, if the Federal Theatre had lasted longer. Even before the final denial of funds by Congress in 1939, the Yiddish Unit suffered smaller but significant losses. Due to budget cuts, many of the Yiddish vaudeville ensemble's actors were given pink slips in June 1937, and director Zvee Schooler was fired in July 1937—changes that add particular poignancy to their revue sketch asking whether Yiddish theatre has a future.[29] "Stars" anticipated the unemployment faced by its own creators; the actors who asked, "Will we make a living?" were talking about themselves, not only about the Yiddish theatre celebrities they impersonated.

Government backing for the Federal Theatre Project and for Yiddish theatre advocates like Benson Inge ceased completely after anti-Communism and opposition to New Deal programs in the arts became more pronounced in Congress. However, the Yiddish Unit of the Federal Theatre did not go under without some resistance. In addition to articulating a troubled future for themselves and their profession in "Stars," Yiddish theatre artists also responded with theatrical acts of protest to fascist politics, and with sympathy for union activism in several Federal Theatre Project plays, notably *The Tailor Becomes a Storekeeper* and *It Can't Happen Here*.

5
The Messiah of 1936

It Can't Happen Here *in Yiddish*

> *So much distress in the country, . . . you get that, anytime, anywhere, with millions vaguely feeling things wrong, and thousands with quack economic nostrums [are] ready to fall for the Messiah with most quaver in his voice.*
>
> —Sinclair Lewis[1]

S inclair Lewis created a false messiah named Buzz Windrip in 1934, when he wrote his novel, *It Can't Happen Here.* The United States elects its own equivalent of Hitler in the novel. Once Windrip, the messiah with the most quaver in his voice, becomes president of the United States, he turns the country into a fascist state. An underground resistance movement struggles against his tyranny, but the book ends before democracy has been restored fully. The future of the country under Windrip remains uncertain, as it was without him in the White House, when Lewis first created the book during the Great Depression.

The resistance against Windrip and his tyranny spread from printed book to the stage, and from English to Yiddish audiences, after Hallie Flanagan invited Lewis to adapt the novel for the Federal Theatre Project in 1936. On October 27th of that year, the new play titled *It Can't Happen Here,* co-authored by Sinclair Lewis and John C. Moffitt, opened simultaneously in seventeen American cities where the Federal Theatre Project was running government-funded unemployment relief programs. Eventually the play was performed at twenty-two different theatres, all under Federal Theatre auspices. The productions differed from one another, as the cutting of scenes, the look of the set designs, and composition of the acting companies changed from one city to another. Actors spoke Spanish in the Tampa production. In Seattle, a Negro theatre company joined a Caucasian company to show minority life under a dictatorship. In New York City, one version of the play opened in English and another in Yiddish.[2]

In *Arena,* her memoir about founding and directing the Federal Theatre Project, Flanagan recalls the night Lewis's play opened. She attended Act One of the American-language production at the Adelphi Theatre in New York City, saw the second act of the Yiddish production in the nearby Biltmore Theatre, and then returned to the Adelphi to see Act Three. She preferred the Yiddish production. In her own words: "Amazing to come into a different theatre and see the same play in another language. Here the continental volubility and gesticulation was in contrast to the quiet playing at the Adelphi. The Yiddish production included several scenes, notably the concentration camp scene, omitted at the Adelphi, and on the whole I thought it a better show."[3]

The *New York Times* did not offer quite the same response, but their critic, William Schack, praised Yiddish actor Julius Adler for his "appealing" performance in the lead role as newspaper editor, Doremus Jessup, while another *Times* critic Brooks Atkinson had reservations about Seth Arnold's American-language portrayal of Jessup, which displayed "none of the fire of a superior thinker."[4] Perhaps the "fire" missing from Arnold's performance was part of the "continental volubility and gesticulation" of Yiddish acting that Flanagan had witnessed at the Biltmore; that acting style would have helped deliver the political oratory and melodrama in the script.

In Praise of Melodrama

Before proceeding further, a word should be said in defense of melodrama. A popular form of entertainment that thrived in the nineteenth century, "melodrama" has acquired another meaning, as a pejorative term used to dismiss events regarded as too emotionally wrought and deficient in nuance. Yiddish theatre critic Moishe Olgin employed this sense of the word in his review of *It Can't Happen Here,* which he hoped would lose its melodramatic elements as the actors became more adept in their roles.[5]

Although the play's dialogue includes some sharp social satire, Lewis and Moffitt's melodramatic plot structure, complete with cumulative suspense and heroic escapes, calls for melodramatic acting. This

Figure 5.1

Spain Rodriguez's comic strip illustration for *It Can't Happen Here. Courtesy of* Jewish Currents *and the artist.*

need not be regarded as a failing. Today the appeal of melodrama has never been greater, as Hollywood films and television employ its conventions. Popular films end their suspense-filled sequences with innocent or unwary characters saved from malefactors by a heroic, sensationalistic rescue. Playwright Joan Holden, who wrote many popular political comedies for the San Francisco Mime Troupe, notes in an essay on the genre that "mass media [in America] have no trouble keeping melodrama up to date, inventing heroes and villains for the '80s, the '90s, and the twenty-first century. . . . The mass audience never seen in theatres lines up for *Fatal Attraction* and *Star Wars III*."[6] In recent years, prominent political leaders have not hesitated to describe the world in melodramatic terms; they see foreign nations constituting an "axis of evil," and the United States as a defender of all that is good and virtuous. Such vivid contrasts are essential to melodrama and, it would seem, to recent political campaigns.

Rather than cede the power of melodrama to conservative mass media, Joan Holden argues for a conscious deployment of the form on behalf of leftist perspectives in popular theatre. Sinclair Lewis and John Moffitt anticipated Holden's proposal, when the Federal Theatre Project offered them an opportunity to reach a large number of spectators across the country. (Sinclair Lewis gave the Federal Theatre rights to his best-selling novel, according to a *New York Times* feature, "because it could best distribute widely the idea of 'It Can't Happen Here.'"[7]) The admission price at Federal Theatre Project sites was low, or free of charge, and Hallie Flanagan wanted a more inclusive kind of theatre, which is one reason she sponsored units performing vaudeville, circus, puppetry, dance, Negro, Spanish, and Yiddish theatre. A political melodrama in Yiddish, social satire included, was not at all out of place in her artistic repertoire.

Imagining the future under fascism, Lewis also anticipated today's politics of melodrama, in which fundamentalist and extremist groups allow little room for compromise and debate. Like Windrip's government, alarmists and extremists today divide the world into two camps, those who are loyal and obedient and those who are not. The world might be a better place if this kind of political imagination could be confined to the stage in melodramas and satires, and if such behavior would be openly questioned when it surfaces in government policy. Lewis's play performed a public service by relocating the melodramatic politics of Hitler and Mussolini and their supporters in an art form where the theatrical bent of fascism, complete with parades, highly decorated uniforms (i.e., costumes for national leaders), and melodramatic public addresses, could be performed by actors rather than high government officials.

That Sinclair Lewis's novel reached the stage at all, let alone in Yiddish, seems remarkable, given that the MGM Studios had initially planned to turn the book into a film, then dropped the project for fear of controversy.[8] MGM's rejection of the project might have scared other producers away; but Hallie Flanagan stepped forward and commissioned the stage adaptation, providing Lewis and the American public with a noncommercial alternative to Hollywood. Though it hardly had Hollywood's budget, the Federal Theatre Project (FTP) could afford to open *It Can't Happen Here* simultaneously at twenty-two theatres across the country. By virtue of its government funds and its widespread theatres, the FTP constituted a national theatre. Because it was a relief program, not a commercial business, and did not depend on box office income or investors (other than Congress, through appropriations), the Federal Theatre Project could risk controversy—until Congressmen began to criticize it. That criticism began at its inception in 1935, but did not become an insurmountable obstacle until 1939.

The play was not universally welcomed when it opened. Flanagan wrote this about the initial reception of *It Can't Happen Here*: "Some thought it proved Federal Theatre was communistic; others that it was New Deal; others that it was subconsciously fascist."[9] She neglected in that passage to add that many critics praised the play and the Federal Theatre Project's decision to produce it. Public interest in the production can be measured by the number of people who attended it. Accountable to the government for all expenses and activities, the Federal Theatre Project kept thorough records of its operations, and the records indicate that the Yiddish production of *It Can't Happen Here* at the Biltmore in New York ran for eighty-six performances, attended by a total of 25,160 spectators. This was a smaller run than the play's ninety-five performances in English at the Adelphi Theatre, which 110,518 people attended. But considering that the Lewis play was not a musical or a star vehicle for Yiddish actors, and was not conceived as a play about Jews, it fared extremely well in its Yiddish form, running from October 27, 1936, to May 1, 1937. The closest rival among Yiddish Federal Theatre productions with extended runs in New York was Clifford Odets' *Awake and Sing,* adapted by Chaver Paver, which ran from

December 22, 1938, to April 9, 1939, several years after the Group Theatre first staged the play in English.[10]

Lewis's play at the Biltmore offered the public several features that deserve special attention, because they were absent from the American-language version of the play at the Adelphi. In addition to its different performance style, with its already noted "continental volubility and gesticulation," the Yiddish production presented one scene set in an American concentration camp, the second scene of Act Three, which was not performed in English at the Adelphi.

Translation of Lewis's script into Yiddish, at a time when Jewish Europeans were fleeing Hitler's anti-Semitism, gave its scenes of the anti-fascist resistance movement and escape from the concentration camp additional meaning for audiences at the Biltmore. Although set in America, the scenes spoken in Yiddish reminded spectators that comparable conversations and actions were occurring, or could occur abroad, in regions immigrant Jewish families had left behind. Americans whose parents fled pogroms for freedom in the United States, as well as German-Jewish refugees, could see a variation of their flight reenacted in their language of exile. Audiences from Germany and Eastern Europe also would have been disturbed by Buzz Windrip's anti-Semitism, expressed at one point in a promise to help America's "downtrodden become the equals of any Shakespeare or any money-wallowing international Jewish banker that ever lived" (Act One, Scene Seven).[11]

The Yiddish- and American-language versions of the play had much in common. Both portrayed the struggle against Windrip's fascist police state. His army of thugs called Corpos arrests and brutally murders opponents. Small-town newspaper editor Doremus Jessup personifies the resistance against Windrip, as the editor joins others to secretly circulate anti-fascist pamphlets, for which crime the Corpos lock him in a concentration camp. After a year there, he escapes to Canada to serve the anti-fascist movement known as the New Underground. Like the novel, the play traces the impact of American fascism on Jessup's family and friends. The stage play ends with a scene in which Jessup's widowed daughter, Mary, and her son (Jessup's grandson) David try to cross the border to freedom in Canada.

Jessup fails to recognize the dangers Windrip's police state poses until he learns about a local merchant's murder by Corpos, and faces government censorship of his own publication. At first he dismisses the fears his co-worker Lorinda raises about Windrip's programs. Lorinda,

Figure 5.2
Doremus Jessup (Julius Adler) tells his grandson David (Sidney Lumet) about
a secret underground publication in *It Can't Happen Here,* Biltmore Theatre,
New York, 1936. *Courtesy of the National Archives.*

more politically aware than Jessup, adds a satiric voice to some conversations. When, for example, she and others picnic with an industrialist
who claims that despite the Depression era's rampant unemployment,
"young fellows with any ability can find something to do, same as I did,"
Lorinda dryly replies, "Start washing dishes and get to be a great manufacturer like you!" The industrialist entirely misses her light humor. Her
doubts about the future that America offers its citizens in a time of crisis become more pronounced as events take a turn for the worse.

Lorinda's early warnings about the advent of fascism begin to make
sense to Jessup by the end of the first act; the editor asks her to resign
from their newspaper, because reporting the truth is too dangerous,
after "one hundred members of Congress and six members of the
Supreme Court have been put under protective arrest." Lorinda replies
with lines that echo the play's title: "I can't believe it! Things like that
can't happen in America!" When she also expresses disbelief that the

government would practice "national censorship," Jessup deploys the sort of satiric language Lorinda has used; he tells her that the full story of the coup in Washington has been held up by "protective censorship." These developments, which occur soon after Windrip's inauguration, embolden Jessup to print criticism of the new president's policies, regardless of the punishment he may face.

Enter Crooks, Exit Democracy

The tyranny shown in *It Can't Happen Here* resembles that exercised by fascist leaders in Europe, but the play was written for and about Americans—whether Yiddish or English speakers—who felt they did not have to worry about fascism in their own country, as long as it was an ocean's distance away. Jessup refers to such citizens in Scene Four of Act Two when he says, "This tyranny isn't primarily the fault of Big Business or of the demagogues. It's the fault of all the respectable Doremus Jessups that let the crooks come in without a protest. I can't blame Buzz Windrip. It's us—the good 'citizens.'" "We're probably doing our plotting about two years too late," Lorinda adds, as she and Jessup prepare to circulate pamphlets critical of the government. By the time they publish their pamphlets and protest forcefully against the dictatorship, such free speech is no longer a constitutional right, but a crime against the state. In 1936, Jessup was not the only one delinquent in his objections to fascism; off stage, across America, public objections to native and foreign fascism were less vocal than they ought to have been, and would be a few years later.

As the U.S. government wages a "war of choice," rather than one of last resort, and reduces civil liberties at home early in the twenty-first century, as leading Members of Congress and White House staffers are charged with criminal offenses, it could be that the kinds of crooks Jessup knew have come back, and entered the government again. Yet, the situations in the play and current-day America differ in many ways. Tens of thousands of citizens marched in public against the invasion of Iraq, before the Pentagon launched the war in 2003. For its incarceration of suspects without due process or a trial date, the Bush administration had to answer vocal critics and respond to lawsuits in court. The Lewis and Moffitt play, written for performance in 1936, does not speak to recent developments with the urgency and directness it offered when responding to tyranny in the thirties; but *It Can't Happen Here*

Figure 5.3

Doremus Jessup (Julius Adler) with fellow prisoner Mike (Morris Dorf) in the concentration camp scene of the Federal Theatre Project's Yiddish production of *It Can't Happen Here,* New York, 1936. *Courtesy of the National Archives.*

stands as a call to Americans to oppose fascism early and often. Its plea not to let "the crooks come in without a protest" in the United States still needs to be heard.

Given the play's emphasis on the need for "good citizens" (actors and directors included) to protest against government oppression, it is surprising that the concentration camp scenes in the novel were completely omitted from the American-language play on Broadway. Deletion of the play's concentration camp scene may be more unsettling, and more historically significant now, than it was in 1936. Although the first Nazi concentration camp was set up at Dachau in 1933, the horrors of German camps and the Holocaust were not fully known in America when *It Can't Happen Here* first opened. Before Nazis developed their camps, the British used the term "concentration camp" late in the nineteenth century to describe centers created during the Boer War. Lewis chose to call the prison in his work a "concentration camp" too. Whether he had the British or the German prison in mind, his stage directions (calling for bunk beds in a cell "low, narrow, unlighted . . . no furniture except a stool and a couple of galvanized iron buckets") set the scene to look more like an American jail than a Nazi death camp. In any case, the prison scene in the play adds to Lewis's portrait of American fascism an important demonstration of injustice under Windrip, and resistance by Jessup.

It Can't Happen Here warned audiences about the potential for American complicity in fascism more than it indicted the leaders of Italy or Germany. Located in the United States, the dimly lit prison cell holds Americans, not Europeans. Perhaps some of the play's producers at the Adelphi found this development—the opening of concentration camps in America—implausible while Roosevelt was president. (Critics of the Federal Theatre Project and the play suggested that its unflattering attitude toward fascism in October of 1936 was meant to scare voters away from Roosevelt's opponents in the November election.) The scene in the camp is not exactly a realistic or journalistic account of prison suffering either, as it melodramatically shows Jessup escaping with assistance from a guard. But the scene should be retained precisely because it shows Doremus Jessup's determination to escape, and to continue his resistance, which his daughter joins in the next scene. With the prison scene deleted, Act Three becomes a simpler story of Mary's flight from the United States; the play no longer offers a sequence of scenes in which the next generation (his daughter and grandson) follows the newspaper editor's example.

While the concentration camp scene with Jessup's melodramatic escape provides no detailed, realistic account of prison life, that may not be a fault. *New York Times* critic Brooks Atkinson observed in his second (post-opening night) discussion of the play that Lewis's "imaginative portrait of America under a Fascist dictatorship is horribly fascinating. But to me it is not very realistic, largely because of the Lewis exuberance which is forever drawing caricatures. Mr. Lewis is such a perfect mimic and satirist that he cannot resist a temptation to make charlatans out of the village orators and villains out of native morons."[12] Atkinson cites this lack of realism and practice of satire as weaknesses in the play; but insofar as the play is a fantasy, a dystopian and cautionary tale, rather than a documentary drama, the "exuberance" and caricature can be seen as assets.

In the novel, Lewis digresses with some literary and political satire that would have been difficult to accommodate in the limited time frame of his stage play. The play does not replicate the novel's humorous, Dantesque assignment of contemporaries to special locations in his vision of Hell. After Windrip becomes president, Lewis informs his book's readers that he follows "the Spanish custom of getting rid of embarrassing friends and enemies by appointing them to posts abroad, preferably quite far abroad. Anyway, as Ambassador to Brazil, Windrip appointed Herbert Hoover, who not very enthusiastically accepted." Fellow social critic and novelist Upton Sinclair was appointed Ambassador in Great Britain. Franklin Roosevelt declined the position of minister to Liberia. The play includes few of these satiric digressions, but through its melodrama it retains some of the villains and caricatures found in the novel.

Brooks Atkinson did not see the Yiddish version of the play or its prison scene, which is not comic, although it introduces villains in roles grotesque and "horribly fascinating," to use Atkinson's phrase. Early in the scene, an inmate named Mike lies dying in his bunk bed, and the nasty resident doctor refuses to supply him with medicine. A guard adds that if Mike is dying, he doesn't need medicine. In the face of this cruelty, Doremus Jessup comforts the dying man, his cellmate. Jessup escapes later, after Mike dies, with assistance from a sympathetic guard. The escapee impersonates a second doctor and leaves the site carrying a doctor's bag, while another prisoner, Pastor Prang, recites prayers. After Jessup's escape, the audience does not see him again.

The concentration camp scene was cut from the New York English-language production after extensive debate over the text by its co-authors, Lewis and Moffitt. Hallie Flanagan notes in *Arena* that, during the writing of the play, Lewis's co-author, John Moffitt, "threatened, if Mr. Lewis did not omit certain scenes and include others, various unusual reprisals."[13] Perhaps the Yiddish translators escaped such demands from Moffitt and Lewis. The *New York Times* reported that during rehearsals "many scenes were scratched out or were written in. Some of the companies in various parts of the country are using early versions, some late versions, with units elsewhere quite happily playing scenes that have been dropped or changed by the parent, or Adelphi group. Mr. Lewis said that would be all right with him." Sinclair Lewis also wanted the opening date of the play postponed for a week, and it was not.[14] He may not have objected to the cut of the prison scene in particular and perhaps "that would be all right with him," but Lewis clearly was unhappy with the Adelphi production prior to its opening.

In retrospect, the Biltmore Theatre version's 1936 portrayal of Yiddish-speaking inmates in a fascist concentration camp seems to be an extraordinarily perceptive depiction of ongoing and future events in Europe. The American-language production of the play at the Adelphi also should have staged this scene in Yiddish, perhaps; it would have attracted attention to the camps, if not won its audience's full understanding.

Morgn Frayhayt critic Moishe Olgin was not particularly impressed by the concentration camp scene. He noted that prisoners were seen lying on beds, but that is all of the camp that was shown. Photographs of the scene preserved in the Federal Theatre Project archives confirm that scenery was spare, the stage almost bare. (The prisoners in one photograph stand upright—they are not in beds.) If anything made the prison scene unusual, it was the language, but here Olgin found the "Yiddishkayt" (meaning Jewishness, or Yiddish attributes) out of keeping with the American character of the story. One exception, Olgin humorously noted, was Julius Adler's portrayal of the editor Jessup, which reminded him of a Yiddish newspaper editor he knew.[15]

Yiddish-Speaking Yankee Farmers

William Schack responded more favorably than Olgin to the New England Yankee "Yiddishkayt" in the production. While he too found the Yiddish-speaking Yankees unusual, Schack praised the new version for going beyond the usual Jewish themes. He judged the production

> significant beyond its merits in that it demonstrates that the American scene readily lends itself to treatment in Yiddish. It has been one of the drawbacks of the Yiddish stage in this country that its playwrights, freed from the confinement of the Old World ghettoes, have voluntarily gone back to them for the material. . . . Rooted in the old environment, they have not been at ease in the new. . . . But in "It Can't Happen Here," Yankee farmers, small-town editors and hoodlums, radio priests and politicians, speak Yiddish as if it were their native tongue.[16]

One could dispute Schack's assertion that anyone was "at ease" in the new world depicted by Lewis and Moffitt; their portrait of fascism showed many characters on stage, like the authors off stage, alarmed by the situation. Although the play was set in America, Yiddish theatre-goers could not easily forget that fascism had already arrived in Europe. Schack's pleasure in hearing Yankee farmers, small-town editors, and radio priests speak Yiddish might have been warranted, as the play extended the capacity of Yiddish theatre to portray American life; but the incongruity of priests and Yankee farmers speaking Yiddish also might have achieved an "alienation" effect—the kind of estrangement effect Brecht sought in his theatre—in which spectators would sense a distance, a strange disjunction, between the story's New England characters and the language they spoke. Perhaps this accounted for the discontinuity that Olgin noted in his review.

Escaping America

Even the scenes retained in both the English and Yiddish versions of the play differed because of new and additional meanings that certain lines acquired when spoken in Yiddish. Hearing the last scene of *It Can't Happen Here* spoken in Yiddish, audiences might well have recalled troubling scenes in their own lives, as they watched Jessup's daughter and grandson trying to cross the border from America to Canada. When a border control officer asks the woman, Mary Greenhill, why she wants to go to Canada, she answers, "Zu makhn a lebn" ("To make a living") and adds that she has relatives there. The question and answer recall exchanges in which tens of thousands of Yiddish-speaking immigrants engaged with customs officials at New York's Ellis Island when they were seeking refuge and economic opportunity. Ironically, the Yiddish speaker in Lewis's play seeks to leave the United States, not enter it, in pursuit of employment. She also seeks freedom, but she can't say that (she is not free to speak), because Windrip's border officers would regard her as a disloyal American. A Yiddish spectator listening to her lines in 1936 could have heard an eerie, unsettling echo of his or her own family's immigration, as the scene set in the future suggested history might repeat itself: Jews might need yet another refuge in the face of American oppression. Lewis's play was not written about Yiddish immigrants, of course; its action intimates that Americans with a wide range of backgrounds and religious affiliations could face the Yiddish ritual of exile and border crossing in the future. If it happened "here" in America, fascism would persecute far more than those who speak Yiddish. But Yiddish-speaking characters were the ones most at risk in the 1936 production of the play at the Biltmore.

Figure 5.4

Mary Greenhill (Jeanette Paskowitch) points a rifle at Corpo Commissioner Swan (Morris Torlowski) while her son David (Sidney Lumet) prepares to go across the border to Canada in *It Can't Happen Here*, New York, 1936. *Courtesy of the National Archives.*

Mary Greenhill and her son David take great risks in the border crossing scene. A high official named Swan becomes suspicious of the mother and son, and suspense builds as he interrogates them. District Commissioner Swan questions the daughter and grandson of the anti-fascist movement's Doremus Jessup, without knowing they are his relatives. If he learns their background, they will be arrested. David, age eight, volunteers to demonstrate his military training to Swan when asked about it. He obeys the drill orders ("Present arms!," "Parade rest") Swan delivers in English. The drill, originally performed by film director Sidney Lumet when he was a young actor, proves that the boy knows how to hold a rifle and understands more than Yiddish. After the drill, his mother asks David to give her the loaded rifle, and she aims it at their interrogator. Swan asks her to "drop the melodrama," meaning to put down her rifle; but his line also suggests that the authors were fully aware of the theatrical genre through which their scene builds its suspense. Threatening to shoot Swan, Mary insists that the officials let her son cross the border. She instructs David to seek out his grandfather, Doremus Jessup, and his Aunt Lindy in Canada. Mary lets Swan hear her say this, so he knows whose grandson is escaping. Jessup's daughter risks her own life to secure the free passage of her son. Swan does not know whether Mary will shoot him as he holds the door open, and the play ends there, with the melodramatic stand-off unresolved. Mary may not survive the encounter and follow her son into Canada, but that seems unimportant to her. Her son's freedom and the continuation of the resistance movement come first. When Swan says he should have killed her father, Mary replies that he cannot be stopped, "Doremus Jessup can never die." Her defiant statement ends the play, and suggests that, if not the man himself, at least the movement of resistance that Jessup represents will continue; younger men like his grandson David will keep the struggle alive.

The closing scene, played for much of the time with a loaded rifle aimed at Swan, turns out to be far from the usual, orderly immigration scene that its opening lines about job prospects lead one to expect. Comparable suspense about border crossing was almost certainly experienced outside the theatre by some of the refugees in the audience. The implication that fascism and the need for flight could develop in the United States disturbed some refugees and some American-born spectators watching the Yiddish performances in 1936. H. L. Fishel, an administrative official with the Federal Theatre's Play Bureau who saw It Can't Happen Here on opening night, confirmed these connections between the play and its audience when he reported, "The reason why the Yiddish business was so important was that we were beginning to get all the refugees from Austria and Germany—the Jewish refugees—at this time. At the Yiddish theatre opening, there were two or three people that fainted. They were identifying."[17]

Credit for unsettling the audience should be given to the play's creators, who fit their political concerns and echoes of events abroad into the structure of a melodrama. Whether performed in English or Yiddish, the scenes of prison escape and border crossing—the suspense-filled plot structure—lead spectators to identify with the heroic resisters of fascism who confront and escape their oppressors. Resistance begins slowly, and gradually increases during the three acts, after Jessup faces censorship and arrest. The performance of the scenes in Yiddish could have heightened the empathy of those who recalled their own flight—or that of their relatives—from Germany, Austria, Poland, Russia, and other locations outside the United States. Even without personal experience of a harrowing border crossing, some spectators might have begun identifying themselves with the refugees because they spoke the same language. Yiddish speech represented their past life abroad, and simply to hear the language of exile spoken by new refugees—Americans, in a New York theatre—might have increased the emotional tension that these scenes imparted.

The play ends with scenes centered around the resistance movement. The anti-fascist struggle, rather than the activities of Buzz Windrip, take center stage. Windrip doesn't appear at all in Act Three.[18] Perhaps the false messiah has not lost all of his following; but in the final scenes, even Windrip's devoted prison and border guards give most of their attention to those resisting fascism—those saving themselves, not waiting for a messiah.

The curtain scene, with Mary Greenhill aiming her rifle at District Commissioner Swan, differed from the ending her character meets in Lewis's novel. There she tries to kill a fascist official by dropping hand grenades from a plane, and dies when her plane crashes. In the play, Mary still lives as the curtain falls. She tells her departing son that she will follow him "when I can." Whether she will join David in Canada is left unsettled. American Yiddish theatre audiences had seen many plays celebrating the "Yiddisha Mama"—and many scenes with a mother protective of her son. But this scene featuring armed protection—rifle cover during a border crossing—was new. Sinclair Lewis and his theatre collaborators had turned the "Yiddisha Mama" into an armed resistance fighter.

6

Pinski's Prelude to a Golden Age

The Tailor Becomes a Storekeeper

T he Tailor Becomes a Storekeeper achieved a special honor late in 1938; it was the only new Yiddish play in the Federal Theatre Project to have its content criticized during hearings of the House Committee to Investigate Un-American Activities. If David Pinski's play was subversive or too radical for Congressman Martin Dies and the committee he chaired, it stood in excellent company; other Federal Theatre works adversely criticized before that committee included Ernst Toller's satire on dictatorships, *No More Peace*; *It Can't Happen Here*, by Sinclair Lewis and John Moffitt (see Chapter 5); the Living Newspaper's innovative productions of *One-Third of a Nation* and *Injunction Granted*; and the children's play, *Mother Goose Goes to Town*.[1]

Testifying against Pinski's play at the Dies committee hearing, witness Hazel Huffman called the satire "pro-union propaganda." That accusation contradicts her summary of the play, which described it as "the story of a tailor who refuses to join the tailor's union and becomes a shopkeeper," but the witness went on to explain that the tailor and his family and relatives "have been thrown out on the streets and are reduced to dire poverty and could get no assistance. Finally, he joins the union and sings happily at the end of the production." Huffman, like the play's main character, sees the union as a last resort, not a first choice—a situation that hardly makes the play resound as "pro-union propaganda." The play's poetic dialogue and expressionistic staging also removed it from the genre of propaganda. Huffman could have more accurately said that she saw "pro-union" tendencies within the play. Whether such tendencies, which depict organized labor seeking fewer work hours per week, constitute "un-American activity" is another question. Her charges led Federal Theatre Project director Hallie Flanagan to defend Pinski's work, along with twenty-five other plays defamed at the hearings, in a lengthy document titled *Brief Containing Detailed Answers to Charges Made by Witnesses Who Appeared Before the Special Committee to Investigate Un-American Activities, House of Representatives*. Flanagan noted in the brief that twenty-six Federal Theatre Project productions in New York City "were cited by witnesses as being 'Communistic propaganda' in whole or in part," and she responded by citing favorable commentaries on the plays provided by critics and theatre professionals outside of the hearings. In the case of Pinski's play, she cited excerpts from favorable discussions of his writing in the *New York Times* and the Yiddish daily, *Der Tog*.

Before Congressman Dies and other conservatives heard testimony about Pinski's play, *The Tailor Becomes a Shopkeeper* had opened at two Federal Theatre Project (FTP) spaces in 1938. The theatre doors were not padlocked by law officers, as happened to another government-funded play, Marc Blitzstein's *The Cradle Will Rock*, in 1937. But federal funding for production of texts like these, and all other FTP plays, ended in 1939, after the Federal Theatre's staff heard from Congressmen the same line of questioning that Sam the tailor in Pinski's play hears from his relatives when he asks them for financial support:

UNCLE: You want us to give you the money?
AUNT: Just like that!
UNCLE: Maybe we haven't got the money . . .
SECOND BROTHER-IN-LAW: Maybe we won't want to lend it to you . . .[2]

Sam persuades relatives to invest in his new delicatessen; then, much like the Federal Theatre Project, Sam is criticized by his backers, whose doubts continue:

AUNT: What did we have to get mixed up in it for? . . . Such a misfortune!

Figure 6.1

The tailor shop in *The Tailor Becomes a Storekeeper,* New York, April 8, 1938.
WPA Federal Theatre Project, courtesy of the National Archives.

The Federal Theatre was no delicatessen, and Pinski did not write his play about the Federal Theatre Project, but rather about Americans like Sam the sweatshop tailor who dreamed of becoming an independent and prosperous businessman. The dream was difficult to keep alive during the hardships of the thirties.

By the end of the play, Sam trades his entrepreneurial dream for union membership. Pinski follows no party line in his depiction of unions and private enterprise, although *Yiddisher Kemfer,* the periodical that published *The Tailor Becomes a Storekeeper* in 1938, was a Labor Zionist journal. The playwright served as literary editor for a Socialist journal when he arrived in New York in 1899, and was a "leader in workers' movements all his life," according to David Lifson, so it is not surprising his play favors unionism.[3] Less expected is the long period of time Sam takes to choose union membership.

The ruined storekeeper arrives at the house of labor when he has nowhere else to go. Unfortunate experiences in the world of private enterprise drive Sam to refuge in the tailors' union. His displeasure with entrepreneurial capitalism, which leaves him adrift, would not have been welcomed by the conservatives in Congress who criticized the Federal Theatre Project; however, Sam gives private enterprise more than one chance before he is forced out of it.

Staged in a decade when American unions were gaining strength through new forms of organization and protest, Pinski's play depicts the birth of a new union in its first scenes. Suddenly, like a divinity in human form, a tailors' sweatshop spokesman creates the union by reciting a few words, in a defiant and comic declaration:

BOSS: Union, union, union! There isn't any union in my place.
UNION LEADER: After our meeting there will be . . .
BOSS: What kind of monkey-business. Who said you could have a meeting?
UNION LEADER: We did.

The Union Leader goes ahead and holds the meeting, which Sam declines to attend. Not opposed to unions, Sam just doesn't want to be a tailor anymore. He tells his co-worker, Redbeard, "A union is a fine thing for the workers. You need a union like you need the right eye in your head." Sam prefers to become an owner, and his own boss.

SAM: I don't want to be a tailor all my life. There's no future in it. A union is alright, a shorter working-day is also alright, and higher wages are surely alright. But there's no future in it.
REDBEARD: And what do you call a future?
SAM: What should I call a future? What do you call a future? Working yourself up to something, getting someplace . . . When I figured it out, I figured it out for myself, and only for myself. If you can't figure anything out for yourself, then you'll be a tailor for the rest of your life.

Sam's plan for "getting someplace" turns out to be one he cannot start or sustain by himself. To fund his combination delicatessen and dance floor, the former tailor needs the support of his family. During his journey into a nightmarish world of private enterprise, the ex-tailor finds little privacy.

As a storekeeper and restaurant proprietor, Sam encounters overdemanding customers who underpay. Charities demand multiple contributions from him. Before long, thieves rob him, racketeers extort protection money, and Sam cannot secure funds to recover from his losses. His struggle to avoid bankruptcy resonates with struggles the

Figure 6.2

Rose Zelaso and Chaim Shneyur are threatened by racketeer. *WPA Federal Theatre Project, courtesy of the National Archives.*

nation itself underwent during the Great Depression. Had Sam been an actor instead of a storekeeper, he might have applied for relief from the Federal Theatre's Yiddish Unit, part of the Works Progress Administration's efforts to put the unemployed back to work.

Instead, Pinski's protagonist seeks relief from an agency that claims to serve American Jews. But the philanthropists turn out to be false messiahs; Sam cannot count on Jewish charity to survive. At first his rescue appears imminent. A member of "S.R.E.L.J.A.N.F.," the Society for the Rebuilding of the Economic Life of Jews of America on New Foundations, declares,

> This cannot go on any longer. The Jews of America are on the very brink of destruction. They are at the end of their rope. The sword of Damocles hangs over their heads. The sea of forgetfulness will

shortly swallow them up. The workers are being thrown out of their jobs. The merchants are squeezed out of their stores. The old ways of making a living are gradually being closed to them.

S.R.E.L.J.A.N.F.'s Board of Governors sleeps through the speech; they are too comfortable to share the speaker's sense of urgency. Pinski derides the society with an absurd acronym; its self-important but abstract philanthropy, removed from the everyday demands Sam faces, cannot help the desperate tailor turned storekeeper. Before sending Sam to another relief agency, one called the "Society for the Help of Ruined Storekeepers," the board members of S.R.E.L.J.A.N.F. tell Sam to take up farming, because "a farmer's never hungry. He always has enough to eat." Sam asks if they'll give him money for a cooperative farm, and hears the reply, "We only give you the plan."

Pinski's satire of philanthropy continues when Sam arrives without an invitation at a luxury fundraiser for the Society for the Help of Ruined Storekeepers. A ruined storekeeper, Sam is just the kind of person for whom the charity ball raises relief money, or so he tells the Society's president. Sam again receives advice instead of money; if he applies for membership, and pays his dues for a year, then he will be eligible to seek relief. Pinski mocks organized charity here (as he does in his play *The Treasure*); but the absurd bureaucracy and impersonality of institutions, not charity or Judaism per se, take the brunt of his ridicule. (Acronyms for Federal relief agencies, such as WPA, NRA, and CCC also became subjects for parody in Modicut's *Dybbuk,* discussed in Chapter 8.)

Dejected after meeting the uncharitable at a charity ball, Sam calls for help out on the street. One photograph of the 1938 New York production shows the downtrodden man lifting himself off the pavement, surrounded by strangers in an expressionistically designed, cartoon-like nightmare of collapsing, two-dimensional tenements. After this brief descent to the lower depths, Sam finds himself welcome only in the union he originally declined to join.

Fellow tailors offer Sam the solidarity he could not find in private business, charity, or family gatherings. Sam joins only after seeing that the alternatives to unionism are worse. The fact that the union still stands open at the end of his misadventures, ready to welcome Sam despite the Boss's objections, constitutes part of its attraction. That the union welcomes him is something to sing about, and Sam sings as the play comes to an end.

Figure 6.3

The storekeeper (Chaim Shneyur, center) prostrate outside a charity ball in *The Tailor Becomes a Storekeeper,* New York, April 8, 1938. *WPA Federal Theatre Project, courtesy of the National Archives.*

An Expressionist Romp

A comedy with songs, *The Tailor Becomes a Storekeeper* was first performed by the Federal Theatre Project's Yiddish Unit in Chicago, at the Great Northern Theatre on Jackson Street. Subtitled "a grotesque comedy in three acts," the play premiered on February 25, 1938, and played in Chicago until April 9; it opened the same month in New York with another Federal Theatre director and cast. Both productions were performed in Yiddish. The play was also translated into English for the Federal Theatre by Elihu Winer. (Winer's unpublished translation is the source of dialogue quoted here.)

William Schack of the *New York Times* praised Pinski's "genial parable," which he found "playfully written and performed as an expressionist romp." The author "believes in unions there is strength," the critic wrote, and he did not hold that against Pinski, as William Edlin of the Yiddish newspaper *Der Tog* did; instead, Schack noted "the author has not lessened [the play's pro-union] force by choosing to deck it out with cap and bells rather than street corner eloquence." Schack did, however, express some reservations. He found "the play less sparkling illumination than a fairly obvious and amusing treatment of a timely theme," and thought director Martin Wolfson had "hardly got beyond the familiar idiom of expressionism" with most of his cast, although lead actor Chaim Shneyur displayed "the right balance between realism and stylization."[4]

Der Tog's critic, William Edlin, found the mixture of realism and stylization in the production unsatisfactory; he wanted a more unified presentation. Edlin also expressed dismay that Pinski ridiculed Jewish merchants and their middle-class lives through grotesque satire, but idealized workers and their union shop. Pinski's "worker-sympathies have not allowed him to be impartial," Edin protested; but his objection can be regarded as an unintended compliment to the playwright, who directed his satire at specific holders of wealth and privilege, as well as bureaucracy.

Although Edlin found fault with Pinski's political satire, his opening statement about the play pays great respect to the author, whom the Federal Theatre Project welcomed into its ranks when he was neglected by "our Yiddish theatres," which served only Yiddish-speaking audiences. Whether or not *The Tailor Becomes a Storekeeper* was one of Pinski's best creations, wrote Edlin, it was significant that a well-known Yiddish playwright had no access to "our Yiddish theatres." The critic paid tribute to the Federal Theatre for giving Pinski a home, and to the playwright himself, for his individuality and avoidance of the "well-worn" path commercial Yiddish theatres followed. "Our stages don't know how to adapt to an original writer," noted Edlin, in a line that may not have endeared him to most of the Yiddish producers on Second Avenue. (Hallie Flanagan, in her defense of Pinski's play against un-American activity accusations, cited Edlin's review, specifically this passage [originally published in Yiddish]: "The fact that for the past thirteen years no play of David Pinski's has been produced is no compliment for our Jewish stage. It is therefore a compliment for the Jewish division of the WPA that they did produce a play by Pinski. . . . David Pinski is one of our oldest and most famous playwrights. . . . Thanks to the American government theatre."[5])

Other plays by Pinski received more attention from critics, and more frequent production than *The Tailor Becomes a Storekeeper.* The prolific author wrote dozens of one-act plays and full-length scripts. Born in Russia in 1872, David Pinski arrived in the United States in 1899, and that year he wrote his first plays, *Yesurim* and *Isaac Sheftel*. From 1949 to his death in 1959, he lived in Israel, but Pinski resided in the United States for the first half of the twentieth century (1899 to 1949). His plays had been staged to acclaim before he collaborated with the Federal Theatre Project. In 1938 his script titled *Yankl the Blacksmith* was turned into a film, *The Singing Blacksmith,* starring the popular performer Moyshe Oysher in the title role.

The list of actors and directors associated with Pinski's outstanding play, *The Treasure,* reads like an honor roll of Yiddish theatre artists. Actors appearing in *The Treasure* over the years included Rudolph Schildkraut, Clara Young, Ludwig Satz, Maurice Schwartz, Bina Abramovitsh, Celia Adler, Ida Kaminska, Menasha Skulnik, and Miriam Kressyn. Max Reinhardt directed the play in Berlin in 1918. The distinguished Polish director Zigmund Turkov staged the work in Warsaw in 1927. It was staged on Broadway in 1920. The Federal Theatre Project also briefly staged Pinski's *The Treasure* in Los Angeles in 1937.[6]

By contrast, *The Tailor Becomes a Storekeeper* had no prior production before the Federal Theatre Project welcomed it in 1938. Its premiere represents a notable development in the Federal Theatre Project Yiddish Unit's history and Pinski's own career. He left the usual Yiddish theatre venues, with their benefits and star system, for the less commercial, more adventurous Federal Theatre Project. (He may have had no alternative, if, as William Edlin of *Der Tog* suggested, commercial Yiddish theatres did not want the play by this "original writer.") The story of the tailor also differs from earlier plays that Pinski set in Eastern Europe and Palestine. He portrays labor conditions that would remind many spectators in New York and Chicago of their own garment industry work. The play was as new as the forty-four-hour work week, about which Congress debated that year.

As mentioned earlier, the Federal Theatre Project's Translations Department director, Benson Inge, wanted to produce new American Yiddish plays, not simply classics, around the country. A 1937 report (unsigned, but possibly written by Inge himself at the time he was affiliated with the Anglo-Jewish Play Department of the FTP) lamented the scarcity of new Yiddish plays, and called Pinski, among others, "passé":

Goldfadden, Gordin and even Hirshbein or Pinski are passé today and few of their creations could be successfully restored.

Except for Maurice Schwartz and the Artef Group there is little hope for development in the commercial field. It is therefore left to the Federal Theatre to bring about a renaissance. And the Anglo-Jewish Play Department is dedicated to this task.[7]

Thanks to the Anglo-Jewish Department's efforts, and Inge's correspondence soliciting new work from Pinski, David Pinski was no longer "passé" in 1938. He became a writer for one of the country's most innovative theatre-producing organizations. As the 1937 report predicted, the new Pinski arrived outside the "commercial field," in subsidized venues where ticket prices were kept low. A poster for the Chicago production of *The Tailor Becomes a Storekeeper* indicates that ticket prices ranged from twenty-five cents to eighty-three cents.

Like the playwright, the artists in Chicago and New York who staged Pinski's new play had considerable experience in Yiddish theatre, and proved they too were not passé in 1938. Adolf Gardner, the play's director in Chicago, had been born in Bucharest in 1879, acted with Yiddish theatre troupes in Europe before entering the United States in 1903, and worked in Chicago's Yiddish theatre for many years before he joined the Federal Theatre. One of his Chicago associates was Muni Weissenfreund, the actor later known as Paul Muni.[8]

Chaim Shneyur, who played the lead role of Sam the Tailor in New York, arrived in America with the famous Vilna Troupe in 1924 and worked with Pinski and other prominent artists before finding employment in the Federal Theatre in 1936. Over the next three years, he appeared in Odets' *Awake and Sing* and *We Live and Laugh,* as well as Pinski's play.[9] Rubin Doctor, who performed Pinski's play with the New York company, had earlier appeared in the Yiddish revue *We Live and Laugh*; he also wrote Yiddish songs, including one popular lyric in which a husband announces, "I Want to Be a Boarder by My Wife." Midwestern actress Jeanette Paskowitch had previously appeared in the Detroit Federal Theatre's production of *It Can't Happen Here* and Boris Thomashefsky's version of *The Yiddish King Lear,* done with a mixture of English and Yiddish.[10]

These artists may have needed the work the Federal Theatre Project offered them in the mid-1930s. But they also must have known the new play was an important addition to American Yiddish theatre. It was not exactly Pinski's escape from neglect, although Edlin in *Der Tog* said the playwright had no productions for thirteen years; a few of his works had been staged earlier in the decade, in New York, Chicago, and Milwaukee. The *Lexicon of Yiddish Theatre* records that Chicago's Yiddish Literary Dramatic Society staged Pinski's four-act satire, *The A.R.Z.A.B.*, in 1932. The Yiddish Dramatic Circle produced his three-act play, *The Conqueror*, in Milwaukee in 1933. *The Power That Builds*, a play about pioneers in Palestine, opened in New York in March 1935. The year before, the same city saw two older plays, *The Treasure* and *The Zwie Family*, given limited productions. But the Federal Theatre Project offered Pinski more visibility and longer runs than the playwright had known for years.[11]

The Tailor Becomes a Storekeeper shares with a number of David Pinski's other plays an expressionistic form, and avoids the melodrama and sentimental realism of more commercial Yiddish theatre. Not all his plays could be called expressionistic. The translator Isaac Goldberg, reflecting in 1918 on Pinski's first twenty-seven plays, said "three manners" of playwriting "appear in rapid succession" in three different plays. Goldberg thought Pinski "first of all, a realistic psychologist" who portrayed "a notable collection of seekers, of souls that have lusted for power and found themselves beaten by powers greater than their own."[12] Sam the tailor also is "beaten by powers greater than [his] own" for a while, but the play's ending takes him into another, more hopeful situation; and the 1938 play's style cannot be called psychologically realistic, as it hardly explores the inner life of its characters.

Writing in *The Tailor Becomes a Storekeeper* recalls the use of the "symbolism and satire" and "bitter comedy" Goldberg attributed to *The Treasure*.[13] Pinski's ability to create nonrealistic, grotesque theatre was noticed quite early in his career by the journalist Hutchins Hapgood. In a 1902 study of New York Jewish "ghetto" life, Hapgood wrote that Pinski is "one of the more wide-awake of the young men of Yiddish New York. He is so keen with the times that he even looks on realism with mistrust."[14] Pinski continued to mistrust realism in later years. From the ghosts that speak at the end of *The Treasure*, written in 1906, to the children of Europe's World War I who survive without their parents in *Little Heroes*, to the "expressionistic romp" of the 1938 play, Pinski can be seen as a rival to masterful Yiddish playwright I. L. Peretz, who brings the dead and the forgotten to life in *A Night in the Old Marketplace*. Unlike the Peretz play and *The Treasure*, both set in Eastern Europe, expressionism in *The Tailor Becomes a Storekeeper* portrays thoroughly American setting and characters.

The Poetry of Delicatessen

Pinski's American characters still speak Yiddish in 1938; but their language has been stripped of its Old World phrases and loquaciousness, which have been replaced by almost breathless, fast-paced speech, suited for a nation where time is regarded as money. Sam and his wife Esther convey a kind of poetry in their delicatessen, as they try to attract customers. But their speech is first of all the language of advertisements and business deals:

> ESTHER: Herring, fresh, right out of the ocean, with the sea-salt still on it.
>
> SAM: Marinierte herring, matjes herring . . . all kinds of herring!
>
> ESTHER: Sardines, anchovies, smoked fish, baked fish, cooked fish, gefilte fish.
>
> SAM: Tongue from fresh-slaughtered calves, marvelous to look at, fine to eat . . . Eat . . . don't be afraid of eating too much. Here you can dance a one-step, two-step, waltz and fox-trot . . .

Where once their family might have peddled fish from carts on Fulton Street, Sam and Esther cry their wares inside their own delicatessen, where customers can also dance to radio music between purchases and swallows of food. Their impersonal language offers the names of the fish for sale, names of dance steps, all words spoken to encourage purchases.

In this scene, at least the fish have names; most of the characters in the play, except Sam and Esther, do not. Here as in earlier expressionist plays (Strindberg's *Dream Play* and Peretz's *Night in the Old Marketplace,* or Pinski's *A Dollar,* for example) instead of personal names characters have titles—"The Boss," "The Uncle," "Third Cousin," "Gangster," and "Racketeer." Even Sam the tailor and his wife Esther have no last name. Pinski gives priority to the social roles people play—summed up by their titles—and their interactions, rather than their personal histories or interior life. Sam's effort to change his profession from "Tailor" to "Storekeeper" constitutes a central action in the play, as the play title indicates; but his dream of a change in categories, from Tailor to Storekeeper, also suggests Sam's imagination remains rather spare and limited.

To live their life of surfaces, where a change in professional titles takes precedence over more personal matters, Sam and Esther jettison almost everything except their dedication to business. The couple's readiness to

Figure 6.4

Yetta Schoengold wrangles over a herring with Rose Zelaso and Chaim Shneyur in *The Tailor Becomes a Storekeeper,* New York, April 8, 1938. *WPA Federal Theatre Project, courtesy of the National Archives.*

sacrifice family life to commerce reaches a grotesque extreme when they threaten suicide until their relatives agree to finance the delicatessen venture. Their relatives then serve as waiters, further turning family life into a business. Business is everything in their world; even pleasure and culture, such as might be found in dances and good meals, become part of the trade, as a dance space is set up on the restaurant floor.

Differences between Old and New World culture can be seen in Pinski's stylistic move from the colloquial dialogue and humor of *The Treasure* to the skeletal plot line and spare language of *The Tailor Becomes a Storekeeper.* The author is not necessarily endorsing the clipped speech or fast-paced profit-seeking of his characters; but like his characters, the playwright too leaves behind the Old World in 1938. Pinski does not embrace the New World idol of commerce. He looks warily at Jews no longer guided by religious precepts or superstition, or by calls for justice and liberation as they were in *The Zwie Family* (*Die Familie Zwie*), but by business interests that become an end in themselves. Sam measures his life's achievement in cash register receipts.

Charity Begins at Sam's

Pursuit of money drives people to extremes in *The Treasure*, as well as in Sam the Tailor's story. Pinski revisits the earlier play's themes and situations without imitating or repeating himself. Consider the grotesque scene in *Tailor*, where Jewish charity representatives, bargain hunters, and racketeers visit Sam's delicatessen in search of funds, and all assume that he can afford to give them a donation.

> VOICES (*those who have entered*): We're here for charity! Agents for the Jewish people! Help the poor! We're good askers. We're good takers! The voice of the people. (*They stand in line.*)
> FIRST PAIR: We're from the Hebrew schools.
> SECOND PAIR: We're from the Yiddish schools.
> THIRD PAIR: We're here for Palestine.
> FOURTH PAIR: We're here for Biro-Bidjan.
> FIFTH PAIR: We're from the burial society.
> SIXTH PAIR: We're from the art theatre.
> SEVENTH PAIR: We're from the Federation of 91.
> EIGHTH PAIR: We're from the Federation of Twice 91.
> ALL (*in chorus*): We take cash . . . we take checks . . . we take coins, that ring! . . . We take a lot . . . we take a little . . . we take anything! We take from the right, we take from the left, it doesn't matter which! From the bourgeoisie, from the working-class, from the poor and from the rich! We take, take, take . . .

The crescendo of these choral lines generates satiric humor and pathos, as a variety of causes ask Sam, the new merchant, for contributions. Some of the fund-raisers represent causes that were quite fashionable in the thirties—including the Soviet region of Birobidzhan designated for Jewish settlement, the art theatre of Maurice Schwartz, and the Zionists seeking a homeland in Palestine. Not a wealthy man, Sam has opened a new store, well-stocked with goods, and that is enough to attract all the latest (and some older) fund-raisers. After the charities leave, thieves and racketeers come for whatever remains. It is almost as if a pack of dogs has descended on some dying animal—in this case, a small business owner without enough experience to survive the financial onslaught.

The short, sharp sentences of dialogue, simple rhymed song lyrics, and quick actions help make the play what the *New York Times* called "an expressionist romp." While the choral lines are less spare and more repetitive in *The Treasure,* there too Pinski created a scene of money-seeking hordes descending on an allegedly solvent man—the gravedigger Khonye. Rich only by hearsay, Khonye cannot escape treasure hunters after his daughter and son find a small sum of money, hardly the treasure imagined by those who ask for a share of it. Khonye's extremely smart and cynical daughter Tilye remarks, "The pack has scented the money." Then a few of the pack confer:

> FIRST MEMBER OF THE VISITING-THE-SICK COMMITTEE: We have an account with Reb Khonye. We are kind of relatives by marriage, you might say.
>
> FIRST MEMBER OF THE DOWRIES-FOR-POOR-BRIDES COMMITTEE: Because you provide work for him [as a gravedigger]? (*All laugh.*) All the same, Reb Khonye will inscribe his first donation in our book. If for no other reason than we got here first.
>
> SECOND MEMBER OF THE VISITING-THE-SICK COMMITTEE: All right, then, you win, what can we do? Let him give you first and give us most . . .

The appeals continue until all that the prospective donor, Khonye, can say is, "My head is splitting. My head is splitting."[15] There is not enough money for everyone in either of the plays. But more elaborate language and cultural traditions are available to the townspeople in *The Treasure*; their Yiddish holds within it the richness—a treasure chest, perhaps—of Old World idioms and folklore. As translator Nahma Sandrow explained, *The Treasure* "takes place in a village in the hinterlands in late nineteenth-century eastern Europe. The characters' religious practices, superstitions, and social organization were all recognizable elements of such a world."[16] Sam the Tailor lives in a fast-paced world of garment factories, tenements, and delicatessens. Folklore and storytelling are replaced by information, as Walter Benjamin observed in his essay on "The Storyteller." *Shtetl* residents in *The Treasure* tell one another stories, fanciful rumors about a fortune buried in the cemetery; the fortune, like the stories, proves to be imaginary. Sam too has no treasure; visitors mistakenly regard his delicatessen with a dance floor as a gold mine. In the thoroughly commercial world Sam enters, even religious texts become proof of financial entitlement in the hands of the American fund-raisers, who employ biblical commentary to secure new money:

> ONE OF THE GROUP [of fund-raisers]: Where there's a storekeeper, then all the needs of the community are placed upon him, says a passage in the Gemarah.
> ANOTHER: Once the store is opened, the owner gives, says the passage.
> SAM (*to Esther*): If it says so in the Gemarah, then we have to give, isn't that right?
> ESTHER: And what if it doesn't say so? We can't send them away without anything.

Not entirely removed from the Yiddish and Jewish traditions of their ancestors, Pinski's characters invoke biblical commentary in an extremely questionable manner; still, they invoke it. They are not yet completely assimilated into American culture.

In their desperation and needs, all the characters in the play, Sam and Esther included, exhibit grotesque behavior about which the Russian critic Mikhail Bakhtin once wrote, "In the grotesque . . . all that was for us familiar and friendly suddenly becomes hostile."[17]

On stage the hostile world Sam encounters can and should be shown through nonnaturalistic acting. The characters need to move as an ensemble of singers and dancers rather than factory workers when they speak and move as a group. In her notes on *The Treasure*, Nahma Sandrow incisively describes an acting style that also would serve some scenes in *The Tailor Becomes a Storekeeper*:

> In the period when Pinski wrote *The Treasure*, expressionist staging used crowds as major presences, moving and speaking as inhuman embodiments of abstractions. . . . Crowd scenes were a means of transforming play texts about individuals into plays about political forces and group will. In this way, successful Soviet revivals of well-known plays by Goldfadn and Sholom Aleichem purported to transform them from humorous portrayals of old-fashioned Jewish life to satires exposing the evils of pre-Revolutionary Jewish capitalists.[18]

Farewell to the Forty-Hour Week

Pinski's 1938 play satirizes not pre-revolutionary capitalists, but a would-be capitalist who cannot adjust to the hostile world's cutthroat behavior. Yet, not all of Sam the Tailor's world proves to be hostile or inhuman. Particularly when characters sing in scenes with the union, and dance in the delicatessen, there are moments of celebration and disclosures of "the potentiality of a friendly world," which Bakhtin also attributes to the grotesque. He notes, "The existing world suddenly becomes alien (to use Kayser's terminology) precisely because there is the potentiality of a friendly world, of the golden age, of carnival truth."[19] In Pinski's play, the friendliest world turns out to be the world of the union, to which Sam returns at the end of the play. The union may not be friendly to the boss, but in striving to improve the lives of its members, it serves them well; and the union's demands provide glimpses of a future golden age, with fewer hours of work, more benefits, and new jobs for the jobless. The Boss thinks the union goes much too far, and it might have been extreme in 1938 to ask for a thirty-hour work week.

UNION LEADER: We're working too many hours.

BOSS: Forty hours a week are too many!

UNION LEADER: Thirty hours are less.

WORKERS (*singing*): Thirty hours, not one more—That's what we're united for!

BOSS: And higher wages too, I suppose!

UNION LEADER: That'll come later.

BOSS: You're going to ruin me!

UNION LEADER: We want to make work for the unemployed . . .

BOSS: I'll close down the factory.

UNION LEADER: You've scared us with that too often. (*Laughter*)

BOSS: I'll move the factory out of town.

UNION LEADER: The union will reach you wherever you are.

These exchanges over work week length and employment opportunities were extraordinarily timely in the spring of 1938. On June 25th of the same year, Congress passed the Fair Labor Standards Act to eliminate "labor conditions detrimental to the maintenance of the minimum standards of living necessary for health, efficiency and well-being of workers."[20] A victory for labor, the act required that the maximum number of hours allowed in a work week be capped at forty in 1940. (The maximum limit was set at forty-four hours in 1938.) Although the play never directly refers to the ongoing national debate over these regulations, the tailors in Pinski's play clearly want to go farther than congressional legislation was taking them at the time.

The union's ambitions for a thirty-hour work week might have sounded utopian, brash, and comic to some spectators in 1938, certainly to Sam's boss; but proposals for a shorter work week to reduce individual workloads and open new jobs to the unemployed found acceptance in Europe—particularly, France and Germany—late in the twentieth century. A thirty-five-hour work week was won by some European unions. Pinski's grotesque comedy discloses this vision of a world potentially friendlier to labor, the beginning of a golden age, shortly before Sam rejoins his shop and sings along with other union members.[21]

Seven decades later, the predictions exchanged between the Boss and the Union Leader have been fulfilled only partially. As the Boss threatened, companies have moved their factories out of towns, and out of the United States, to nonunion locations, rather than pay for improved working conditions and benefits, which would reduce profits. Since 1938 all too few unions have developed a strong national and international movement that can reach bosses and owners wherever they move. Here too, Pinski's vision seems to have been ahead of its time; what was said half in jest, as part of his grotesque comedy, reveals a potential for union strength through an international movement that has not yet been built.

When Sam enters during the closing exchange between the Boss and the Union Leader, stage directions note, "Sam enters the door with bowed head, stands meekly, then joins in the singing, directing, barely noticeable, with both hands."

Sam's former boss says he won't rehire the tailor. The union leader responds, "We'll decide that." Sam's future depends on the union's strength in bargaining with management. Given that the union in the play won its earlier demands, Sam's rehiring seems quite probable. Asked to sing along with the other workers (their refrain is "union, union, union, union"), Sam agrees, and exhibits none of the reluctance shown in Act One.

REDBEARD (*to Sam*): Sing! Sing!
SAM: You're telling me! Don't you hear me!

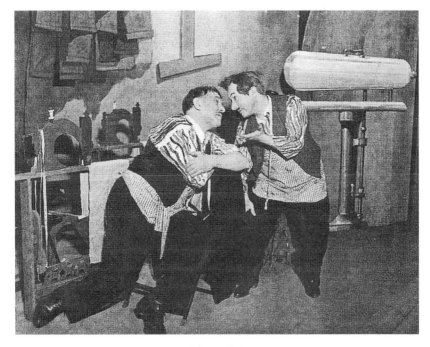

Figure 6.5

Two tailors portrayed by Chaim Shneyur (left) and Eddie Pascal debate the life of a storekeeper in *The Tailor Becomes a Storekeeper,* New York, April 8, 1938. *WPA Federal Theatre Project, courtesy of the National Archives.*

The tailor's return, which begins with a song, situates him in a carnivalesque event, not exactly the same kind of celebration Bakhtin described, but one of collective activity that provides Sam with more community support and hope than he had in his ill-fated storekeeping. The last moments of the play reverse the earlier plot and the play title's prediction; the storekeeper becomes a tailor again.

Finally, in a remarkable sequel to Pinski's play, its lead actor joined a garment industry union and became a presser. In 1941, a union of pressers invited Chaim Shneyur to direct its drama circle, where he staged David Pinki's *Yankl the Smith* and other plays. Shneyur became a respected professional presser in Dress Presser Local 60; for twenty years he worked in the union shop, and continued producing plays there, along with ironing.[22] His role in Pinski's play, *The Tailor Becomes a Storekeeper,* may well have influenced his decision to stay with a garment industry union, as Sam the Tailor did. Shneyur's later years contain the story for a new play that should be titled: *Pinski's Actor Becomes a Presser.*

Pinski's play also further developed the genre of the messianic satire seen in Nadir's *Messiah in America.* The tailors' union brings its members closer to a golden age for labor, although its goals are far from fulfilled when the curtain falls. Another comic play that portrays militant Yiddish union activity, *Getzel Becomes a Bridegroom,* featured the comic actor Menasha Skulnik as a strike leader. Skulnik's character is more of a *schlemiel* (or fool) than a messiah, but messianic behavior is not entirely free of folly either.

7

Menasha Skulnik Becomes a Bridegroom

Popular Yiddish Theatre Reconsidered

Popular Yiddish entertainment known as *shund*, or literary trash, thrived during the thirties. Leftist criticism of the genre hardly deterred audiences from enjoying the musical comedies featuring Menasha Skulnik, Molly Picon, Aaron Lebedev, and Leo Fuchs. Opposition to such entertainment placed a leftist in the curious position of renouncing theatre events attractive to the masses. In "On Shund-Theatre," written in 1943, Nathaniel Buchwald objected to *shund*'s banal plays with formulaic situations and characters, to the genre's acceptance of the status quo, and to the happy endings and stage fools offered by these plays at a time when Buchwald felt the world desperately needed social change.[1] Buchwald, a founding member of Artef, the highly accomplished Yiddish-speaking worker's theatre, was not merely writing from theory; he had a vision schooled in practical and laudable stage experiments. His vision of socially engaged theatre was not necessarily the one that audiences expected from popular performances by Picon, Skulnik, and Fuchs; yet their characters and the songs and dance these Yiddish actors presented in *shund* also constituted a kind of social criticism, and offered the audience a better life for a few hours through vicarious pleasures.

Shund and progressive political comedy coexisted in the 1932–33 Hopkinson Theatre production of *Getzel Becomes a Bridegroom,* starring Menasha Skulnik. Before turning to that example of *shund*'s response to social crisis, the genre itself warrants further discussion. *Shund*'s long life in Yiddish theatre and its continued popularity during the past century attest to qualities within the genre that its audience also exhibited: a sense of humor, optimism, perseverance, and an ability to survive poverty and prejudice. Its opponents would have preferred to see Yiddish versions of Ibsen, Shakespeare, and Jacob Gordin on stage, serious and elevated stage art, instead of the melodramatic tragedies and musical comedies that constituted *shund*. Among the most fervent early opponents of the so-called literary trash were the great Yiddish actor Jacob Adler and the playwright Jacob Gordin. In 1902, journalist Hutchins Hapgood reported that Adler, a "belligerent promoter of the original and serious Yiddish drama," "tried to introduce Gordin's plays and the new spirit of realism and literature into his company . . . [but] the old style is still strong in popular affection, and Adler's company rebelled." Gordin and Adler had to compromise. "Adler is now [in 1902] associated with a company which presents every kind of play known to the [Yiddish-speaking New York] Ghetto, and Gordin has had to introduce horseplay and occasional vaudeville and comic opera into his plays."[2] Hapgood did not call that "horseplay and occasional vaudeville and comic opera" *shund*, but Gordin and Adler incorporated these forms of *shund* into their offerings to please their actors and audience.

Moishe Nadir acknowledged the attractions of *shund* in a humorous monologue he wrote for the "average" Yiddish theatregoer, as noted in an earlier chapter. His imaginary theatregoer complained that critics "won't let me get any pleasure out of life. . . . When a play really does please me because there is dancing and singing in it and it's lively, they [the critics] come along and say that it doesn't even begin to please me, that it is trash and that it revolts me."[3] Nadir also wrote one musical, *Tsutsik,* still unproduced. He incorporated popular entertainment forms in his own plays: a boxing match and a sideshow in *Messiah in America,* and popular songs in "Prisoner 1936," the sketch he wrote for the revue, *We Live and Laugh.*[4] He also wrote a puppet play, *The Other World,* performed by his friends Maud and Cutler. Nadir knew such popular forms exerted a powerful attraction for spectators, and humorously acknowledged them in his satire of warring theatre producers, and the revue sketch in which a courtroom judge admits popular songs as testimony.

The term *shund* remained loaded with bias against popular entertainment when Buchwald objected to the genre in 1943. Today there is no need for a *shund* anti-defamation league, because Yiddish plays of that kind and any other are rarely staged; but the genre still deserves some defense. The prejudice against *shund* was not shared by many theatregoers and actors. The so-called literary trash of operettas and comedies provided opportunities for some of the Yiddish theatre's most popular actors to clown around and display a wide range of emotions onstage. Audiences flocked to see the lead actors in these plays, not necessarily the scripts of *shund*. With awe and delight, they watched Menasha Skulnik, Aaron Lebedev, Molly Picon, Leo Fuchs, and Jennie Goldstein; if the rest of the cast performed compelling scenes too, that was an additional gift. The admittedly trivial and diverting plots of *shund* would not have been so welcome without popular actors performing them; but these plays also provided the enthusiastic audience with portraits of its own community, Jewish history, and social concerns in its own language, Yiddish, which could not be heard in many other American entertainment venues. (Yiddish films and radio programs offered comparable diversions, but without the attraction of stars live and in person.) Even the strongest objections to *shund* have within them hints of the qualities for which the genre was appreciated by Yiddish-speaking audiences. Buchwald's antipathy to the genre's happy endings and stage fools undervalues the possibility that clownish Yiddish characters, in particular, displayed more than simple acceptance of the status quo in their society; they introduced a naïve questioning of Old World traditions in the New World, and some questioning of the New World's practices too.

Many of the topics addressed in *shund* by once popular Yiddish comedians remain timely. Their antic references to exile; their dreams of success, marriage, and assimilation; and their physically demanding and clownish, slapstick experiences of hardship and cultural difference resonate with struggles encountered today by newer groups of American immigrants from Asia, Latin America, Africa, and the Mideast.

As a *schlemiel*—a naïve, unlucky comic character—onstage, Skulnik or Fuchs often portrayed a newcomer ("greenhorn") or an outsider, a Jew who was impoverished, inexperienced, or denied success. The displaced and disadvantaged character might have the same background as members of the audience; only onstage he or she was less knowing and funnier.

Dreams of success in marriage and professional life eluded the comic character or led him or her to make extreme and sudden choices, seemingly irrational behavior that became a source of laughter.

While *shund* on stage did not often achieve the resourceful literary humor and folkloric mastery of Sholem Aleichem's stories, some popular Yiddish stage comedies portrayed fools who were as deluded, and then as disillusioned, as Aleichem's great, optimistic clown, Menachem Mendel. Menasha Skulnik and Leo Fuchs both were cast in plays where they portrayed this *luftmentsch,* a man who lives on air. Menachem Mendel dreams of winning his fortune in the stock market, then as a matchmaker; but he miscalculates, and a series of entrepreneurial pratfalls follow. (The Menachem Mendel plays featuring Skulnik and Fuchs are discussed in the Appendix.)

Most of the *shund* in which Yiddish actors performed remains unpublished and untranslated; unlike Sholem Aleichem's stories, the stage scripts have not become great literature. There is an ironic twist to this development. When Maurice Schwartz produced Yiddish theatre early in the twentieth century, before he started the Yiddish Art Theatre, he used to dismiss some literary works as *a buechel*—meaning, as David Lifson explains, Schwartz the play director felt "such a book [*a buechel*] belonged in the library, not on stage."[5] Nearly a century later, almost all Yiddish plays are *a buechel,* and found primarily on library shelves, not onstage. (Many copies of unpublished *shund* scripts now rest in the rare book archives of the Library of Congress and YIVO Institute for Jewish Research.) Even the once popular *shund* is *a buechel.* In that sense if no other, the genre shares the shelves with the great classics, *The Yiddish King Lear, The Dybbuk,* and *God of Vengeance.* But the genre deserves reconsideration for other reasons too.

The Wedding *Shtick*

Yiddish actors became famous for signature songs, dances and monologues, routines, and solo turns that in Yiddish would be called *shtick.* Like clowns in a circus ring, the actors often broke through the imaginary fourth wall between them and their audience, speaking direct addresses and asides, and stepping out of character. Other attributes of this nonrealistic, comic acting style were noted by *New York Times* critic Lewis Funke in 1950; reviewing *In Sadie Is a Lady,* he observed that "Miss [Molly] Picon is not the only one [in the play] who can make a Second

Figure 7.1

September 1933 Yiddish newspaper advertisement for Menasha Skulnik's *Menachem Mendel*. *Courtesy of the Forward Association.*

Avenue audience laugh. Clowning in able support are such players as Max Bozyk, Henrietta and Irving Jacobson. These are not inhibited players. They play for laughs and anything goes, disheveled costumes, broad gestures, and even plain burlesque brawling."[6]

Uninhibited, freewheeling delivery by Second Avenue actors might be traced back to the origins of Yiddish comedy in wedding celebrations, in which Eastern European *badchanim* (jesters) performed. The *badchen* mocked newly married couples and their wedding guests with comic poetry, songs, jokes, and dances. The guests would have been uninhibited themselves, if given enough wine, food, and music before the jester arrived.

Badchanim are seen far less frequently now than they were from the Middle Ages to early in the twentieth century. But their successors, Yiddish comedians in *shund* stage plays, continued to joke about weddings through at least the first half of the twentieth century. In times of joy, as in times of emergency, comedy is wanted, particularly since weddings often precipitate a crisis. Jennie Goldstein, who usually sang in Yiddish, recorded one humorous American-language tune entitled, "Look! The Rabbi Is Waiting, Here Is the Bride, Where Is the Groom?" (The groom never arrives in her song.) Ludwig Satz as a bridegroom seeking to reconcile with his new wife in the film *His Wife's Lover* puts on a top hat and swings a cane before going to bed with her—a fitting vaudevillian end to a romance that began in a Yiddish theatre where Satz's film character, a popular actor, met his future partner. In marriage, as in *shund* comedies, Yiddish stage clowns are liable to see disaster approaching, and respond with song, dance, and a sense of humor—arts that help them keep their wits about them and survive.

In the musical comedy *Getzel Becomes a Bridegroom*, Menasha Skulnik portrayed a bridegroom; but his character also led a labor union to victory with almost messianic fervor. Skulnik, famous for his timid, "little man's" demeanor, displayed incongruously comic boldness when his character called for a prolonged, ten-year strike. Courtship and the wedding dominate early scenes in *Getzel*, but since the strike is directed against the bridegroom's new brother-in-law, it too can be seen as a family affair, a movement from one union to another. These comic affairs lasted nearly the entire 1932–33 theatre season, as the play toured the United States and Canada after its acclaimed opening at the Hopkinson Theatre in Brooklyn.

Menasha Skulnik Married on Stage

Playwrights preparing a script for Menasha Skulnik are said to have included the stage direction, "Menasha enters," followed by pages of white space, which permitted the comic actor to insert his own, special material.[7] The improvisations and physical comedy he brought to the title role in *Getzel Becomes a Bridegroom* are lost; no film of the work exists, and short of Skulnik miraculously coming back to life, this play's script may be as close as we can come to sensing how *shund* provided the actor and his audience with a source of socially conscious popular entertainment. Between the lines of dialogue, in stage directions, in later interviews with the actor, and in a memoir or two, clues to his physical comedy can be found.

For much of his stage career, from one Yiddish comedy to another, Skulnik (1892–1970) moved with his famous *schlemiel,* a character who wore a hat too small for his head, walked with hesitant, stiff-legged steps, hunched his shoulders, and spoke with a nasal and braying voice. This crowd-pleasing behavior enabled the actor to turn almost any Yiddish comedy in which he appeared into his character's play. Skulnik first fully developed this character in *Getzel Becomes a Bridegroom.*

Hardly a conventional lover, Skulnik's naïve bachelor gets married—to the wrong woman—in the play. The *schlemiel* he portrays meets a matchmaker and a prospective wife early in the story. That the timid, inept man becomes a bridegroom is not completely surprising. It was difficult for a comic Yiddish actor not to appear in a play about marriage. Over and over again, Yiddish stage comedies celebrated marriage: from the meeting of young lovers to the objections or blessings of their parents, to the wedding celebration under the *chuppah* (wedding canopy). Occasionally wedding arrangements made by parents would go awry with tragic consequences, as they did in *God of Vengeance* and *The Dybbuk.*

The frequent repetition of marital themes in Yiddish theatre led critic A. Mukdoiny to dismiss such *shund* as a genre. To quote David Lifson's English paraphrasing of Mukdoiny's Yiddish, *shund* is "without literary worth, without reflection of a folk spirit, with no reasonable continuity or development of a plot, limited by a coterie of five or so librettists and with a lesser number of plots or devices which revolved around the need for each presentation to have a grand wedding scene."[8]

Weddings on stage did more than simply perpetuate the species known as Yiddish comedy. In *Getzel Becomes a Bridegroom,* the wedding and its aftermath provide an occasion for criticism of arranged marriages and unfair labor practices. The play offers its social criticism indirectly. Through his behavior, Skulnik's *schlemiel* initiates a series of wedding jokes, with him at their center, as he is led to the *chuppah* by a matchmaker and a brother of the bride eager to see her married. If among other things a *schlemiel* is, in Leo Rosten's words, "anyone who makes a foolish bargain," Getzel easily qualifies.[9] He agrees to marry Selba without knowing she already has two children by another marriage, and he learns almost nothing about her, except her name, before they stand together under the *chuppah.* He is even mistaken about her name early in the play. "This is her. . . . Her name I already know," Getzel says when introduced to Eva—but he thinks she is his bride to be, Selba.[10] He spends much of Act One conversing with Eva, the matchmaker's attractive daughter. Since she never denies she will be his bride or says that she is already married, a comedy of mistaken identity follows. Getzel doesn't get to know his bride until they stand under the *chuppah,* and he doesn't seem fully aware he has wed Selba until after what he calls the "accident" of marriage.

Early in the play, Getzel claims to be a "maven" (expert) on prospective wives, because he has spent eight years looking for a bride. Events that follow prove he is no maven. His claim to such a title is immediately undercut, and made comic, by his own admission that eight years earlier he promised his mother he would find a "kosher girl" in America. The expert's bride has to meet his mother's approval. Surely *badchanim* told such jokes (and better ones) in the past. Getzel finds less humor in his own disappointing marriage arrangement, after he learns more about the bride in Act Two.

Not simply a medley of wedding jokes, the play also features songs, dances, a strike by a union of kosher chicken cutters, and a dream of a Turkish harem. The fact that Getzel's misadventures have Coney Island as their setting makes it tempting to see the scenes as sideshow acts, with the *schlemiel*'s mismatch as the featured event. (In fact, no references are made to Coney Island's sideshows or amusement rides in the play—unlike some other Yiddish comedies located there, notably the film, *The Great Advisor,* and the play, *Messiah in America.*) But Getzel's standing changes during the course of the play; before the story ends, he moves from the margins of his community into a position of union leadership.

His eccentricity ends—or at least diminishes—when his solidarity with the labor movement begins.

The wedding and the strike later in the play have more in common than the brother-in-law against whom Getzel leads his strikers. The simple man at the center of both events displays a naiveté that can be seen as a kind of messianic faith in others, in humans if not in a divinity. If more indication than Skulnik's own acting is needed to establish his character's naiveté, the play's text provides it when Getzel first arrives on the scene. As he arrives in Coney Island to meet matchmaker Israel Aitch and the bride, the *schlemiel* sings about his home in Chelm, the Polish town said to be populated by fools. He does not see himself as a fool, but his Chelm-like innocence becomes apparent when the matchmaker's wife, Feiga, greets Getzel after his first entrance:

FEIGA: Who are you looking for?

GETZEL: A bride.

FEIGA: Ah, then you are the young man, the bridegroom?

GETZEL: Yes, that's me, Getzel Kukeruza from Steverka. . . . This is really Coney Island?

FEIGA: What, you're in Coney Island for the first time?

GETZEL: Yes, the first time. I said a blessing as soon as I sighted the hot dogs.

FEIGA: You never swam in the sea before?

GETZEL: Never, because I hear women bathe in the same sea.

FEIGA: Well, so what?

GETZEL: Oh, I'm very shy. My mother had a lot of trouble with me when I was a child.

FEIGA: Trouble? What was the trouble?

GETZEL: I was ashamed to be born.

FEIGA: Why were you ashamed to be born?

GETZEL: I didn't want to be born naked. Are you really the bride?

FEIGA: God forbid! You're mistaken. I'm the matchmaker's wife.

GETZEL: I meant, you're still a girl.

FEIGA: God forbid, the bride's a little more of one than I am.

GETZEL: Yes, I'm glad that I wasn't too far off.

The bridegroom's newness to Coney Island, his inability to recognize his bride, and his fear of undressing provide opportunities for *badchen*-like jokes and physical humor. His shyness about seeing naked human bodies, including his own, and his blessing of the hot dogs are comic attributes of the naïve character whom Menasha Skulnik conveyed through tentative, hesitant movements and slow, deferential speech rhythms. In an interview Skulnik once revealed a technique for achieving such deference and modesty; discussing a humorous line in a play, he told Arthur Gelb, "I say it now so naïve that I myself don't know I'm saying it. It gets a laugh."[11] There was art and rehearsal behind his innocence, and the actor knew more about his character's world than his *schlemiel* did. As he told Gelb in the same 1953 interview, "I play the little guy—the *schlemiel*—against the world." (Skulnik convinced himself that he was an innocent offstage too, according to Gelb. The comedian told the *Times* writer, "I don't know anything outside the theatre. And when I'm not onstage I'm just an ordinary person like you or me." But the confession doesn't sound as funny as his *schlemiel*'s lines onstage.)

By the time he analyzed his character for the *New York Times,* Skulnik had moved from Yiddish- to English-language stage productions. In 1953 he opened on Broadway in *The Fifth Season.* The next year he would appear there in Odets' *The Flowering Peach,* and star as the grandfather (*Zeyda*) in *The Zulu and the Zeyda* in 1956. Skulnik also portrayed Uncle David on the CBS television comedy, *The Goldbergs,* in 1953. Popular outside Yiddish theatre circles during that decade, the actor who first visited theatres and the circus as a boy in Warsaw became the most successful *schlemiel* in the United States.

In his memoirs, Herman Yablokoff, another actor in *Getzel Becomes a Bridegroom,* recalled that this new musical marked a breakthrough for Skulnik. Previously the comedian had "resorted to devices that made him appear different in each role. But now, on his own, he decided to stick to one type of lovable patsy who is still smart enough to know what's best for him."[12] Skulnik's future career as a *schlemiel* onstage was shaped by his role in *Getzel.* Although the lines of dialogue are credited to Isidor Friedman and Isidor Rosenberg, jokes like "I was ashamed to be born . . . to be naked," sound like Skulnik's own, so close are the role of Getzel the naive bridegroom and Skulnik's future roles as *schlemiel.* By 1936, his character had become familiar enough that *New York Times* critic William Schack, describing "our favorite nitwit" Menasha Skulnik and his play titled *Schlemiehl,* wrote, "For years now, as Getzel, Yeckel, Yankel, Berel, Schmerel, [Skulnik] has made it plain that he is no intellectual giant, that his plans always go wrong, that he just can't make a living."[13] Skulnik's character, whatever his name onstage, whatever the playwright's name, was recognized as his own creation, and made a living as the man who can't make a living.

The Bronx Casanova

Skulnik's *schlemiel* becomes less naïve and shy in the second half of *Getzel Becomes a Bridegroom*. He displays boldness in his union activism and also when Eva, the matchmaker's daughter, enters as a Turkish princess. Her exoticism, her beauty, and the attractive costume worn by the actress tempt Getzel to kiss her. He forgets his arranged marriage to Selba. His unfaithfulness may be only a dream, but the bridegroom also enjoys talking to Eva when he wakes up. Before she wakes Getzel up, Eva's role resembles that of the Turkish harem women who love a *schlemiel* in Skulnik's song (not sung for the *Getzel* play), "Cordova, the Bronx Casanova." In that song, Cordova lyrically boasts, "I once spent a weekend in Turkey, showed the Sultan a thing or three. And when I flew back to my little Bronx shack, the whole darn Harem followed me."[14] The milquetoast sound of Skulnik's voice undermines the boast of prowess; but in his dreams and his song, the timid man—a Yiddish Walter Mitty—finds himself drawn to Turkish temptresses.

Eva also appears to be carried away by the pseudo-Turkish romance. She considers leaving her husband and becoming Getzel's lover, until her husband dissuades her. The imagined exoticism of the Orient may inspire Eva's actions to some extent; but she also suspects her husband of infidelity with a Russian immigrant woman. Eva prepares to leave her spouse because, in her words, she would rather have a husband who is a fool (Getzel), and be the smart wife, than have a wise husband whose wife (meaning Eva with her philandering husband Sim) is a fool. Whatever the reason why Eva admits an attraction for Getzel, her admission briefly overwhelms him. With comic abandon—of his language, not his wife—the *schlemiel* cries out in English, "She loves me!" Ultimately, however, Eva and Sim reconcile. Getzel, his philandering thwarted, ends up accepting Selba and her children as his own family.

Getzel's dream of a Turkish princess and the accompanying ensemble song and dance in the production introduce a Yiddish version of the phenomenon Edward Said terms "Orientalism." Highly critical of Western subjugation of Asians and Mideastern people, Said defines

"Orientalism" as a construction of cultural and imperial fantasies by Westerners who would dominate non-Westerners.[15] The fantasies of domination to which Said refers are generally less innocent than the dream sequence in *Getzel Becomes a Bridegroom*. Still, Getzel's fantasies of illicit love and infidelity are not wholly innocent or devoid of sexism and racial and class biases. The compliant "Turkish woman" makes herself available for bigamy in Getzel's dream. "Why wasn't I born a Turk?" asks Getzel. Knowing he already has one wife, he adds, "a Turk can have as many wives as he wants." The play criticizes his fantasy to some extent by denying its reality when the *schlemiel* wakes from his dream.

The play, however, does not introduce comic geopolitical references to Turkey and Palestine, as Sholem Aleichem did in one of his stories about Kasrilevke, a story titled "Homesick." Aleichem's character wonders, "What could be easier than buying Palestine from the Turks? Let's face it—what could block it? Money was no problem. . . . One Rothschild (if only he wanted) could buy up not only Palestine and Istanbul, but all the Turks to boot."[16] Getzel's Oriental fantasy looks far more restrained, by comparison.

His dream of a "Turkish" woman in a harem, with him as the Sultan, also hints at a minor rebellion against arranged marriages among Jews. Bridegroom Getzel, as noted earlier, reports that for eight years in America he looked for a "kosher girl." You would not expect the Turkish girl of his dreams to have been raised kosher, but since Eva's father works as a kosher chicken slaughterer as well as a matchmaker, Getzel turns out not to be too profligate; he doesn't stray from kosher women even in his sleep. Still, he rebels against arranged marriage in his own way, and his dissident nature surfaces again when he calls for a strike by the chicken slaughterer's union.

Two Celebrated Unions

Getzel Becomes a Bridegroom portrays two unions: one created through marriage, one created through labor organizing. The subplot introduces a strike by the chicken slaughterers who form a union to protect their wages. This combination of the plots transforms what would otherwise be another Yiddish wedding comedy into a play with a thirties social conscience, and a few moments of comic messianism. When the *schlemiel* portrayed by Skulnik first enters, he informs his new friends in Coney Island that he is a chicken-flicker. He hopes that after marriage he will

Figure 7.2

"Skulnik on Strike." Comic strip illustrated by Spain Rodriguez. *Courtesy of* Jewish Currents *and the artist.*

learn the practice of kosher slaughtering—and advance from plucking chickens to killing them in an approved manner. Although hardly a rampant careerist, the man wants more from life than chicken feathers. (In 1938, comedian Leo Fuchs played the role of Getzel. Fuchs also performed a song about a chicken-flicker, but that song doesn't appear in the original script of *Getzel*. Another Yiddish union, one composed of matchmakers, surfaced in Fuchs's 1940 film, *American Matchmaker*.)

The depiction of union organizing and a strike by slaughterers within the play includes Getzel's selection as union president. His comrades assume no speech from the bosses will move Getzel to compromise—their fancy words will go right past him, if not over his head. The newly appointed leader tries to be a fiery political activist, but with the usual ineptness of a *schlemiel,* he has trouble coming up with a plan for the union to follow.

> GETZEL: I want to see blood!
>
> ALL: Blood?
>
> GETZEL: I don't mean blood from chickens. I want to see your blood!
>
> NAHUM: God be with you, Getzel.
>
> GETZEL: I don't know about you, but I will see blood. Take for example Russia. What has Russia done? Do you know what Russia did?
>
> ALL: No.
>
> GETZEL: I don't know either. But I know that Russia has a five-year plan. We Hebrew chicken slaughterers need a better one, we need to make a ten-year plan. We need to strike for ten years.
>
> ALL: No, we want to eat!
>
> GETZEL: I don't mean we should make a revolution right away; we've already gone on strike.
>
> ALL: So what should we do now?
>
> GETZEL: Pray . . . (*They begin to pray in Hebrew.*)

Not a revolutionary, Getzel quickly runs out of steam and advises the union to try prayer. Life as a *schlemiel* with a naïve faith in others, including God, has its advantages. The scene, however, should not be mistaken for an anti-union comedy. (Many Yiddish actors in New York were members of the Hebrew Actors Union.) The parody's critique of union activism takes aim at extreme and self-defeating measures, and if anyone knows about self-defeating measures, it should be a *schlemiel* like Getzel. The fact that his union wins its strike in the play suggests that the comedy and its creators sympathized with union struggles, and did not regard marriage as the only turbulent event fit for comedy during the Great Depression. Elsewhere in the play, when an anti-union character calls the strikers "Bolsheviks," the comedy mildly mocks red smear tactics as unjustified vilification.

While hardly a leftist play like those staged by Artef, *Getzel Becomes a Bridegroom* celebrated the labor movement and, briefly, comically cast Skulnik as a messianic leader. Getzel can lead the strikers in part because of his imperviousness to the odds against him. His absurd proposal to strike for ten years parodies Soviet planning, but Getzel knows too little about the impracticality of such a plan to let it stop him. He commits the union to a long struggle—if only for a few moments, until the strikers protest against his proposal.

In his short-lived, parodic calling as a revolutionary, Getzel displays some of the messianic character traits that critic Ruth Wisse attributed to *schlemiels*: "The figure of the simple man continued to be used . . . to demonstrate the real advantage of faith, than which nothing in the modern world seems more foolish, over reason and intelligence. . . . The schlemiels are committed to Messianic truth, and if need be they can reinterpret, distort, or obviate immediate reality when it contradicts their ultimate ideal."[17] Wisse was not referring to Skulnik when she wrote these words; but his call for prayer and his fiery words to strikers might well be described as a triumph of "the foolish, over reason and intelligence." Getzel even briefly, comically assumes the mantle of secular messianism, insofar as prayer is his fallback position; a workers' struggle, more enduring than Russia's, his first choice.

The union strike receives less attention than the wedding in the play. But its triumphal course accompanies the other festivities—the marriage and its aftermath. Skulnik's anecdotal introduction of a ten-year union plan and (elsewhere in the play) his history of avoiding service in the Tsar's army introduce us to the bridegroom's character as a wedding jester might through his jokes, only here the bridegroom himself is the most humorous speaker.[18] The role of the *badchen* has been wedded, as it were, to that of the chicken-plucking, strike-supporting *schlemiel*.

Where once the *badchen* joked about the bridegroom, the bride, and their celebration, in *Getzel Becomes a Bridegroom* the bridegroom becomes the jester. The wedding provides an occasion for comedy about other momentous events in his life too: a labor strike, war, overcoming the temptations of a Sultan's harem. Comic *shund* on a stage is not exactly the same as a Jewish wedding offstage; but the theatre's audience members become celebrants of a kind, as they laugh and applaud the premarital and postmarital adventures of newlyweds. Leon Kobrin in his 1925 memoirs of Yiddish theatre recalled that, early in the twentieth century, audiences and actors were boisterous. Sometimes the actors would get married on stage, and invite the audience to witness their matrimonials. Even without such marriages, recalled Kobrin, "the theatre had the atmosphere of a Jewish celebration, where the *bodchins* and dancers entertained the roistering public, rather than the atmosphere of an art temple."[19] That celebratory spirit survived in *Getzel Becomes a Bridegroom*, too, with Menasha Skulnik featured in two unions.[20]

8

Prosperity's Crisis on Stage

The Yiddish Puppetry of Maud and Cutler

> To speak of a puppet with most men and women is to cause them to
> giggle. They think at once of the wires; they think of the stiff hands
> and the jerky movements; they tell me it is "a funny little doll." But
> let me tell them a few things about these puppets. Let me again repeat
> that they are the descendants of a great and noble family of Images,
> images which were indeed made "in the likeness of God."
>
> Gordon Craig, "The Actor and the Über-Marionette"[1]

When the English stage designer and director Gordon Craig
published a manifesto praising marionettes in 1907, he
spoke with great reverence for the art of puppetry and
its animated objects. Craig would have been distressed by the arrival
of the Yiddish puppeteers Yosl Cutler and Zuni Maud two decades
later, as their practices contradicted almost everything he advocated.
Craig wanted to banish human actors from the theatre, and replace
them with puppets; Maud and Cutler gave human forms smaller and
more comic features, but still represented them on stage through
puppets. Craig wanted to revive the sacred impulses of ancient puppetry; Maud and Cutler satirized religious icons and legends. In one
of their Yiddish puppet plays, God appeared, mainly to demand that
others praise His greatness. If the appearance of God, or other acts
performed by the Yiddish puppeteers, caused men and women to
giggle at religious figures, and not take them seriously, Maud and
Cutler would have been pleased; they were satirists, after all. Their
popular entertainments were not the future of puppetry Gordon
Craig envisioned. But they moved puppetry in new directions, where
their friend Moishe Nadir also proceeded, to create anti-religious
and secular messianic satire in Yiddish.

Thousands of spectators applauded Modicut, the puppet troupe to which Zuni Maud and Yosl Cutler each gave half of their last name. Their partnership extended from 1925 until 1933. During their years together, Maud and Cutler toured with their Yiddish puppet plays in London, Paris, Warsaw, Vilna, Moscow, and the Catskills, when not at their own theatre on Manhattan's Lower East Side. Their popular art prompted laughter at images of questionable wealth and authority. They turned Franklin Roosevelt and William Randolph Hearst into comic wonder rabbis, whose powers to bless and curse they then mocked. Rather than celebrating great leaders on their tiny stage, Maud and Cutler portrayed the struggles and triumphs of "little" men and women, ordinary, working-class characters more likely to read eviction notices than prayers during the Great Depression.

When not inside their own theatre, Modicut's puppeteers sometimes performed at Yiddish Communist cultural events in New York, in collaboration with Nadir and Artef. Yosl Cutler first met Moishe Nadir at the playwright and poet's summer hotel at Lake Sheldrake in 1919. Later Nadir's Artists' Café in New York sold tickets to Cutler and Maud's theatre. The friendship continued through 1933, when Cutler designed scenery for the Artef premiere of Nadir's *Messiah in America,* a benefit for the Communist Party's Yiddish Bureau. Their shared satiric, left-wing outlook spurred the puppeteers on to their finest productions, including performance of Nadir's *The Other World*—in which God bullies the angel Gabriel—and their parody of Ansky's Yiddish classic, *The Dybbuk.* Cutler dedicated his last version of *The Dybbuk,* published posthumously in 1936, to his "dear comrade Moishe Nadir."[2] While influenced by Nadir, one of Modicut's Yiddish puppet plays also acknowledged the political activism of the Communist "Unemployed Councils," which sponsored rent strikes in the thirties to benefit apartment tenants.

Simche and His Wife

In *Simche and His Wife,* Yiddish-speaking Simche, and wife, Sheyne Pesi, face eviction from a New York apartment when their landlord gives them a "dispossess." Made of cloth and wood, Simche sports a thick black beard and a worker's cap. Sheyne Pesi wears a large headscarf. She cries out "Oy" and "Oy Vey Iz Mir," words of distress, when Simche tells her the landlord gave them an eviction notice as a Sabbath gift. The local Unemployed Council comes to their rescue, armed with picket signs, and soon the husband and wife celebrate their victorious stay in the apartment with song and dance. In this miniature musical comedy, Simche sings about how he lost employment as a locksmith, then lost his job as a clothing presser, and couldn't pay the rent when winter arrived. His wife accompanies Simche, as they sing about the arrival of the Unemployed Council's pickets. Their cheerful references to the rent protest are so fleeting that modern spectators probably would not know the Council was a Communist-led organization. Even Sheyne Pesi has never heard about the "Employment Council" (sic) until asked by her husband to run and notify them that the landlord has given the couple a "dispossess."[3] The Council members never appear on stage; we only briefly hear about their triumph. For Sheyne Pesi, and anyone who sees the performance of the play preserved on film, the Unemployed Council might as well be the new messiah, who also arrives unrecognized, according to legend. The Council solves the crisis like a magician whose art eludes human sight. The struggle between a cold-hearted landlord and rent strikers, who keep an evicted family off the street, stays offstage. There is an innocence about the puppets and their rescue, a joy and absence of party line slogans, which makes the play suitable for children as well as adults—provided they speak Yiddish.

Modicut's adult spectators would have known more than Sheyne Pesi about the Unemployed Councils. The *Morgn Frayhayt*'s front pages often reported on struggles against rent eviction; on January 4, 1933, for example, the Yiddish Communist newspaper featured a lead story about a demonstration against evictions at 1433 Charlotte Street in the Bronx, and another story about a rent strike on Franklin Avenue. If spectators had not already witnessed confrontation between rent strikers and police before going to the theatre, they could see such conflict more fully portrayed in a play by Cutler titled *Out and In*.[4] Its crowd scene with many characters might render *Out and In* less effective on a small puppet stage than the simple, two-character song and dance of *Simche and His Wife*. But like Simche's story, the longer play ends with a triumphant song and dance.

Joyful song and dance and the naiveté of Modicut's plays recall Brecht's writing on the need for fun and new views of the world in theatre;[5] perhaps Modicut shared Brecht's epic theatre aesthetics as well as his politics, although the puppeteers never called themselves Brechtians. Their spirit of playfulness renews the Yiddish traditions of *Purimshpiln* (plays that celebrated Jewish victory over the tyrant Haman) and of wedding

Figure 8.1

Modicut puppet theatre card with the Master of
Ceremonies, illustrated by Zuni Maud. *From the
archives of the YIVO Institute for Jewish Research, New York.*

jesters, whose antics the puppeteers would have known from their child-
hoods in Eastern Europe.[6] (Maud emigrated from Russia to the United
States in 1905, and Cutler emigrated from the Ukraine in 1911.)

The two men also drew cartoons for various Yiddish journals. Their
expertise as visual artists led director Maurice Schwartz to hire them in
1924 for his production of Goldfaden's *The Witch*; they designed scenery,
costumes, and their first puppets. Their own puppet theatre followed in
1925 with *King Achashverus,* a play based on the traditional story of
Purim. Another play in their first repertoire portrayed Jewish pepper
merchants who tell bears not to eat them, because they (the salesmen)
are too peppery; the bears let their guests go, and the Jewish merchants
survive danger, a harbinger of later comic survivals by Modicut puppets.
From fables Maud and Cutler moved on to topical satire with a version

of *The Dybbuk* in September 1926. They kept changing its text to comment on current events over the next decade.

Billing itself as the first Yiddish puppet theatre in America, Modicut created innovative, satiric theatre throughout its eight-year life.[7] Although some of their plays might be classified as Yiddish Communist theatre, Maud and Cutler had no rivals. Far different from the full-length plays of the Artef collective in New York and Goset, the state Yiddish theatre in Moscow, their repertoire consisted of short musicals and satires that fit onto a small stage. Freed from the need to support a large ensemble of actors, Maud and Cutler's mobile shows reached a widespread audience—thousands of adults and children—through travels in New York and abroad. It could be argued that Yiddish Communism of the period never achieved its international goals. But Maud and Cutler successfully practiced their own internationalism, through performance of radical Yiddish puppet plays welcomed in many locations. They distributed their own wealth of humor and song, their own models of social justice and artistic engagement around the world.

Their vision of a world improved by Yiddish Communist activism was not entirely imaginary. As noted already, the rescue of Simche and Sheyne Pesi from eviction had a counterpart in Communist-led rent strikes. Communists associated with the newspaper *Morgn Frayhayt* not only "were the folks who came to put your furniture back in your tenement after you were evicted for being late with the rent one month," as Yiddishist Dovid Katz notes; they also "were the people fighting for the rights of the poor, the unemployed, the disenfranchised, the victims of all sorts of prejudice, not least racial and religious." On the domestic front, New York's Yiddish Communists developed their own local responses to events, and did not have to follow a line from Moscow. Their foreign policies advocated laudable positions at times too, as Katz suggests; they "took the lead in exposing Hitlerism for what it was from the first moment. . . . The unrelenting exposure of the Fascist threat was no mean feat in the early and mid-1930s."[8] (One of Modicut's contributions to the anti-Nazi movement was a Hitler puppet that bared its fangs when one arm rose in a "Heil" salute.[9])

Communist journals such as *Morgn Frayhayt* and *Der Hamer* also provided space for Maud, Cutler, and their collaborator Nadir to publish some of their finest satire, where it remains available in archives today. Modicut's theatre now can be glimpsed in rare documents of its achievements: a seventeen-minute film, photographs, a few Yiddish stage texts, and cartoons the two men drew. Few of their scripts survive. Most of the world they created on stage can no longer be seen. Even when the puppeteers first performed their plays in the early part of the twentieth century, some of the offstage world to which they referred was disappearing, as critic Samuel Tenenbaum noted in "Puppets that Speak Yiddish," an essay B'nai B'rith Magazine published in 1934:

> The like of the puppets which the Modicot Theatre presents has never been seen before. They act as Jews, they think as Jews, they look like Jews. The troup [sic] includes rabbis, matchmakers, malamdin (Hebrew teachers), Jewish clothing bosses, the Maggid, the anti-Semite, the luftmentsch—types that are rapidly disappearing from Jewish life.[10]

As Eastern European immigrants in America, Cutler and Maud postponed the prospective loss of traditional, Old World Jewish characters in a period of social change, by preserving on their stage images of the matchmakers and luftmentschen (men of "air," who lived on dreams and speculations). Their shows were not simply acts of cultural conservation, however; the puppeteers mocked some of the old and legendary Jewish traditions, including the Old Testament God, and jested about new, progressive politics and popular artistic developments, such as FDR's New Deal and the 1926 (then new) New York stage versions of Ansky's Yiddish play, The Dybbuk.

He Wants to Know the Truth

In the early thirties, for all of the Roosevelt administration's innovations, the federal government had not yet resolved America's economic crisis, and Maud and Cutler still regarded the USSR as a promising alternative. They visited the Soviet Union twice, and performed their puppet shows to acclaim in Moscow and other Russian cities. One short play written by Yosl Cutler, and performed for Artef in December 1933, re-creates in comic form a debate he and his associates heard (or engaged in) during the period. The play He Wants to Know the Truth opens with a husband and wife debating whether life would be better in the Soviet Union or Palestine.[11] (Palestine at that time was under

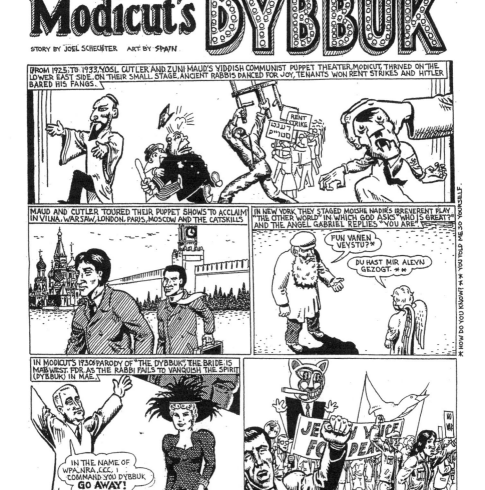

Figure 8.2

Modicut puppet theatre comic strip illustrated by Spain Rodriguez. *Courtesy of the artist and* Jewish Currents.

British rule, not yet the sovereign nation and homeland for Jews that Israel has become.) The husband tells his wife she would be better off in Palestine, where he wants to retire, and if he were in Russia he would be tortured. The wife says he has heard lies about Russia. Then she sees Yosl (the author) passing by, and since he has just returned from a visit to the Soviet Union, she wants to hear his report. She asks if he was there for a long time.

> YOSL: It depends what you mean by long and short. For one person three weeks in Russia can be long, for another, three years in the Soviet Union can be short.
> HE [Husband]: Oh, Yosl's already playing his tricks. [His *shtick*.] What did you hear in Russia? How're the Jews doing there?

Yosl does not condemn Russia for its treatment of Jews. His casual, comic answers suggest that Jews in Russia are just as fully employed, and just as idle, as other residents of the country. The husband clearly wants to hear that Russian Jews are beaten, and presses Yosl to admit it. Eventually Yosl agrees, "They used to beat the Jews. For." The Yiddish word used here could mean "for" in the sense of "pro" or "in favor of," but Yosl's interrogators hears the word "fur."

> HE: Aha, I understand you now. You want to say they beat Jews in fur coats.
> YOSL: That's correct, only not completely.
> HE: Tell me everything, please.

Next Yosl employs a pun on the words "for" and "schlagen" (to beat). Together, as "forschlagen" they constitute the verb "to propose." Yosl says it has been proposed that Jews travel to Birobidzhan, an autonomous Jewish region in the USSR. This comic wordplay disappoints Yosl's colleague, as it deprives the red-baiter confirmation of Soviet Jewbeating that he wanted his wife to hear.

Cutler's scenario finds humor in the anti-revolutionary position, and the puppeteer plays with words rather than unequivocally agreeing that the Soviets mistreat Jews. He goes his own merry way, as suggested by the Yiddish title of the book (*Muntergang*, or *Merry Way*) in which he printed the play in 1934.

In this dialogue, with its focus on the position of Jews in the Soviet state, Cutler's contrarian view of Communism appears to be inseparable from Yiddish culture (including puns in Yiddish). Like his interrogator in the playlet, Yosl too sees a special relationship between Jews and the Soviet Union, but Birobidzhan rather than anti-Semitic brutality is the link. Yiddish culture and language are shown to be not only part of a larger group of cultures and beliefs but also a distinct, identifiably different part of the whole: "correct, only not completely."

Cutler's openness to change and diversity here anticipates in his own comic way an understanding of cultural diversity expressed in 1947 by the Yiddish author and journal editor Itche Goldberg: "cultural democracy today means full co-existence of the various cultures . . . by which each culture creates and builds for itself and simultaneously enriches the general culture of our land. . . . [T]he U.S. has never been a land of one language."[12]

Preservation of a separate, distinct language or culture within a more general culture would guarantee an independent identity to the preservationists. They would not wholly lose themselves or sacrifice all to the state, whether it is Russia, Palestine, or the United States. This could explain why Modicut chose to ridicule popular Yiddish culture, popular American figures, and fixed ideas about the Soviet Union. The puppeteers felt free to mock all sides—like Chonon, the deceased man whose spirit lives on in their new versions of *The Dybbuk*; the learned man defies all the rabbis who would exorcise him and end the heterodoxy his free spirit represents. The puppeteers, who side with the dispossessed in their rent strike plays, favor the possessed (Leah, the woman possessed by Chonon's wild, unruly spirit) in their *Dybbuk* parody.

Nishka

In a number of Modicut plays, creativity thrives on a spirit of dissent, at times almost childlike in its refusal to conform to expectations, or leap onto a bandwagon. Cutler's poem "Nishka," published in a 1934 collection, contains this playful defiance in its title and lyrics. "Nishka" is the name given a character who is "Not." Instead of the old vaudeville routine about "who's on first," and "what's on second," the poem suggests that "Niskha" is "not" many things.

Guess who he is!
You don't know?
You can't catch him.
So take it slow.

Ask a question.
What kind of fish?
I'll tell you
What he isn't.

He's not a carpenter.
He's not a farmer.
He's not a tailor.
He's not a builder . . .

He's not,
And that's it.

And though he is none
Of these things,
Even so,
He can do everything.

When a furrier
Needs to make a coat.
He takes a pelt
And makes it.

But when Nishka
Needs to make a coat
He takes a pelt
Along with a furrier
And makes it . . .

When a writer wants to write
A new poem
He takes a pen
And a bit of paper
And then composes it.

When Nishka wants to write
A new poem:
He takes a bit of paper, a pen
And a bit of a writer
And then creates it . . .

He's whatever's in the cards:

A racer, a guzzler,
A laugh, a buyer,
A grabber, a whirlwind,
A taker, a creeper . . .

Nishka gets on tolerably well.
He simply lives on earth.
And he's immensely happy
That his mother
Gave him birth.[13]

Cutler's verse recalls the nonsense poetry of Lewis Carroll, Edward Lear, and Bert Williams' song, "Nobody," and anticipates the Beatles song, "Nowhere Man." The poem celebrates an absence of a fixed, constant identity; but Nishka's lack of a profession he can call his own and his dependence on the work of others are not so surprising, given the widespread displacement and scarcity of jobs in the thirties. Millions of other Americans were not carpenters, or farmers, or tailors, or builders at that time, though they had been, before the Depression. Others who were unemployed may have shared Nishka's condition, if not his name. They too were ready to do anything, and take whatever was in the cards. Such uncertain standing in American society was nothing to sing about, unless you sang the blues, or Yiddish lyrics like Cutler's, later set to music for a chorus by Jacob Shaefer.

The Crisis Dybbuk

In the course of reshaping the world to fit their satiric, small-stage versions of events in the twenties and thirties, Modicut's puppeteers turned their attention to *The Dybbuk* in 1926. They continued to perform different parodies of Ansky's classic through 1935, and updated the dialogue to reflect changing cultural and political conditions. They turned the *Hamlet* of Yiddish theatre, Ansky's classic tragedy, *The Dybbuk,* into a comedy on the Modicut stage. The world as they saw it was not tragic, despite the economic and social crises of the period.

In Maud and Cutler's *Dybbuk,* the scholar Chonon falls in love with Leah, dies, and enters her as a spirit when denied a chance to marry her; this much, and the arrival of rabbis to exorcise Chonon's spirit from Leah, can be found in the original version of the play written by Ansky in 1914. But Modicut's lovelorn Kabbalist resists all entreaties to cease and desist; he refuses to be exorcised.

An English-language synopsis Modicut published to describe its 1926–27 parody of the play summarized the plot this way:

1st scene—The Prologue

The scene represents the last moments of Sh. Ansky's Dybuk [sic]. The Dybuk reenters Leah and she dies. In this play, however, the Yiddish messenger calls up a well-known theatre critic (a Ph.D.) on the telephone, asking him to save Leah, so the Dybuk may live [in her]. The critic arrives through the telephone. Crying "Holy, Holy, Holy," he brings Leah back to life. Happy that this Dybuk has been saved for some more chasing, all sing "Dybuk, Dybuk, Dybuk."[14]

Although their chant could serve as a happy ending, the puppet play does not end there. In the second scene, we are told, "after eighteen years of being chased we discover Chonon the Dybuk and Leah in their apartment on Delancey Street [on New York's Lower East Side], where daily both the Yiddish, and English theatre casts come to drive the Dybuk out of Leah. The same today. The Dybuk has grown used to it and lets them chase him out, only to go into Leah and out of her, with great nonchalance, whenever he pleases."

In the third scene, the Epilogue, rabbis who have failed to expel the Dybuk summon Chonon's father, Meth Thoar, from his grave. The corpse of the father and the dybuk son are reconciled, and the father vows to "put out the Dybuk." The play ends as "[t]he Dybuk enters Leah for the last time. Ensemble sings, 'Dybuk, Dybuk, Dybuk.'" The play ends with Chonon still a Dybuk in residence, inside Leah.

In the 1926 version of Modicut's parody, rabbis attempting to exorcise the dybbuk in Leah arrive from local, New York casts of the play. At the time, Ansky's play was being presented locally by several Yiddish theatre companies—the Vilna Troupe, the Yiddish Art Theatre, even the English-language Neighborhood Playhouse. Maud and Cutler mocked the vogue for Ansky's drama by placing the different versions in competition, and having all of them fail in their attempts at an ancient ritual of exorcism.

In a later version of the evolving parody, a Herbert Hoover puppet, wearing a rotten apple for a head, appeared as a rabbi.[15] (Apple sellers could be seen on many street corners during the Depression; why shouldn't the nation's leader carry an apple on his shoulders, especially if he didn't have much else up there?) By 1933, after Franklin Roosevelt became president, a puppet representing him entered the play as the miracle-working rabbi who might end the crisis. The dybbuk continued to resist its would-be conquerors; the result was a triumph of the spirit of resistance, a spirit created through satire and social criticism.

Edward Portnoy in his superb essay on Modicut rightly calls its early parody of *The Dybbuk* "a satire on popular Yiddish culture," with its "welcome comic relief" for theatregoers "who had tired of the many productions of *The Dybuk* that season [1926]."[16] The later version with parodies of FDR and Mae West extended the satire to include American popular culture and politics. In a June 1936 introduction to Yosl Cutler's revised scenes of the play, published in the journal, *Der Signal,* Moishe Katz noted that the political satire represented the crisis of the Depression as a dybbuk trapped inside "Prosperity."[17]

The full title of the 1936 version was *Der Dybuk in Crisis Gestalt* [*The Dybbuk in the Form of a Crisis*]. "Prosperity" in Cutler's play is the name given to the attractive, sensual Leah, who speaks at one point like Mae

West.[18] Soon after the parody's devout student, Chonon, announces he will die for love of Leah, he falls down. As the synagogue's caretakers, Shames and Beadle, try to revive Chonon with brandy, they recall that Leah's wealthy father, Sender, earlier called the student a dybbuk, a crisis, and poverty in human form. But the attendants are not terribly alarmed. The Beadle notes there are plenty of rabbis available to drive away a dybbuk, and he names a few, including newspaper moguls Abe Cahan and William Randolph Hearst. (Cahan edited the Yiddish *Forward*; Hearst owned a chain of papers and was also a friend of Hitler, one puppet noted.)

In the 1936 version of the play, Chonon's delirium might be due to his rigorous mystical meditations or his love of Leah, but more likely, he faints and dies because he has hardly eaten since 1929. His own poverty and hunger parallel those of the nation. Before his demise, Chonon analyzes the nation's crisis in a parody of Kabbalistic number interpretation. He announces, "The 9 signifies: united, and 40 signifies: front. This signifies: that the Yiddish poor with the goyish crisis have to create a united front."

Although it originates in a parodic Kabbalah reading, Chonon's vision of a "united front" formed by those in crisis recalls far more serious Communist-supported plans for an anti-fascist Popular Front after 1935. Heeding his character's call, and mocking it at the same time, Cutler facilitates a comic union between Jews and powerful *goyim* (non-Jews) later in the play, when Chonon becomes a dybbuk whom Franklin Roosevelt must exorcise from a woman resembling Mae West.

The puppet figure of FDR tries to exorcise the spirit by chanting "WPA, NRA, CCC," waving overhead a Blue Eagle, symbol of the National Recovery Administration, and commanding the Dybuk to go away[19]; just as FDR fails, the satire implies that New Deal programs cannot solve everyone's problems. In fact, the New Deal's litany of acronyms for its new programs, and the programs themselves, did not immediately or magically solve the economic and social crises of the Great Depression; problems persisted, like the Dybuk's presence in the play. Nishka's refusal to be a farmer or tailor or carpenter in Cutler's poem has a sequel in Chonon's refusal to yield to the panaceas represented by the abbreviations WPA, NRA, and CCC.

The bride in the play also rebels in her own way. In the scene where she meets Chonon, Leah displays an extremely funny, irrepressible sensuality. She first visits the synagogue with her grandmother and kisses the holy Torah. Traditionally Jews gently kiss the sacred scroll in a tribute to the divine words it holds. Cutler's Leah refuses to let go of the Torah; she continues to hold and kiss the scroll until pulled away. "Let up, woman," the synagogue caretaker implores. The Beadle in the room informs her, "A Torah is not a sweetheart." As if to prove she knows a sweetheart when she sees one, Leah as she exits eyes Chonon (distracted by her, unable to pray), and offers him Mae West's famous line (transliterated into Yiddish): "Come up and see me sometime." If Chonon were not already infatuated with her, this could drive him over the edge. The Mae West incarnation of Leah displays less modesty than the bride in Ansky's original version of the play, although there too, Leah rather affectionately kisses the Torah in the synagogue. Ansky's stage directions say that she embraces the holy scroll, "presses her lips against it. Kisses it passionately."[20] Cutler does not wholly invent the young woman's sensual behavior, but renders it more comic with his homage to a Hollywood star.

Another variation on the original version of Ansky's play occurs when Leah's father provides a banquet for the poor. Traditionally, a Jewish wedding's host would invite poor people to celebrate and eat. In Ansky's *Dybbuk,* some of the poor complain about the meagerness of the offerings. Far bolder in Cutler's parody, the poor march in with placards and recite slogans demanding unemployment insurance. They complain that the rich have eaten their fill, like pigs, and left only crumbs for the poor. The bride's father, Sender, says he will grant their request for insurance. Then the police rush in and chase away the protesters amid shooting and beatings. Cutler's scenario for a poor people's protest enacted by puppets brings the street life and political demonstrations of the thirties into "classic" Yiddish theatre.

Other topical references in the 1936 *Dybbuk* concern a blue bird—not the bluebird of happiness, but the blue eagle mentioned earlier, which represented the National Recovery Administration (NRA) under Roosevelt's administration. Roosevelt's hoisting an eagle aloft during the exorcism, and lines spoken by the eagle needed no footnote in the mid-thirties. Pictures of the bird could be seen across the United States between 1933 and 1935, as thousands of businesses that agreed to the NRA "blanket code" displayed the bird's image.[21] Businesses accepting the code paid workers a minimum of twelve to fifteen dollars a week, abolished child labor, and granted blue-collar workers a thirty-five-hour work week. Agreement to these terms entitled the businesses to waive antitrust laws. The NRA also permitted laborers to seek improved working conditions through unions. But leftists like Cutler and Maud had doubts that the NRA and its blue eagle conferred benefits on workers, particularly after businesses failed to negotiate in good faith with the unions and physically intimidated strikers.

The "blue bird" appeared in the constantly evolving puppeteers' version of *The Dybbuk* as the NRA neared its end, which came in May 1935 after the Supreme Court ruled the NRA code system unconstitutional. The eagle would have been remembered—and not fondly—when it spoke in Cutler's 1936 version of the parody. First the synagogue Shames and Beadle discuss rabbis capable of conducting an exorcism. Their candidates include *Forward* editor Abe Cahan and newspaper magnate William Randolph Hearst ("friend of the richest magnates of industry, friend of war, friend of Hitler"). "But the greatest rabbi," says the Beadle, "is Rabbi Roosevelt," who works with a little blue bird. His avian friend sometimes is invisible, sometimes entirely devoted to business, we are told. The reference to the bird as an invisible person—"roye-ve eyne-ni-re" in Yiddish—involves a pun, and echoes of "N.R.A." can be heard in it. The joke hints that the blue eagle, the National Recovery Administration it represents, and their relief cannot be seen by everyone; later the eagle himself speaks and suggests he has no interest in the poor, only the rich.

After Cutler's Yiddish-speaking puppets refer to Leah as "Prosperity," who is possessed by a "Crisis," Rabbi Roosevelt and the blue eagle of his National Recovery Administration do not remove the Crisis from Prosperity. Instead, Roosevelt gives the eagle to Sender as a wedding present, and tells the father of the possessed bride that with his gift Sender can do business with all lenders. (The rhyme works in Yiddish too.) Sender wants his daughter to marry J. P. Morgan's grandson. She prefers Chonon, another reason to equate the student with a Crisis.

Roosevelt's eagle speaks and inadvertently offers an explanation for Maud and Cutler's discontent with the NRA. In rhymed Yiddish lines (with the rhyme lost in translation) the eagle says,

> I am the bird
> from the song of songs.
> I'm no good for the poor
> And I've sickened the rich.

"The Song of Songs," which Chonon sings earlier in the synagogue, includes reference to the eyes of a dove, and hair black as a raven's, but no praise for blue eagles. Perhaps the blue bird sees himself as a dove or a raven, or simply claims credit where it is not due. In any case his words, spoken before the eagle dances to klezmer wedding music, accurately sum up the antagonism business owners and conservative politicians expressed toward many of Roosevelt's programs, including the NRA. Labor unions and Communists were not pleased by the NRA either; they saw the program doing little for the poor and the working class. The labor movement found new forms of activism, such as the sit-down strike, more effective than the NRA in winning concessions from management.

The ingenuity shown by Cutler and Maud in modernizing *The Dybbuk* would be difficult to match today. In the thirties, they could count on their audience knowing Ansky's Yiddish play and political issues of the day well enough to enjoy the topical references. As Yiddish Communists, the puppeteers were not prepared to welcome Roosevelt's New Deal and his blue bird in the thirties any more than they would welcome a traditional rabbinical council of exorcists to save them. They had reservations about capitalist democracy as well as Jewish ritual, and satirized both in their versions of *The Dybbuk*. Like Nadir's *Messiah in America*, Modicut's *Dybbuk* satire called into question the promise of modern saviors at the same time as the puppeteers revived and mocked traditional Jewish images of redemption.

The Other World

Another comic invocation of Old World miracles can be seen in the brief puppet play, "Kosher Dance."[22] A puppet representing an old rabbi almost staggers onto the stage, with Yosl Cutler's unobtrusive helping hand. Barely able to see through his long white hair, the rabbi promises the audience a miracle, and then proceeds to create it by forgetting his decrepit status and dancing. His miracle is self-made, human in form (although cloth and wood in content). It requires no praise or invocation of a higher order, no Comintern or new laws, as the rabbi slowly lifts his feet in time to a traditional Jewish tune, with percussion added as Simche (from the earlier rent eviction play) comes out and beats a drum.

The dance is a small miracle, to be sure; on Modicut's puppet stage everything is small, except the implications of the acts shown. They take on extra dimensions, as the scenes become poetic metaphors for larger and more difficult struggles to survive and keep dancing. In their miniature stage world, Modicut's artists fulfilled an artistic tendency that writer Hannah Arendt once attributed to Walter Benjamin, when she observed, "For him the size of an object was in an inverse ratio to its significance. . . . The smaller the object, the more likely that it seemed it could contain in the most concentrated form everything else. Hence his delight that two grains of wheat should contain the entire Shema Israel, the very essence of Judaism, tiniest essence, appearing on [the] tiniest entity."[23]

For Maud and Cutler, not a prayer praising God, engraved on a grain or two of wheat, but rather God Himself, reduced to the miniature form of a Yiddish-speaking puppet, took on large significance. A graven image of God, or a puppet representation of divine form might be regarded as blasphemous in some circles (including those who observe the Ten Commandments). For Gordon Craig, quoted earlier, puppets were "descendants of a great and noble family of Images, images which were indeed made 'in the likeness of God.'" Modicut's reduction of God to puppet size on stage was accompanied by a comic inflation of His ego, if a divinity might be said to have an ego. In Moishe Nadir's puppet play, *The Other World,* which Modicut first staged in 1926, God keeps asking a devil and the archangel Gabriel to tell Him that He is great and powerful. Either this large marionette with a golden beard needs reassurance, or simply enjoys seeing others follow His commandments, which in this case are commandments to praise Him.

> GOD'S VOICE: Hey, Gabriel.
> GABRIEL: His voice. What is it, God?
> GOD: Who is great?
> GABRIEL: You.
> GOD: Who is smart?
> GABRIEL: You.
> GOD: Who is powerful?
> GABRIEL: You.
> GOD: Who is eternal?
> GABRIEL: You.
> GOD: How do you know this?
> GABRIEL: You told me yourself.
> GOD: That's right.
> GABRIEL: All day, all day he bores me with these questions. And
>   I have to answer. What can you do? I'm in His hands.[24]

The satire here refashions some of the most sacred Hebrew prayers, including the Kaddish, which praises the Lord repeatedly. In *The Other World*, God insists on his subjects repeating their praise, as if they will not do it without prompting. God's subjects are only puppets, after all. The Creator also appears to be a creation in *The Other World*.

Nadir's play declines to see divine order everywhere, and instead sketches an unpredictable, unjust world—in short, a world much like the one in which he lived. Here God speaks Yiddish, the language of everyday life, rather than the Hebrew associated with religious services. Here religion is a series of commands more resented than willingly honored. Like Maud and Cutler's other puppets, in Nadir's play the sinner, the righteous man, the angel, the devil, and the Almighty display everyday human qualities— pride, boredom, envy—even if their behavior recalls one of Groucho Marx's wisecracks to his brother Chico: "it's human to make mistakes, and you're only human. However, no one would know it to look at you."[25]

Reviewing Modicut's staging of *The Other World* in 1926, the *Frayhayt*'s critic praised the play for its "Moishenadirish" humor and "pranksterish" qualities,[26] but he complained that an angel puppet lacked the traditional six wings (two to fly, two to cover its face in the presence of God, and two to cover its cloven feet). In his call for traditional representation of a religious figure, the Communist newspaper's critic missed the point: Modicut's representations of the divine had human features and human failings, as if they were created by human beings (which they were). If he couldn't sense this in the design of the puppets, the critic might have found the human-like failings of "the other world" in Nadir's comic dialogue and in the plot that sends a sinner to Heaven and a righteous person to Hell, with everything determined by chance, rather than divine ordination.

> GABRIEL: It's the way we do things now. They used to have bookkeeping, with cash bonuses. But God changed the system, when he saw the expenses were too great. He started a new system: knots. When someone dies and comes here, God holds in his hand two ends of a handkerchief. At one end there's a knot. If someone chooses the knot, he goes to Hell. If he avoids it, he goes to Paradise.[27]

There's no divine justice, only a divinely ordained game of chance in Nadir's vision of *The Other World*. The situation calls to mind a Hasidic saying that in the world to come, everything will be arranged as it is here, only a little differently.[28] In fact, Modicut's own performances rarely lost contact with life as it is "here," in human form. The faces of Cutler and Maud occasionally would pop up inside their small stage frame during the show. A short film featuring Yosl Cutler has him conversing with his well-dressed puppet master of ceremonies. According to Yiddish novelist Chaver Paver, Modicut's Master of Ceremonies puppet was so carefully modeled on Zuni Maud that "[w]hen Zuni worked this puppet, addressing the audience at the same time, it was hard to escape the illusion that the puppet was Zuni Maud himself."[29] (Maud does not appear in the only film that records Modicut's work, so it is difficult to compare him to the puppet Master of Ceremonies; but the puppet in the film does not look like most photographs of Maud—perhaps it is not the representation to which Paver referred.)

The Master of Ceremonies acknowledged other human forms, those of the audience too. Chaver Paver writes, in his fictionalized memoir of visits to Modicut, that the Master of Ceremonies would turn to the audience and ask, "Is so and so here?" as he named someone. "If the audience laughingly answer 'Yes,'" Paver reports, the puppet would reply, "All right, let him stay here." This comic acceptance of the human presence implied that the puppet could decide who stayed or left—a power exceedingly difficult to enforce, given his small size. An anecdote also recounts a performance in which Modicut's Master of Ceremonies introduced Chaver Paver to his future wife, a woman in the audience he had never met before; the Modicut puppet became matchmaker for a day.

Some of Modicut's characters—the Almighty in *The Other World,* the landlord who evicts Simche—appear cruel and unreasonable. But most of the puppets display a disarming joy in life. They are liable to break into song and dance during a rent strike, and even the factory owner puppet in the play *Business* sings about his rebellious employees.[30] (He sings a parody of the popular Rubin Doctor song, "I Want to Be a Boarder by My Wife." To the same tune, the boss chants, "I want to be the boss of my own shop," and complains the workers won't let him make all the decisions and enjoy his wealth.)

Such open displays of cheer, even from a selfish boss, could account for the popularity of the puppets on tour in Moscow, Warsaw, Vilna, Paris, London, and the Catskills. Modicut's cast employed several international languages—Yiddish was one, but laughter, dance, and highly visual humor were others. Those, along with the theatre's portability, the capacity of most of the cast to fit in one steamer trunk, enabled the international Communist troupe to travel inexpensively around the world. Like Eastern European immigrants who fled the injustices of Russia or Poland, Maud and Cutler traveled across Europe and America, only in reverse immigration—unsettling audiences with humor and iconoclasm, bringing a new American Yiddish culture and politics to people from the Old World. The wonder rabbis so famous in Eastern Europe were also welcome on Modicut's New York stage: but satire, not piety, not miracles, won them a devoted public.

9

Leo Fuchs, Yiddish Vaudevillian in "Trouble"

Everywhere you go, you hear people yelling woe.
These are troubled times.
   —Leo Fuchs, singing in *I Want to Be a Boarder*

L eo Fuchs lived in troubled times. The Yiddish actor immigrated to New York from Eastern Europe during the Depression. Unknown to American audiences, unable to perform in English, his future uncertain, Fuchs told producer Herman Yablokoff, "I'm going back to Poland. In Poland, I'm the greatest, but in America, I don't stand a chance."[1] Yablokoff persuaded the gifted comedian to stay around for his 1936 production of *Cigarettes* (*Papirossen*), which won acclaim on Second Avenue. Fuchs stood a chance, after all. In the New World, where immigrants once imagined that the streets were paved with gold, the comic actor had ample opportunity to see people like himself move from anonymity to fame, from poverty to wealth, and back again during the thirties. A vast array of unstable income levels and cultural identities coexisted in New York. Fuchs often depicted scenes from that world in Yiddish plays and films; his characters walked, then raced between different languages, different income levels, and different identities, sometimes changing identities within the course of a song.

His protean characters with multiple personalities passed from everyday life into a dream world—which the New World was for many immigrants. In the 1937 film *I Want to Be a Boarder*, Leo Fuchs portrays both a greenhorn—an unassimilated immigrant—and a successful, beloved nightclub entertainer, two distinct characters who may have represented halves of the actor's own life. Transforming his greenhorn apartment boarder into a nightclub star, and returning to his immigrant persona in the same act, Fuchs physically embodied some of the abrupt changes in class and wealth that Americans experienced during the Depression. He is not remembered as a cultural activist or social satirist, but one of Leo Fuchs's best song and dance numbers, "Trouble," in the film *I Want to Be a Boarder,* demonstrates how his vaudeville entertainment could bring political and cultural criticism onto the stage. The act shows the possibilities for social transformation in his own comic character transformation.

Fuchs also jubilantly, but briefly moved wealth and poverty into the same neighborhood with a song titled "Der Millionaire fun Delancey Street." The "millionaire" from Delancey Street on New York's Lower East Side, where many Jewish immigrants lived, walks with Rockefeller—"it's no joke," Fuchs sings. As Rockefeller smokes cigars, "I walk behind him and inhale all the smoke."[2] In the song, he and wealthy socialite Gloria Vanderbilt talk; when the millionaire from Delancey Street goes into the park, she asks if he'll take her little dog for a walk. Though not exactly intimate with the upper class, his character shares the streets with them. Wall Street is not that far from Delancey Street, even if vast financial and social differences remain between their inhabitants. The fact that Fuchs sang in Yiddish about being "the millionaire from Delancey Street" was part of the joke. Without a translator, Rockefeller and Vanderbilt couldn't have conversed with the Yiddish "millionaire," or understood his musical dream of sharing their world without giving up his language and his Eastern European background. (Now a Rothschild might have understood.)

Fuchs's vision of a promenade with millionaires on New York's streets is not exactly what Irving Howe had in mind when he wrote that "the streets [of New York] are crucial . . . [as] the training ground for Jewish actors, comics, and singers."[3] Howe observed Jewish comedians learn "to hold an audience, first on the stoops and sidewalks, later in vaudeville and legitimate theatres." In the Delancey Street song, Fuchs holds a sidewalk audience of wealthy citizens, not Lower East Side immigrants; but he is dreaming aloud, imagining a land so friendly and golden even Rockefeller frequents the training ground of Yiddish comics.

He brought immigrant greenhorns and debonair New Yorkers closer together still, by embodying both groups within his own dramatic repertoire, and joining them in one character. Film critic Judith Goldberg sees a double world in Leo Fuchs's Yiddish film, *American Matchmaker* (*Amerikaner Shadchen*). She notes that its characters live in both "the English speaking [world] outside [the house] . . . and the closed world of Jews, albeit successful ones, wherein one speaks Yiddish and may relax."[4] In the film Fuchs portrays a wealthy Jewish New Yorker named Nat Silver, who, like his uncle before him, has trouble finding a wife. Like his uncle, Silver becomes a matchmaker. A hybrid of Old World *schadchen* (matchmaker) and modern businessman, Nat Silver falls in love with one of his clients. A camera flashback to his uncle (Fuchs in beard) briefly suggests Nat Silver's relative looked like him, only unshaven. The two characters even sing similar, wistful Yiddish tunes, and through this double identity Fuchs represents different Jewish generations with one body—his own—and one beard.

During the thirties, Fuchs performed in Yiddish vaudeville houses and in plays on New York's Second Avenue and starred in a few notable Yiddish films. Artef's politically engaged stages and the Federal Theatre Project's Yiddish revues were not his performance spaces; yet Fuchs's vaudevillian sensibility and his multiple role playing contained within them a timely comic response to the economic hardship and displacements of the period. Through his song and dance, Fuchs acknowledged those still struggling to survive in the promised land.

The Yiddish Fred Astaire

His fantastic Yiddish songs and dances, not any particular social concerns, won praise for Fuchs early in his American career. He was called the Yiddish Fred Astaire and was also praised for his dazzling imitation of Charlie Chaplin, but Leo Fuchs was far more gifted than Astaire and Chaplin in one respect. While they could match him in physical comedy and eccentric dance, they could never sing Yiddish songs as eloquently as the actor from Lemberg, Poland. Because he performed for many years in the language East European Jews imported to the United States, Fuchs's stage art has not been widely discussed in English. He became one of the most popular Yiddish stage comedians in America; and his name deserves the same honors—admittedly limited so far—that Sigmund Mogulesko, Aaron Lebedev, Ludwig Satz, Molly Picon, Menasha Skulnik, and Yetta Zwerling have been accorded in the annals of theatre history.

Fortunately some of the comic performances by these Yiddish actors have been preserved on film. Fuchs can still be seen in the short film titled *I Want to Be a Boarder*, where his comic repartee, as well as the song and dance number "Trouble," amply demonstrate the vaudevillian talents that made him an extraordinary actor. Fuchs's performance of "Trouble" also represents a fascinating Yiddish response to the misery suffered by Americans of every variety during the Depression years.

I Want to Be a Boarder is hardly the culmination of Fuchs's career, since the film was released in 1937. He continued to perform in America for five decades after his New York debut in 1935. An Eastern European born with the name Laybl Springer in Lemberg, Galicia (Poland), in 1911, Fuchs began acting when he was five years old, and won praise at Warsaw's Que Pro Quo theatre at age seventeen. Still performing at the age of seventy-nine, four years before his death in Los Angeles, he portrayed an Eastern European immigrant in the film *Avalon*; it was a role Fuchs knew quite well and played with many variations throughout his life. The comedian spoke his lines in English in *Avalon*. Earlier in his American career, he joked and sang in Yiddish, with a few English sentences mixed in, as can be seen in the full-length Yiddish films *I Want to Be a Mother* (1937) and *American Matchmaker* (1940). The actor also performed in a television production of Clifford Odets' play, *Awake and Sing* (1970), and the Hollywood, American-language films, *The Story of Ruth* (1960) and *The Frisco Kid* (1979).

Beginning with his New York stage debut, and for many years following, Leo Fuchs won high praise from critics for his clowning in Yiddish stage plays, such as *Lucky Boy* (1935), *Cigarettes* (1936), *Give Me Back My Heart* (1937), *Sammy's Bar Mitzvah* (1938), *Bei Mir Bistu Schoen* (1961), *A Cowboy in Israel* (1962), *My Wife With Conditions* (1963), and *Here Comes the Groom* (1973). The plays themselves are not well known or available in print, and even at the time they first opened, they served primarily as vehicles for Fuchs and other Yiddish actors to display their comic art.

Throughout Fuchs's long career on stage, he never abandoned the songs (or *kupléts*, as they were called) and comic turns of Yiddish vaudeville. New York and other American cities had a Yiddish vaudeville circuit that presented variety shows composed of short sketches, songs, and dances. But Fuchs and other Yiddish actors did not need the vaudeville houses to perform vaudeville acts; they were able to insert their own, special songs, impersonations, and comic dances within the structure of full-length plays. Actor and producer Herman Yablokoff recalled

Figure 9.1

Leo Fuchs comic strip illustrated by Spain Rodriguez. *Courtesy of the artist and* Jewish Currents.

that when Leo Fuchs hesitated to take a role in *Cigarettes,* "to please him [Fuchs], I [Yablokoff] padded his part with special material suited to his own unique style."[5] Inclusion of such "special material" and solo turns in Yiddish plays allowed actors their own equivalents of Commedia dell'Arte *lazzi* or circus clown *entrées,* forms of an unwritten, orally transmitted repertoire that popular theatre artists developed as signature pieces and repeated in different shows.

Vaudeville itself receives only passing mention in most chronicles of Yiddish theatre, which focus on full-length plays, not performers of novelty songs or "special material." In his book *Klezmer,* music historian Henry Sapoznik suggests that popular Yiddish recordings on vinyl provide "an unparalleled glimpse of a typical Yiddish vaudeville show. These three-minute distillations of what Yiddish audiences clamored to see are dependably formulaic: a bit of a skit, a song, and some brisk closing music with which to dance off into the wings."[6] In this respect, vaudeville and stage plays were similar for Fuchs and other leading Yiddish actors; in both arenas they sang *kupléts* and performed comic monologues. Nahma Sandrow notes in her chronicle, *Vagabond Stars,* that Yiddish musical comedy *kupléts* often were only peripherally related to the plot of the play, and they "took the clown out of the play framework, reasserting the primacy of the relationship between the individual and the audience. For the moment, the play resembled the vaudeville of the era, both Yiddish and American (and the English music hall), with its intense rapport between performer and public."[7] Occasionally the audience was invited by Fuchs to sing along with him, which increased the contact between the singer and his spectators.

The insertion of vaudeville diversions into stage plays allowed Yiddish actors to carry their most popular acts into different dramatic plots and different theatres. The practice of departing from the plot to perform a favorite novelty song, impersonation, or comic monologue may have developed because many Yiddish actors were wandering stars. Why give up a good routine, just because you change plays or cities? Actors like Fuchs and Molly Picon also imported their special numbers into films when the opportunity allowed. The right song and dance act would fit in vaudeville houses, stage plays, and films.

Fuchs the vaudevillian can be discerned in a description of his role in the Yiddish stage production of *My Wife With Conditions* (1963). *New York Times* critic Richard Shepard remarked:

[T]he irrepressible Leo Fuchs . . . does not let his role—a young man driven by deception into destitution and alcoholism—distract him from the business of comedy. His very presence is laugh-provoking and he tells even the oldest of jokes with style, even, as in one, when he missed a word and the audience corrected him. Mr. Fuchs doesn't stand still for a second. He slips, slides, struts, fiddles, dances, and for a too-brief second does a dazzling imitation of Charlie Chaplin.[8]

Needless to say, Fuchs was offering his audience far more than the play's text required; the fact that he staged this production allowed him certain liberties with the script, and he took them. Shepard wrote that *My Wife With Conditions* had "a plot of sorts if you want to follow a story, but you don't really have to. In summary, it's about blighted love, con men, and the decline, fall, and rehabilitation of the hero who really couldn't have cared less." Clearly the critic did not care much for the story; Fuchs, and not the plot, was the main attraction, even when he was playing the role of "a young man" at the age of fifty-two. (By 1963, the average age of Fuchs's Yiddish-speaking audience members may have been high enough to make a fifty-two-year-old appear young by comparison. The Yiddish theatre audience did not grow younger, or gain many newcomers after World War II.)

Fuchs first performed in New York when Yiddish theatre there still had a considerable following. Its Golden Age ended after World War II, as assimilation of American Jews into the cultural mainstream and the destruction of Yiddish-speaking communities in Europe sharply reduced the prospective audience. Arriving in the United States in the thirties, Fuchs brought with him a consciousness of immigration that much of his audience shared, either as first-generation immigrants or their children. Yiddish vaudeville acts and *shund* still attracted Jews who spent long hours in garment industry sweatshops, department stores, and open air markets and struggled to pay the rent for their crowded apartments. Some who had arrived from abroad without money earlier in the century, and had improved their living standard, struggled once again with economic hardship in the thirties. Whether new immigrants or newly unemployed New Yorkers, when they could afford tickets, they turned to Yiddish theatre for relaxation; but the plays and vaudeville evenings also provided the audience with reflections and celebrations of its own condition. Leo Fuchs's comic depiction of a boarding house tenant in *I Want to Be a Boarder*, for example, was inspired by the need many families had to take in boarders for extra income.

In this film, as in *American Matchmaker*, Fuchs wears a false beard and removes it. Again two disparate worlds meet, more fantastically this time, when Fuchs sings and dances to the tune of "Trouble." The song is part of a dream sequence in the film.[9] Fuchs first portrays a Yiddish-American immigrant who looks like an early version of Nat Silver's uncle in *American Matchmaker*. Quite Eastern European in appearance, the character wears unflattering, over-large eyeglasses; a false goatee and moustache; ill-fitting coat, hat, and trousers; and a worse fitting marriage. After quarrelsome conversation with his wife, portrayed by comedienne Yetta Zwerling, both characters agree the husband might fare better if he became her boarder:

HUSBAND [Fuchs]: Tomorrow, I move out.
WIFE [Zwerling]: Wait, I have a better plan. Be my boarder . . .
HUSBAND: I'll be your boarder.
WIFE: Ya.
HUSBAND: But then treat me like a boarder, not a husband.

Zwerling, zany as Fuchs in her waywardness, briefly contemplates marital fidelity, then warmly welcomes the new boarder's overtures, and drives her husband to jealousy (of himself) with thoughts of divorce and new romance.

HUSBAND (*as boarder*): Mrs., can I hope that you will be mine?
WIFE: How can I? I'm married. I'll get a divorce. Or perhaps become a widow.
HUSBAND: I have sleepless nights. Eating, I see you on my plate. Walking in the park, you hang from the branches. Bathing, you appear in the tub. Do you think I have no heart, no feeling?
WIFE: Such dear, sweet words. My husband, I hate him. Come into my arms, my beloved boarder.
HUSBAND: So, you love your boarder, eh! Beautiful, really lovely.
WIFE: And you, you make love to your landlady. As my husband you never made love to me. That's why you want a divorce.

The boarder's words of praise ("you hang from the branches") simultaneously evoke images of a haunting love and lynching, of a sensuous body and an overcrowded bathtub. No wonder his partner becomes suspicious. With her manic demeanor, comedienne Zwerling was a fine partner for Fuchs, even if her character, the wife, was not. She also appeared with him in the film *I Want to Be a Mother,* and in the Yiddish stage musicals, *Give Me Back My Heart* (1937) and *Sammy's Bar Mitzvah* (1938). Like Fuchs, she performs delightful transformations of character; she turns from bitter wife into charming landlady in a moment.

Comedy about boarders and landladies was not unique to this act. As Richard Shepard and Vicki Gold Levi note in their book on Yiddish culture in America, early in the twentieth century, when young male immigrants from Eastern Europe boarded in New York, "the institution of the boarder provided an endless source of plots for novels and plays, and was equally valuable for stage comics, who would delight and scandalize audiences from Chrystie Street to the Catskills with ribald tales of intimacies between boarders and their landladies."[10] Still, the film version offers a unique and innovative variation on an old story, when Fuchs begins his song and dance.

After flirting with his new landlady (his ex-wife), Fuchs's character drinks some liquor, falls asleep, and dreams of himself as a debonair, clean-shaven nightclub singer adored by a crowd of young women. He still speaks Yiddish, but he is a different person, almost unrecognizable. His voice has lost its gruffness and is now smooth; his demeanor, modest, almost bashful. It is as if Groucho Marx shaved, lost his comic stoop and leer, and assumed the top-hatted elegance of Fred Astaire. Fuchs's new character, the debonair singer, has a second, lower class identity hidden within that of the elegantly dressed entertainer. He serenades the nightclub women with lyrics about the Great Depression, about how the world has gone to hell and businesses are turned upside down, with woe and trouble everywhere. He sings of an unhappy bridegroom about to marry a hunchback, while his own hand, curving from behind him in a clownish trick, appears to be someone else's, a pickpocket's perhaps, and reveals that his trouser pocket (or, the lyrics suggest, the pocket of the bride's father) is empty. Though the singer wears a tuxedo, he temporarily becomes a destitute man, who knows the financial troubles of which he sings. Despite the high society costume he wears, Fuchs links his identity with that of the poor and forsaken—a dowryless hunchback bride and her father.

The Singing *Schlemiel*

Fuchs's filmed vaudeville number is replete with dream imagery, intoxication, and "bodily innervations" that Walter Benjamin once ascribed to surrealist art. The immigrant whom Fuchs portrays not only falls asleep and dreams after drinking liquor; his intoxication induces the grotesque comic song and dance that unwittingly fulfill Benjamin's calls for surrealist actions in which "no limbs remain unrent" (or at least unstretched to their limit in this number).[11] Several times during his song, the otherwise stately Fuchs breaks into a crazy eccentric dance, full of rubber-limbed footwork and doltish facial expressions, as if he can no longer stand still or remain calm in a poverty-stricken and chaotic world. His elegant, restrained character turns into a rubber-legged clown who dances and finds joy in the moment, intoxicated by dizzy dance steps if not by liquor. The women in the nightclub audience cheer for his dance, despite the distressed state of the world and the ill-fated wedding he describes. The number recalls Irving Howe's description of the Marx Brothers and their "gleeful nihilism . . . [which] made a shamble of things, reducing their field of operations to approximately what a certain sort of East Side skeptic had always thought the world to be: *ash un porukh,* ashes and dust."[12] Or as Fuchs sings, "Everywhere you go you hear people yelling woe." But he keeps singing.

Like Chaplin's resilient tramp, Fuchs's would-be boarder cannot be kept down for long: he literally bounds back to an upright position after his legs nearly fold under him during the "Trouble" number. Of course, the dancer superbly controls his balance in this movement. Unlike the *schlemiel* Leo Rosten once described as a simpleton who "falls on his back and breaks his nose," Fuchs breaks his fall, and returns to a state of grace as he croons about catastrophe.[13] He is more like the *schlemiel* Walter Benjamin described when he wrote about the 'genius of failure' and noted, "Chaplin or Schlemihl. The schlemihl takes offense at nothing; he just stumbles over his own feet. He is the only angel of peace suited to this world."[14]

Whether or not Fuchs is a "genius of failure," he finds in failure—a world of woe and trouble—something about which to sing and dance. As Brecht once said, in dark times, there will be singing about the dark times. Fuchs in his double identity of suave singer and dancing dolt, and in his comic dialogue as husband who would be a boarder, proves himself a clown who can speedily pass between high and low life, and find stately grace and intoxicated abandon in the process. His vaudeville act bridges the distance between assimilated and greenhorn Jews, and Fuchs delights in leaping between their different worlds. He plays one world against another—but both are within his character and his ample imagination—two sides of a larger American schism between dreams of luxury (or luxury itself), and the uncomfortable, entry-level struggle known to so many newcomers in the United States. The comedian moves from one extreme to the other in a few deft face, hand, and foot maneuvers, literally descending to the lower depths and rising again to high society demeanor in the course of his dance. He offers a graphic confirmation of Yiddish cultural historian Henry Sapoznik's thesis that, for immigrant performers in vaudeville, "the way to ascend the ladder of entertainment success was to portray someone farther down that ladder."[15]

At the same time, Fuchs's transformations in character and social standing convey the possibilities of another, better life developing out of that which already exists. It has been suggested that *Yiddishkayt*, Yiddish culture itself, represented to many Jews the geographical location of a *shayner, besser velt* (more beautiful, better world); while anarchist critic B. Rivkin's reference to this better world in *Yiddishkayt* originally meant a world of socialism, it might be argued that in Fuchs's Yiddish vaudeville, there is also a better world: one of humorous song, dance, community, and the promise of change wrested from the throes of economic hardship and woe.[16]

When the song ends, the dreamer wakes (actually his wife wakes him), and has to choose one identity: either he will be a flirtatious boarder or an unhappy husband in his own home. The film ends with the boarder cheerfully escorting his alleged landlady out of the apartment. Their quarrelsome marriage, somewhat like the wedding in the song, has dissolved. The dream of the nightclub entertainer turned into a dancing fool, his suavely sung Yiddish lyrics about the Great Depression and the eccentric dance cross other boundaries too. Fuchs's contortionist twists to music are similar to dances African Americans were performing in vaudeville and nightclubs around the same time; it suggests a crossover between Yiddish American and African American cultures.[17] Fuchs was no Al Jolson, not exactly a jazz singer, but there is an uncanny confluence of interests in his eccentric dance steps and those of African American vaudevillians such as the Nicholas Brothers. In fast-paced, comic moves, the dancers seem to be set free, or free themselves, from the culture of Old World dance steps.

In his memoir, *Der Payatz* (*The Clown*), Herman Yablokoff recalls that once when Fuchs "went into his eccentric dance, doing double-jointed twists and corkscrew turns . . . the crowds wouldn't let him off the stage. And, since he would not repeat his bag of tricks to satisfy them, the only solution [to end the act] was to drop the curtain."[18] The dance was quite literally a show-stopper in the 1938 musical, *Sammy's Bar Mitzvah,* which Yablokoff produced in New York. Much as the Marx Brothers decimated the logic and dignity of polite conversation through their barrage of puns, Fuchs could destroy a certain kind of social club elegance and demeanor through his wild dance. Further movement (going on with the show) became difficult, and counterproductive of the sensational effect already created. All one could say in response would be *genug shoyn* (Yiddish for "enough already").

Here I am tempted to compare Fuchs to the Elizabethan clown, Will Kempe, whom that great friend of popular theatre, Peter Thomson, praised as a "people's clown." In his own way, Fuchs too was a people's clown. His show-stopping eccentric dances were modern sequels to Kempe's stage jigs, which, as Thomson observed, brought the Elizabethan comedian "a playhouse status that would have been immediately recognizable in the responses of [the] audience."[19]

In his history of Yiddish cinema, J. Hoberman describes the filmed vaudeville act *I Want to Be a Boarder* as "a kind of missing link between the Marx Brothers and the Yiddish stage" and "a small classic of Jewish surrealism."[20] Although Fuchs doesn't portray four brothers, only three different men in the film, his identity transformations recall the moment when Groucho Marx steps out of character to face the camera in *Animal Crackers* and says, "Pardon me while I have a strange interlude." In *I Want to Be a Boarder,* Fuchs also revels in strange interludes, surreal transformations, and disruptions of situation and character, as he and Yetta Zwerling keep changing their identities.

The eccentric dances that Fuchs performed during such songs as "Trouble" led the *New York Times* reviewer of *Lucky Boy,* his 1935 American stage debut in Yiddish comedy, to say that Fuchs "has half a dozen loose or double joints, but he is not merely a contortionist. He is a nimble dancer, but he is not only a dancer. He can put over a song; he can fiddle, and he is a subtle character actor."[21] Two years later, another *Times* review proclaimed Fuchs "an extraordinary comic. His clowning, contortions, dancing and miming are full of grace and esprit."[22]

Even in *Avalon,* the Hollywood film that required more traditional, realistic acting in English, Fuchs's nimble timing stole a scene. At the age of seventy-nine, Leo Fuchs did none of his famous vaudeville dance steps in the film, but he engaged in fast-paced, vaudevillian repartee. Director Barry Levinson's portrait of Jewish family life in Baltimore shows four aged immigrant brothers sitting lazily on a couch in one scene. Sam Krichinsky (played by Armin Mueller-Stahl) asks the other brothers, "What was the movie we saw with the stagecoach? A very good movie."[23]

Fuchs's character, Hymie Krichinsky, responds without hesitation, "*Stagecoach.*" He is not fully understood as the dialogue continues.

SAM [Mueller-Stahl]: The movie had a stagecoach.
HYMIE [Fuchs]: *Stagecoach.*
SAM: Very good actor, John Wayne. The movie had an outlaw, but he was not an outlaw.
HYMIE: *Stagecoach.*
SAM: That's what's I'm saying, *Stagecoach.*
HYMIE: *Stagecoach.*
SAM: *Stagecoach.*

Fuchs's character, Hymie, wryly and quickly repeats the correct answer until Sam accepts it. Hymie's Eastern European accent adds a touch of humor to each repetition of "*Stagecoach.*" With his Old World knowledge of Hollywood cowboy films, accurate from the start, Hymie never wavers, and his voice sounds slightly more amused each time he correctly answers the question.

Shalom, Cowboy

How could a Jew from the Galicia be so confident about cowboy lore? Decades earlier, Fuchs explored that question in his Yiddish stage musical, *A Cowboy in Israel.* The billing for the play by Louis Freiman and Chaim Tauber credited Fuchs as the author of "special material," and his opening line, "Shalom, Partner," was also the title of a Fuchs record album. He sang about a Jewish cowboy named "Hop Along Knish"; although Knish, named after a special Eastern European dumpling, was not as famous as television's Hopalong Cassidy, his lyrics promised, "My reputation's getting bigger, I can even outsmart Trigger" (Roy Rogers's horse).[24] The actor also once performed a role on the television series, *Wagon Train*. Fuchs knew from Yiddish cowboys, although in the 1962 musical, the American cowboy he portrayed ended up in Israel raising a herd of Goldsteins instead of Holsteins. The actor found comedy in the meeting of Old World and Wild West, and Hollywood cast him accordingly. Before *Avalon,* Fuchs portrayed a Chief Polish Rabbi in the film *The Frisco Kid.* From within his huge white beard, the Rabbi called one of his least learned talmudic students (played by Gene Wilder) "cowboy," and sent the young man from Poland across the American plains to San Francisco. (In this film role, Fuchs was permitted few lines and gestures; he was much freer on the Yiddish stage.)

Besides Yiddish cowboys, his repertoire included a Yiddish detective, the "Private Oy" named Friday in William Siegel's parodic play, *Yiddisher Dragnet.* Later in his career, between films in Los Angeles, he also took some stage roles in American, English-language musicals and comedies, including a 1956 parody of Tennessee Williams titled *Katz on a Hot Tin Roof.* (Fuchs portrayed Danny Katz, a character who marries his landlady's daughter in Havana, and then discovers that one of his ancestors was an Irish "Leapracohen," with emphasis on the Jewish name Cohen.[25]) But in his finest hours on the Yiddish stage and on film, Fuchs displayed the gifts of a popular variety artist. He excelled in parodies of film genres, jokes based on ethnic identity, as well as songs, dances, circus-like contortions, and impersonations, all part of his vaudevillian repertoire. This genre of live entertainment lost much of its audience as film culture became more prevalent in the United States. Ironically, when Fuchs's film *Amerikaner Shadchen* (*American Matchmaker*) opened in 1937 at a Yiddish theatre in Brownsville, New York, it could be seen daily along with eight live Yiddish vaudeville acts.[26] Even if Fuchs was not onstage in person at the time, he was still playing to a vaudeville house.

On stage, live in front of a Yiddish-speaking audience, Fuchs was able to improvise each night, and perform in and out of character more freely than he could on film. (As noted earlier, the Yiddish plays in which he appeared did not all have compelling plots to begin with; it may be no accident that he was tempted to digress from their plots, or forget the plot completely, as subsequent generations have.) The absence of a compelling plot, and his delight in digressions, probably led Fuchs to step out of character late in his career, and offer his stellar impersonations of Maurice Chevalier, Menasha Skulnick, and Jimmy Durante in a stage play titled *Here Comes the Groom* (1973). But earlier in his career,

Fuchs was just as prone to step out of one character and into another, to play multiple roles within plays and films.

In 1962, when Fuchs stepped onto a New York stage in a ten-gallon hat and said "Shalom, Partner!" he was still a half-assimilated American, half-Yiddish immigrant in his opening line, in two cultures at once, three decades after leaving Eastern Europe. Here too, he was incapable of leaving behind his vaudeville custom of offering the audience a novelty song, even if it had no special relevance to the play on stage. Fuchs was reported by *Times* critic Richard Shepard to have left the script "when needed, as in his seizure of the happy chance to do his popular chicken-flicker song in which he is unable to dissociate any thought or dream from his job of plucking chickens."[27] The Yiddish cowboy Leo Fuchs was still a vaudevillian in 1962, perhaps the last Yiddish vaudevillian able to stop a show with a song about chicken-flicking. As S. J. Perelman once said in praise of a talking chicken, it might be said of Leo Fuchs too—that as a comedian versed in Yiddish humor, chicken-flicker songs, and vaudevillian variety acts, he "reached a pinnacle undreamed of in poultrydom."[28]

The African American actor and writer Anna Deavere Smith, in the preface to *Fires in the Mirror*, a play in which she portrayed twenty-seven culturally diverse Hasidic Jewish and Caribbean American characters in 1992, noted that "in America, identity is always being negotiated."[29] Fuchs's roles offer earlier evidence of the ongoing negotiations. The half-assimilated characters he portrayed, like the actor himself when he threatened to return to Poland, could not readily adjust to their new country. American dreams turned into surreal comedy featuring misfits, or at least incompletely assimilated Americans: a Yiddish cowboy, a Yiddish private oy, an obsessive chicken-plucker, a marriage consultant whose modern practices united a union of old-fashioned matchmakers (*shadchanim*) against him. Moving between prosperity and poverty, nightclub and tenement, wife and landlady, adjusting to the changes with great speed, Fuchs acted out economic and social negotiations that continue within American culture today as new immigrants enter the country. The lyrics to his 1937 song about troubled times now might be appreciated in many other languages besides Yiddish.

10

Yetta Zwerling's Comic Dybbuk

She began to dance in her mother's stomach before she was born, Yetta Zwerling once said. The comic actress continued to dance and sing through her years on stage and in films, notably *Motel the Operator, I Want to Be a Boarder, The Jewish Melody,* and *The Great Advisor.*[1] Unlike some of the other theatre creators introduced in this survey, Yetta Zwerling (1894–1982) cannot be described as a messianic artist. She was first of all a free spirit, although her father once said a dybbuk (a spirit beyond her control) possessed her. Perhaps Zwerling's independence kept her from joining a messianic movement, but like other Yiddish comedians, she often portrayed characters trying to move beyond poverty, misfortune, and social marginality. To do this as a woman and remain independent, Zwerling's characters would defy men and act unconventionally in other manners, which may be why she was so often called an "eccentric" actress. Her comic portrayal of troublemakers also qualifies her for inclusion in any list of comic Yiddish dissidents.

In the film *Motel the Operator,* as Zwerling's character, Chana Bella, prepares to go to her daughter's wedding, she dances joyously, flounces her large white dress, and holds the edges of the gown out as if she is about to take a bow or take flight, with the extended dress serving as wings. She can't wait for the wedding. She is celebrating in advance, and her pleasure spreads to her husband Joseph (portrayed by Seymour Rechtzeit), who constantly smiles and joins her dance. They sing about klezmer musicians playing at the wedding, and about relatives at the ceremony. Zwerling's lyrics verge on gossip, as she declares,

> Look at Aunt Leach
> She gives everyone advice.
>
> Aunt Mala doesn't let anyone
> Mix in. She sits up on high.

Even in the midst of joy, Zwerling's comic character is something of a *yenta*—a gossip and a social critic. She delivers her critiques in song and revels in the disclosures, which suggests a recurrent tendency in her comedy: Yetta takes delight in trouble—reporting it, creating it, and surviving it.

Zwerling's role as troublemaker may have begun, as she recounts in her 1951 memoirs, when she first discovered that she was a "komiker," or comedian, on stage. Her partner, who had hired her, was singing a song, the same song for the third night in a row. Zwerling, hardly the center of attention, began to make funny faces. She winked seductively, turned her head toward someone else besides her partner, and the audience laughed at her diversion. Later her partner asked what the actress did on stage. (He had been too preoccupied with his own performance to notice her.) At first she felt guilty about her improvisation, but when the partner offered her a raise of $20 a week if she would repeat the routine each night, she realized she was a comedian.

The Komiker's Tears

Her shedding of tears was also quite humorous, at least in one episode Zwerling recounts. That it occurred during her life offstage does not reduce the humor of the situation. If one of her stage or film characters did not suffer the same situation, they should have—it would have been one of Zwerling's best scenes. In her 1951 memoir, the actress writes that she went to the funeral of a doctor she knew; at least she thought it was the doctor's funeral. She recognized no one, and the nose on the corpse was longer than she remembered it. Before long, she learned she had gone to the wrong funeral—a taxi driver's, not a doctor's. She left and went to the funeral of her doctor friend. But Zwerling was unable to cry at his funeral; she had shed all her tears over the taxi driver. Crying for a stranger was not out of character for her, nor was running out of tears.

Monkey Business

In her memoir, Zwerling tells of another event in her stage career that inadvertently provides a metaphor for her art. When she performed at the Grand Theatre in New York, the manager of the Yiddish vaudeville show arranged for Zwerling to go on after the monkey act. Goldstein, the manager, was fond of his monkey act, or told Yetta Zwerling as much. After the public has seen the monkeys, he promised, the actress would enter to great applause. It was the best spot for her in the program, he said. A friend in the circus (Jeff Raz, a clown currently in Cirque du Soleil) tells me that it is not an especially great honor to go on stage *after* a monkey act; that gives the following performer the role of "second banana" or worse. Zwerling did not stay at the Grand Theatre too long, but she created her own monkey business in other performances.

Years after her life with monkeys, the actress performed one remarkable comic scene with other animals in the film, *The Jewish Melody*. As an unmarried daughter longing for a husband, her character helps her father perform *kapores* in their kitchen. The ritual traditionally completed before Yom Kippur, the holy Day of Atonement, involved waving a rooster overhead, so the creature took on the holder's sins before it was sacrificed. Jews performed the ceremony in the hope that peace, happiness—and in the case of Zwerling's character—marriage would follow.

But Zwerling's rooster refuses to cooperate; the bird flutters above her head like an exotic, live hat and then flies out the window to freedom. Zwerling's character next tries to complete the ceremony with a live carp. The carp has been swimming in the kitchen sink while waiting to become gefilte fish. Removed from the sink and briefly held aloft by Zwerling, the sacrificial victim wiggles free from its captor and leaps off-camera. Clearly the would-be bride is not meant to continue her family's old, traditional way of life in the New World. How the actress managed to train a rooster and a fish as her comic partners remains a mystery, but the scene humorously carps on the foolhardiness with which Zwerling's character seeks a husband. She portrays a young woman desperate to marry, and at the same time mocks her character's attempt to secure a man as her partner.

One man was not enough for her, at least on stage. After leaving the vaudeville partner who ignored her, Zwerling found other partners who turned out to be the best comic Yiddish actors around, including Leo Fuchs, Menasha Skulnik, Itzik Feld, Irving Jacobson, and Julius Nathanson. Her continuing loss of stage partners had a comic counterpart in roles where the actress portrayed a widow.

The Zwerling Zetz

In the film *The Great Advisor*, as a widow seeking a new husband, Zwerling admits, "I'm a widow five years already, you may call me Miss." The man who wants to find her a companion (and be paid for his service) responds, "The size of your bank account warrants addressing you as Madam." His arrogance amuses Zwerling's character; she takes as much pleasure in her eligibility and the attractions wealth confers on her, as the man who would match her to a bridegroom. Her enthusiasm for romance waxes so fervent in a dance hall that she pokes a man in the ribs with her elbow, gives him a *zetz* (punch), and almost pushes him to the floor to express her zeal. The comic excess of Yetta's energy may cause spectators to question the woman's behavior and wonder if she poses a danger to society, but the widow never consciously knocks down those near her. She just has strong emotions and expresses them with her whole body. The critic Stark Young's praise for Yiddish theatre could well apply to Zwerling. He saw in Yiddish acting an "expressiveness of hands and eyes and shoulders . . . tremendous and inexhaustible vitality. . . . It has the realism of intense feeling, and a deep respect for that feeling."[2]

Funny With Money

Some of Zwerling's funniest Yiddish characters could be considered archetypal: the rich widow, the once poverty-stricken wife whose husband is newly rich, and the unmarried woman who wants a rich husband. In these roles, wealth does not make her characters forget the poor; quite the contrary, her women tend to remember the poverty and struggle from which their families departed, and display concern for those less fortunate.

One exception to this rule of remembering her working-class background could be found in Zwerling's role as Shimele the tailor's wife, Eti Meni, in Sholem Aleichem's *200,000*. When her husband becomes rich, Eti Meni easily forgets her impoverished past. She berates the family's new maid as if she owned the woman. Zwerling performed in a version of Aleichem's play, retitled *Twice 100,000,* when it was staged at New York's Public Theatre in November of 1934. The play was done for one night only, as a benefit, and most of the *Times* critic's attention was devoted to the play's director, Menachem Rubin, who also took the lead role of Shimele the tailor. Sholem Aleichem wrote the play long before Zwerling became an actress, but a few of the lines sound like they were written for her. When Eti Meni tells her newly rich husband, "For me you're still the same as you were," he replies, "That's the whole problem. You could at least have a little respect." A new woman now, the wife responds, "Wait, I'll take off my hat," and here one can imagine Zwerling slowly, ostentatiously removing an ornate feathered hat. No account survives that can confirm this speculation about her role. But if she took off her hat, perhaps she also inadvertently removed her *shaytl* at the same time. Losing her wig onstage was another one of Zwerling's *shtiklech* [stage routines].[3]

Her character displays far more respect toward the working class in *Motel the Operator.* There Zwerling as Chana Bella, the nouveau riche New Yorker, exits from a cab with her husband, Joseph, silently grabs his arm, gestures to the cab, and holds Joseph until he tips the driver. She knows they can afford to pay more than the fare, and she's not forgetting the cabbie, despite the expensive, high-flying feather hat she wears. Her husband is more concerned about lighting his cigar (with a match struck on his shoe sole—he has not yet adopted all the manners of the rich) than paying the cabbie a tip. Joseph (formerly Yosl) was once a struggling sweatshop tailor himself, not the wealthy pants manufacturer he has become. But the memory of poverty, the tribute of a tip to a working man, begins here with his wife's comic, stubborn hold on Joseph's arm.

Zwerling's character in *Motel* is one of a series of women whom she portrayed as insistently good-natured, determined to be cheerful and friendly to others even if it requires humbling her husband or herself.

The Dybbuk in the Actress

Part of the humor in Zwerling's elbow-inflected enthusiasm for life may reflect her father's fear, expressed when she was a young woman, that "the dybbuk of the theatre" had entered his daughter. Although he did not want Yetta to become an actress, she did so, and stayed on stage despite objections from her husband after she bore several children. It was not easy for her to be an actress, wife, and mother at the same time—but perhaps a dybbuk drove her to it. Her dybbuk was more mischievous than evil; and if it drove the actress into moments of madness and hysteria, it also drove her audience into fits with comedy. If there was no dybbuk (who says her father was right?), Zwerling's determination to continue acting, despite objections by her father and later by her husband, further attests to the independence of an actress who mocked a number of man-hungry women through her comedy.

In his review of the 1936 Yiddish comedy *Love for Sale*, *New York Times* critic William Schack described the actress as "the ever-man-hungry Yetta Zwerling"[4]; it is not clear whether he was referring to her character in the play, or the actress's recurrent performance of such roles. (The play's title refers not to prostitutes, but to prospective marriage partners, Zwerling among them.) In one film the strength of her character's drive to marry or begin a new relationship with a man nearly becomes lethal— comic *eros* as *thanatos*. More than an elbow in the ribs awaits her future husband in *The Great Advisor*, when the wealthy widow portrayed by Zwerling promises, "I was a good wife and erected a big tombstone for my first departed. If the Lord helps me I'll erect a larger one for my second husband."

Does she expect to outlive her husband or kill him? This is no idle question in the filmed vaudeville act, *I Want to Be a Boarder*, where Leo Fuchs plays the roles of husband *and* apartment house boarder, and proposes marriage to his landlady (see Chapter 9). Zwerling responds to the proposal as a landlady who happens to be the same man's wife: "How can I? I'm married. I'll get a divorce. Or perhaps become a widow." Fuchs's bachelor character encourages her plotting, and recommends that if her husband won't divorce her, she should "do away with him. Use a knife, a revolver, hit him on the head, kill him." The lady consents, not in rage, but out of undivided love for her boarder: "My Romeo, I love you, I can't live without you. You're the only man in my life." In one sense, her love is undivided. The man Fuchs portrays *is* the only one in her life, because the same actor portrays both husband and boarder. To "do away" with the husband here only means abandoning one of his roles, and one of hers (as his wife). In the end, he chooses to be the boarder; she, the landlady.

The high caliber of comedy in film scenes that Fuchs and Zwerling performed together could also be seen on stage, if the review of *Semele's*

Figure 10.1

Leo Fuchs and Yetta Zwerling in the 1937 film, *I Want to Be a Boarder. Courtesy of the National Center for Jewish Film.*

Bar Mitzvah written for the *Times* is an indication. On January 17, 1938, William Schack praised the "amusing comedy relief served up by the madcap Yetta Zwerling and the inimitably eccentric Leo Fuchs."[5] The "madcap" and "eccentric" couple also performed together on the Yiddish vaudeville stage in New York a number of times.

The performances by Fuchs and Zwerling in *I Want to Be a Boarder* recall Bertolt Brecht's expectation that in theatre and elsewhere people should be able "to take pleasure in the possibilities of change . . ."[6] Zwerling visibly takes pleasure in her character's transformation from wife to landlady, and (in *Motel the Operator*) from struggling tailor's wife to wealthy pants manufacturer's wife, and (in *The Great Advisor*) from widow to remarried wife. She smiles, almost laughs at her rich husband when he calls her by her adopted, *nouveau riche* name, Anna Bella, instead of the Old World Chana Bella, in *Motel the Operator.* The change of names, like her change in fortune, becomes a source of amusement to Zwerling's character, as her husband keeps forgetting her new name, in their strange, new world of wealth.[7]

The actress displays more than her character's pleasure here. A Brechtian comedienne without knowing it, Zwerling plays herself and her character at the same time. Her consciousness of role-playing, revealed through the delight she takes in singing, dancing, and responding to others, resembles the double consciousness Brecht advocated for epic theatre actors. The showman, or in this case show-woman, "does not disappear [from the character] whom [s]he is showing." The actress's own "opinions and sensations" are not swallowed up by the character, to paraphrase Brecht further.[8]

Zwerling was not consciously practicing Brecht's acting techniques, but her Yiddish comedy shared with Brecht's approach to theatre a playful consciousness of and visible pleasure in the art of acting. She demonstrates these qualities in her memoir, when she recalls unobtrusively listening to audience members discuss her act after a show. She plays a character and herself at the same time, but this time not onstage. In a restaurant near the theatre, she overhears admirers discuss the actress, "Oy, how Zwerling plays." "She's has spirit." "Her dancing." "Her singing." Then comes the line her own character, the independent woman, would have been most delighted to hear, or might have spoken herself, although someone at another table speaks it for her: "How long has Zwerling been on the stage? She's no spring chicken." Take it as a comic tribute to her endurance, which kept her onstage past the age of sixty in the 1950s. The humorous *chutzpah* of that question ("How long . . .") also characterized Zwerling, onstage and off.

Popular Theatre, Popular Actress

By the mid-thirties Yetta Zwerling was a star in Yiddish theatre; her name, an attraction in advertisements for plays and films. People came to see her, and her equals in theatre, more than they came to see particular plays. It is no accident she acquired her fame in Yiddish theatre by portraying women who display initiative, women not easily embarrassed, women who push their male companions forward or go on without them. Often her character behaved more aggressively than the men accompanying Zwerling.

Her nerve came across as comic—a Komiker's *chutzpah*. While audiences laughed at the women Zwerling portrayed, laughed at the naiveté and the brashness of her character, her women were usually amused too, delighted by their own forward behavior. (By coincidence Zwerling published her memoirs in the Yiddish *Forward*!) Her determination gave comic form to the ambitions of an immigrant generation of women on the move, in search of opportunities for themselves and their families. Curiously, although she spoke English when she played the American vaudeville circuit early in her career, and later sang in American-language musical comedy with Leon Errol, Zwerling became a star by performing in Yiddish.

Eastern European Jewish women usually were not given the advanced education men received in the Old World. Wives and daughters were not taught to read Hebrew; Yiddish, the language of everyday conversation, was their language. Yiddish language was regarded as inferior by some Eastern European Jews, because women spoke it, while men knew Hebrew if not German or Russian. Sholem Aleichem in his memoirs writes that when he was a child, Yiddish was "a jargon good only for women. A man would be ashamed to be found with a Yiddish book in his hands."[9] Zwerling's films and plays portrayed a new world where Yiddish spoken by a comedienne like her could become part of popular culture, a celebration of a country in which women as well as men were advancing socially and culturally, becoming not only seamstresses and shop girls but also stars of stage and screen. When Zwerling performed on stage, the Yiddish language became "good for women" in the best sense of the words. Her lines made the woman speaking them, and her comic art, more popular wherever Yiddish was spoken.

11

Menachem Mendel's False Profits

Sholem Aleichem and the Communists

If only you had listened to what the Bible says, you would never have believed in False Profits.[1]

—Tevye the Dairyman to himself

"Is it my fault, I ask you, is it my fault if I'm applauded by Communists and revolutionaries?" Sholem Aleichem never asked himself this question, but plays featuring his characters were welcomed by Yiddish-speaking Communist theatre audiences in New York and Moscow after the Russian revolution. His plays deserved the leftist praise, not only because some of the most innovative actors and directors in Yiddish theatre staged them but also because Sholem Aleichem was, in his own satiric way, a radical critic of injustice and oppression. His stories, and the plays based on them, portrayed survivors of poverty and persecution, Jews who dreamed of a better world and humorously spoke, in the Yiddish Aleichem gave them, about the inadequacies of the existing world.

"For Russian Communists," J. Hoberman observes, "Sholem Aleichem was the most important Yiddish writer . . . the only Soviet Jewish culture-hero who never fell from grace. . . . As the province of the poor and disenfranchised (not to mention a secular alternative to Hebrew), early Yiddish literature was *a priori* politically correct."[2]

Sholem Aleichem (1859–1916), born Sholem Rabinovich, son of a Ukrainian business agent and storekeeper, was no Marxist. He married the daughter of a wealthy landowner, after which he became a full-time writer using the pen name of Sholem Aleichem. While living

Figure 11.1

Caricature of Sholem Aleichem in New York, printed in *Kundes,* December 1914.

in Kiev, he lost a fortune in the stock market crash of 1890; a local pogrom, not the crash, convinced him to leave Kiev. International success as a writer enabled him to support his family, and live for some years in New York. In 1916, more than 100,000 mourners attended his New York funeral. After Sholem Aleichem's death, his books and plays remained popular, although some Americans know his characters only through the musical comedy *Fiddler on the Roof.*

While not a Communist himself, his satiric portraits of stock market trader Menachem Mendel, Shimele Saroker the tailor, and the financially poor but daughter-rich dairyman Tevye attracted several of the twentieth-century's leading leftist Yiddish theatres. Goset, the Moscow State Yiddish Theatre, and Artef, the New York proletarian theatre collective, both adapted Sholem Aleichem's writing for the stage, and produced some of his original one-act plays, to satirize what Tevye once called belief in "False Profits." As Edna Nahshon notes in her landmark book on Artef, the company "appropriated [Aleichem] not only because of the advantage of his enormous popularity, but also because he portrayed characters largely as products of their social environment, a perspective that lent itself easily to Marxist interpretation."[3] That Aleichemesque social environment included homes of affluent Jews with servants, and impoverished East European *shtetls* where Jews like Tevye dreamed of becoming rich.

Stage versions of Sholem Aleichem at Artef and Goset deleted and de-emphasized religious references voiced by his characters. Faith in a messiah and God became less central to the plot than faith in the "False Profits" and false hopes placed in financial speculation. Aleichem's Tevye and Menachem Mendel meet and collaborate in one play, *Nit Gefidelt* (*Not Fiddled*), which Chaver Paver wrote and Benno Schneider directed for the Artef studio's 1935–36 season. While it was not a full-length or main-stage production, *Nit Gefidelt* enlarged the Aleichem repertoire for Artef's actors and their audience. The demand for plays by Sholem Aleichem was unending; and if the Yiddish master who died in 1916 could not write more plays, they would be written for him, especially by authors with access to the appropriate means of production (actors and a thea-tre). The new authors created new scripts with an old cast of characters found in the humorist's short stories or in his own plays. Gifted stage directors at Artef and Goset sometimes didn't even need a new script; they edited, cut, and improvised from existing Aleichem plays, in rehears-als with an ensemble of Yiddish actors, and came up with something distinctly their own, suited for a period of revolution and Great Depres-sion. Traditionalists may object to the textual changes; but the altera-tions kept alive Aleichem's characters, as well as his social consciousness and humor, by presenting them in a new *mise en scène*.

Chaver Paver's American Plan

Paver's *Not Fiddled* combines several Sholem Aleichem stories, so that after Teyve the Dairyman tells his family about recently earned money, the entrepreneur Menachem Mendel invites him to become his partner in a matchmaking business.[4] Tevye declines, and Mendel then offers to find a bridegroom for one of Tevye's daughters. Needless to say, for those who know Mendel's disastrous history as a businessman in Aleichem stories, he makes mistakes. In Paver's play, as in one of Aleichem's stories and the 1925 Soviet film, *Jewish Luck*, the matchmaking brings together two brides and no groom, much to the dismay of the wedding parties. Before this error, Mendel speaks of creating an enormous matchmaking business, which he plans to run with a partner named Reb Osher. He wants his partner to specialize in finding eligible young men, while Mendel specializes in young women. In Paver's play, Mendel refers to his scheme as "an American plan," because it will speed up production, like a Detroit assembly line. He doesn't mention Detroit assembly lines, only a speedup; but the lines about American efficiency are Paver's, not Aleichem's, and they make the adaptation of the East European stories more topical and appropriate for a New York, worker-supported theatre like Artef. The speedup has hardly been mentioned before the business falls apart through Mendel's mismatch-making.

By combining several stories in his play and having Tevye, his daughter, his wife, and Menachem Mendel interact more than the original stories did, Chaver Paver creates an ensemble piece, in which no single character becomes the protagonist. The social relations among the characters, their business relations, and their exchanges of dialogue are more important than individual portraits, although individual traits can be seen.

Chaver Paver's playwriting suited the performance training of Artef members, whose ensemble differed from the "star" system of other, more commercial Yiddish and American theatres. Sharing the spotlight as a group, the performers placed more emphasis on collective creation in their work. This may be one reason few names of actors in the company are well known today, or discussed in histories of Yiddish theatre.

Benno Schneider also directed the one-act play, *Motl the Cantor's Son in America*, for Artef's studio collective during its 1933–34 season and again in 1938. Chaver Paver's adaptation of Sholem Aleichem's novel about Motl enlarged one episode about a worker's strike. Created in a period when unions across America were initiating picket lines, marches, and factory occupations, the new play would have been quite timely when first staged. Like Sholem Aleichem, Chaver Paver finds innocence, humor, and increasing commitment to the union movement in the adventures of Motl and his family. Young Motl, new to the United States and the American language, displays a naiveté and eagerness to learn about labor relations. Before the play ends, he volunteers to join a picket line and fight against scabs. His initiation into the world of unions might have served as a comic primer for Yiddish-speaking audiences, if they were as unfamiliar as Motl and Brokheh (his brother's wife) were with English-language terms like "overtime" and "scab." These terms have to be explained during the play, and discussion of them comically criticizes bosses and sweatshops.

Chaver Paver, born Gershon Einbinder in Bessarabia in 1901, left Romania for New York in 1924. The situation of the newly arrived East Europeans in Sholem Aleichem's tale about Motl may have recalled to the adaptor his own immigrant experience. As an author of children's stories, Chaver Paver also was well prepared to make young Motl's viewpoint central to the drama.

Waiting for his older brother, Elye, to return from a job in a sweatshop, Motl questions his brother's friend Pinye, a clothing presser, about work in America. Pinye either doesn't know the answers, and doesn't want to admit it, or thinks his understanding adequate; in either case, his etymology of labor terms is quite amusing. The American labor movement derived all its key words from Yiddish expressions, in Pinye's view. While Yiddish labor activists formed and influenced American unions, their native language was not quite as influential as Pinye imagines. Asked where the word "boss" comes from, Pinye traces its derivation back to the Yiddish *balebas,* a word that does mean landlord or boss; but Pinye's etymology proves to be more entertaining than accurate. He informs Motl that Americans shortened the Yiddish word *balebas* to "boss" because they love speed and accelerated speech. Asked about the origin of the word "picket," Pinye attributes it to another Yiddish source. When workers walk out of a shop to go out on strike, says Pinye, the spleen of the boss is burst, or *tsepicket* (poked) in Yiddish; hence a "picket" line.

Later when the boss visits his employee's apartment, Pinye naively asks him whether justice is available to workers. The boss replies, "My eye! Justice stayed in Europe. Here in America, the President has hated strikes. They can still ship you back to Europe." His threat of deportation intimidates Pinye and Elye for a while. Motl overhears the threat, and reluctantly reports it to Elye's wife, Brokheh. The most radical labor activist in the family, Brokheh urges her husband and Pinye to go on strike, despite the boss's warning. When the employer returns to intimidate Elye and Pinye further, Brokheh pours a cup of water on him, rebukes the man, and he retreats. Motl reminds his friend Mendel that he had predicted Brokheh's ferocity. With these words, the innocent young man displays newly gained confidence and understanding of the resistance his own family can demonstrate against injustice.

Earlier in the play, Elye acknowledges a need for improved conditions in his sweatshop. As he describes his day at work, Motl's older brother recites a speech that union activists had delivered in the shop: "Brother and sister workers, you've suffered enough already, enslaved in these hard conditions, you've already had the souls chased out of you. We strike! We strike!" The brief speech echoes late nineteenth-century romanticism in its Yiddish. Perhaps Paver's activists had been reading the sweatshop poet Morris Rosenfeld prior to delivering their oration. Rosenfeld's poem, "The Sweatshop," begins with a reference to an old house "at the Corner of Pain and Anguish," where men and women toil on the windowless third floor "with their spirits broken, and their bodies spent."[5] Paver's dialogue evokes that romantic spirit, Sholem Aleichem's sense of humor, and the union activism of his own day.

This is not to say Paver fully brings Motl into the 1930s. The writing adds new dialogue and a larger comic lexicon of American labor terms to the original story. But the play does not promote Aleichem as an advocate of thirties unionism; rather, through enlargement of the story, Paver creates a continuity of Yiddish cultural concerns from Aleichem to Artef. Motl's innocence belonged to an earlier period, as did Elye's fear of being shipped back to Europe if he went on strike. Several decades after Aleichem wrote about Elye's sweatshop, improvement of working conditions through the American labor movement was still needed; Chaver Paver and Artef acknowledged this through their continuation and renewal of the social consciousness and humorous stories Sholem Aleichem brought into Yiddish culture. Reviewing the 1938 production of the play, Nathaniel Buchwald found it "fresh and ebullient" and "played in the style of a farce." He had special praise for Chaver Paver's English and Yiddish word play, executed in Sholem Aleichem's popular manner.[6]

Chaver Paver was no Sholem Aleichem in other respects. His own short stories, collected under the title *Clinton Street*, received a full, mainstage production by Artef in 1939, but the production was not as popular as the company's staging of full-length Aleichem plays. *New York Times* critic William Schack said Paver's depiction of New York Jewish ghetto life in *Clinton Street* offered "nothing more than a stock bare bones melodrama. . . . Living language gives place to cliché."[7] Perhaps the stories collected in *Clinton Street*, and informed by Chaver Paver's own experience as a Yiddish-speaking immigrant, did not lend themselves to stage dialogue. The stories in his book contain few of the lively monologues—readily usable as stage speech and the basis for detailed character acting—found in Aleichem's prose. Yiddish critic Itche Gold-berg, in his praise of the *Clinton Street* story collection, refers to "an ever present sing-song rhythm of the narrator's voice, eagerly carrying the story-thread forward."[8] That may have been part of the problem on stage; a narrator also spoke in Artef's *Clinton Street*, where self-explanatory dramatic action might have been preferable. By contrast, Chaver Paver needed no narrator in his Sholem Aleichem adaptations, where the char-acters spoke for themselves, although their speeches were improved behind the scenes by the playwright.

Artef's Winning Ticket

In 1936, Artef staged *200,000* (also known as *The Big Win*), a masterful, full-length comedy about a tailor who wins the lottery and then loses his fortune to swindlers. The play that Aleichem wrote in 1914 needed no rewriting in the 1930s. By the time Benno Schneider directed the pro-duction, he already had staged Sholem Aleichem adaptations by Paver and Nadir, and interpolated his own additions into Aleichem's one-act play, *People* (retitled *Aristocrats* and transformed into a three-act drama at Artef). His directorial expertise at bringing Aleichem's characters to life on stage, in a comic, stylized manner, had been widely acknowl-edged before rehearsals of *200,000* began.

200,000 may be Aleichem's finest play, and Artef's staging of it was hailed as "a work of great artistic significance."[9] Nathaniel Buchwald initially greeted Schneider's production with those words, but later expressed reservations about Artef's Sholem Aleichem presentations. In his book *Theatre*, Buchwald recognized that Artef's adaptations of Aleichem led to great "artistic and material success," but he also thought that such plays offered only a pale and distant echo of ongoing class struggle.[10] He regretted that newer, more topical plays in the Artef rep-ertoire were not winning as much acclaim as the older texts. As gifted as Moishe Nadir and Chaver Paver may have been in their original writ-ing for Artef, Sholem Aleichem remained their unrivaled predecessor.

In *200,000*, a dream of riches leads the tailor Shimele Saroker to buy a lottery ticket. He wins the drawing in Act One, and confidence men then promise the ex-tailor more money through making an investment in Hollywood; they win him over by throwing in free admission to the movies. Inexperienced in handling large sums, Saroker blithely invites the shady businessmen to fill out the check he signs. The error costs him his fortune, but leads him to see that wealth isn't everything. His daughter marries a poor apprentice tailor, the father welcomes the son-in-law into his family, and the play ends with a celebration.

Besides ending the comedy with a wedding, as so many Yiddish authors did, Sholem Aleichem fortuitously chose to portray a few variations on American dreams with which people still identify today. Hollywood success stories and high-stakes lottery drawings continue to command press coverage. The dream of winning a lottery still helps some Americans endure their poverty, as it did when Aleichem wrote his play. In 1936, the play also could be staged as a critique of capital and those it corrupts, although reviews suggest that Schneider's comic direction was not heavy-handed or propagandistic, quite the opposite.

Success with *200,000* led to some curious contradictions in Artef's standing as a theatre for workers. The play attracted rich and famous spectators, and the theatre company's publicity staff did not hide celebrity visits. One advertisement for Artef's *200,000* (see Figure 1.2) listed the names of "rapturous admirers of this play," including Fanny Brice, Moss Hart, Ben Hecht, Jed Harris, Lillian Hellman, Sam Jaffe, Frederick March, Clifford Odets, Irwin Shaw, William Wyler, and Ernst Toller.

Like the tailor in the play, Artef's success drew Hollywood film people into its house. The advertisement, published in English, could be viewed as one of Artef's endeavors to reach a larger theatregoing public, including an English-language audience for its Yiddish productions. By several accounts (one of them by Emanuel Eisenberg was quoted in Chapter 1), the collective succeeded in its outreach by presenting Sholem Aleichem's work, and won praise from people who didn't know the language they heard spoken. This development deserves consideration in any discussion about the future of Yiddish theatre, as well as its past. Within Artef's performances of *200,000*, certain qualities of acting and stage direction helped American-language spectators transcend language barriers. These qualities, visible in highly physical comic stage performances, reflected the economic and social standing of the characters—standing that influenced human behavior in Aleichem's own stories and plays, as well as in Artef's interpretation.

The inspiration for the comic, socially based acting style becomes clearer in Aleichem's stories and plays when they are viewed through the lens of 1930s leftist Yiddish theatre productions. Characters in the stories suffer from secular and economic problems, but their difficulties are not all due to *shtetl* poverty or anti-Semitism. Some losses are self-inflicted. Rather than wait for the Messiah to improve their lives, Tevye the dairyman and Menachem Mendel at least briefly place their faith in financial transactions. Money proves to be a false messiah, as the men lose their worldly wealth, and spectators acquire a sense of the characters' folly. The warning Tevye gives himself not to believe in "False Profits" comes too late; he has already given Reb Menachem Mendel one hundred rubles, and Mendel loses it in speculation. In another regard, however, the pun occurs just in time, as it alerts Tevye to the fact that Menachem Mendel is no prophet. Tevye more fully comprehends his associate's inability to predict the future when he arrives at the financial district in Yehupetz and sees from the look on Menachem Mendel's face that his fortune is lost, "the principal's gone with the profit and all that's left you is troubles!"[11]

In Sholem Aleichem's story, "Tevye Blows a Small Fortune," Tevye hears Mendel confess his ill luck, and then begins to feel sorry for the loser: "I stood there looking at the *schlimazel* pressed against the wall with his hat falling off, every sigh and groan of his breaking my heart." Generous, philosophical, even religious in his acceptance of the loss, the dairyman tells unlucky (*schlimazel*) Mendel: "If we blew a small fortune, that's only because we weren't meant to make a big one . . . the more man plans, the harder God laughs."[12] Here in abbreviated, folkloric form Tevye outlines a comedy of cosmic proportions—a universe in which the speculations and dreams of two Yiddish-speaking Jews who dared to believe in "False Profits" prompt divine laughter. The creators of the comedy are Mendel and Tevye on one level, Sholem Aleichem, on another; no doubt Aleichem would have said that he too has a Maker, who laughs at the dreams and delusions of others in that comedy called *Life on Earth*.

The Anti-Capitalist Aleichem

The divine comedian plays a smaller role in the Goset and Artef adaptations of Sholem Aleichem. Characters like Tevye and Mendel acquire new significance as would-be capitalists in a system that ill serves them, and needs a revolution if its injustices are to end. Aleichem lived in a world different from that of his pro-Soviet adaptors, if only because he died before the 1917 revolution in Russia. But a curious parallel arises between the world that waits for a messiah and the world that needs a revolution. Walter Benjamin saw a correspondence between messianic and Marxist worldviews when he wrote about moments in history that present "the sign of a messianic cessation of happening, or, put differently, a revolutionary chance to fight for the oppressed past."[13] The "messianic cessation of happening" provides an opening for intervention in history, a conjunction of events that allow a chance for revolutionary action or recovery of a lost, oppressed past through revision of history. In a sense, the theatres of Goset and Artef engaged in recovery of the past—cultural and political archeology—as their productions of Sholem Aleichem found within his world of "False Profits" and non-arriving messiahs a critique of continuing privilege, wealth, and the congregants who regard capital investment as their secular messiah.

Benjamin saw in Brecht's epic theatre a gestural language through which actors could create signs, if not of "messianic cessation," then of social transactions in tableau—a theatrical equivalent of cinematic freeze-frames and close-ups, which allow spectators to see and hear situations, and judge imagery and words in a new way.[14] Benjamin never explicitly calls Brecht's "quotable gesture" a theatrical form of "messianic cessation" or a chance "to fight for the oppressed past"; but with highly stylized acting, with physical movement as repeatable and decontextualized as a quotation, such theatre provides a means for visually and orally recovering fragments of past life and thought, and bringing them into the present tense of theatre. Brecht's own brief comments on Yiddish theatre, written after seeing Artef's New York production of *Haunch, Paunch and Jowl*, criticized an actress because she spoke about a leg wound "as if it were something perfectly natural." Instead, he suggested, the actress "needed a special technique which would have allowed her to underline the historical aspect of a specific social condition."[15] Artef's staging of Aleichem plays appear to have offered less "natural" portrayals. Even without a special acting technique, *200,000* underlined moments of social change through its story of "unnatural," extreme change in social conditions, as the tailor went overnight from poverty to wealth, then abruptly lost a fortune. The experimental stage direction and acting also made the tailor's change "unnatural."

Through nonnaturalistic, grotesque presentation of Aleichem's characters at both Artef and Goset, the ensembles' actors, designers, and directors turned the theatre into a kind of secular synagogue congregation, an assembly of Yiddish-speaking Jews and other guests for whom "messianic cessation" and "a revolutionary chance to fight" were the order of the day. Instead of promising a messiah's arrival, these performances portrayed followers of "False Profits" such as Menachem Mendel engaged in comic class struggle as part of the "oppressed past," where privilege and profit, or the lack of them, were central concerns. Non-naturalistic styles of presentation placed more emphasis on the frivolousness of the aristocratic figures and the indignities suffered by the underprivileged. Once Shimele Saroker the tailor wins the lottery in *200,000,* he tries to adopt a new, upper-class lifestyle too. The absurdity of his nouveau riche pretensions surfaced in a highly physical, Chaplinesque comedy of manners that attracted to Artef the likes of Fannie Brice, Jed Harris, and Ben Hecht. These spectators and others could follow the actors' body language, their dances, and clowning, even if they could not follow the Yiddish words.

Chagall's Aleichem

One visual language highlighting the grotesque humor in Aleichem's stage characters came from Marc Chagall's paintings. The Soviet critic Abram Efros, writing about Goset's 1921 *Sholem Aleichem Evening,* said that the presentation "was conducted, as it were, in the form of Chagall paintings come to life. The best places were those in which [the director] Granovskii [sic] executed his system of 'dots,' and the actors froze in mid-movement and gesture, from one moment to the next."[16] Benno Schneider, who collaborated with the Habima Theatre in Moscow before joining Artef in New York, could well have known Granovsky's approach to Aleichem, which was imported to Brooklyn in 1931 when a Russian actor restaged the 1923 Goset version of *200,000.*[17] If Schneider did not try to follow Granovsky's example in his own work, at least he led his acting ensemble to perform Aleichem with comparably stylized, highly physical comedy. The mid-movement freeze-frames inserted in stage performances also might be regarded as a variant on the "messianic cessation" about which Benjamin wrote.

While Chagall's painting greatly influenced the visual and kinetic style of Goset's Aleichem stage works, the playwright's important social and political views of "past Jewish life, condemned to disappear in our country," showing "the ruins of the old [and] great social hopes," were also acknowledged by the Soviet actor Solomon Mikhoels, who portrayed Menachem Mendel for the Moscow State Yiddish Theatre (Goset), and became the theatre's artistic director. Mikhoels spoke of a "method of scenic social analysis" in a 1928 interview:

Instead of the individual's moods, half words, half tones—explicit, burgeoning social feelings; instead of isolated heroes with private, purely subjective, limited experiences—joyful mass movements, with their noise, their dancing on the ruins of the old, their great social hopes and rational activities; instead of types—social figures that convey the breadth of large human masses, of human collective; instead of family conflicts, instead of "Chekhovism," instead of sadness and melancholy—large social contradictions which create the background for the whole action on the stage. . . . Looking for the means, how most sharply and conspicuously to uncover the tragic content of past Jewish life, condemned to disappear in our country, the theatre showed a great diversity in evoking new stimulae in its development. To hone the characters, to perfect the stage devices, uncover new social kernels hidden in the atrocious, often-anecdotal classical figures—this was our continuing path. Isn't tragicomedy one of the phenomena typical of our contemporary epoch?[18]

Mikhoels, Brecht, and Chaplin

Mikhoels's description of his theatre's "joyful mass movements . . . dancing on ruins," and figures drawn from the "human collective," recalls some of Brecht's and Benjamin's approaches to socially conscious play creation, although Brecht and Benjamin would rarely if ever call for exploration of "past Jewish life" through tragicomedy. A memorable example of Mikhoels himself representing tragicomic Jewish life in Russia has been preserved in the Soviet film *Jewish Luck*, where he portrays Menachem Mendel, under the direction of Goset founder Alexander Granovsky. The film is silent, with subtitles in Yiddish (and now in English), so his voice cannot be heard. Also, the camera tends to isolate the actor and show close-ups of his face in a way that separates him from other actors; in this respect, the film continues the drama of "isolated heroes" that Mikhoels wanted his theatre to avoid.

However, in some scenes ensemble movement reveals a great deal about Mendel's character. A surreal, grotesque dream sequence in *Jewish Luck* begins when Mendel falls asleep. His dream of becoming a world-famous matchmaker rolls across the screen.[19] A telegram implores Mendel to "save America" through his matchmaking, by shipping a boatload of Jewish brides to the nation that desperately needs them. As the brides are transferred from railroad boxcars to an ocean liner heading to the United States, Menachem Mendel gazes with triumph on his greatest achievement. The great fame bestowed on Mendel in his fantasy releases the dreamer from the abject misery he suffers in his waking hours. At the same time, it is sad, if not tragic, to see that his dreams of business success require unmarried women to be treated like livestock, shipped in mass and sorted by weight, and then to see his professional success as matchmaker disintegrate after he wakes and erroneously matches two brides to each other. Here the crowd's movements, the exit of the brides from boxcars, and the gaze of admiration a crowd directs at Mendel the dreamer reveal his own interior life, and its limits in reality. Mikhoels's Menachem responds to the crowd scenes with brilliant, visually compelling physical expressions, from abject, silent pleading and discomfort to delusional, grandiose postures of pride and wealth. At times his dejected Mendel, in bowler hat and business suit, recalls Chaplin's down-and-out Little Tramp; but aside from moments inspired by the prospect of money-making, Mendel is less jaunty than the Little Tramp, who can take delight in the beauty of a flower, and other small pleasures.

On stage, Mikhoels's character and others adapted from the Aleichem stories would have been integrated in crowd scenes much of the time, amid acrobatics, choral song, and scenic spectacle. The crowd becomes a central character in *Jewish Luck* when Menachem Mendel oversees the exportation of a massive numbers of brides. This kind of group scenography was integral to Granovsky's direction, as Jeffrey Veidlinger indicates in his description of Granovsky's 1923 Goset production of Aleichem's *200,000*:

> Granovsky shunned any psychological complexity, preferring to portray characters as social types. The sharp contrast between the reformed [nouveau riche] Shimele and his working-class background was emphasized by a split stage which placed workers on ladders effortlessly floating above the bourgeoisie, whose obesity made them ever aware of the pull of gravity. A matchmaker parachuted onto the stage, alluding to a literal interpretation of the ubiquitous *luftmentschen* [men of air, dreamers, schemers].[20]

Goset's *200,000* and other stagings of Aleichem plays at Goset and Artef, presented characters as part of a social group: nouveau riche, poor working class, and other variants associated with either the *shtetl* or urban Jews. Earlier, Mikhoels was quoted saying that "instead of types" his theatre offered "social figures that convey the breadth of large human masses, of human collective." Different vertical and horizontal movement sometimes expressed the group's identity. Menachem Mendel, in this case not portrayed by Mikhoels, lived on air and his ethereal schemes set him up for a fall, a flight Granovsky literally depicted by the parachuter in *200,000*. Artef's production of *200,000* directed by Benno Schneider achieved comparable nonrealistic character movement through dance, clownery, and musical comedy choreography. *New York Times* critic William Schack wrote of this production, "Lines aren't merely spoken— they are half-sung; the characters do not merely move across the stage— they half-dance. When a swell comes in to have a suit measured, it isn't a perfunctory piece of business but an occasion for epic clowning."[21] *Morgn Frayhayt* critic Nathaniel Buchwald also praised the production's "clowning and elements from low comedy . . . and original stage compositions," even if he wasn't entirely pleased to see the play's period of history so far removed from contemporary class struggles.[22]

Moishe Nadir criticized Granovsky's production of *200,000* for immersing actors in a lot of acrobatics and *tummel* (Yiddish for "noise").[23] This component of Granovsky's direction was described more favorably by the Russian writer Abram Efros in 1928:

Had it only been by imitation of *shtetl* daily life, by a naturalistic counterfeit of the countenance and life of the everyday Jew, even with a light admixture of a Jewish anecdote, that traditional consolation of both the friendly and hostile citizen—so be it! Ultimately, it would have been acceptable to everyone, and you could have pitied them, "Poor people . . . How good it is that history, nevertheless, moves!" But Granovskii demanded something entirely different. . . . The long hems of the *capotas* and fringed undergarments, the curls of beards and hair, the curves of noses and backs hovered over the space of the stage in Granovskii's theatre, if one can say so, as absolutes. The singsong, guttural speech, squeaking at the ends of sentences, entered the ear like a molded, finished, self-sufficient system. The scattered, hurried movements and gestures, interrupting each other, ran like a counterpoint of beads. Granovskii turned the features of small daily life into a theatrical *device* and a stage *form*. From this moment, the Yiddish theatre came into being.[24]

Granovsky's transformation of Yiddish speech into sound effects, or a device in which sounds conveyed the sense, enabled non-Yiddish-speaking Russians to appreciate the performance, although they may not have understood the words Aleichem wrote. The journalist Leon Dennen wrote that half the audience watching Mikhoels recite a Sholem Aleichem story did not understand Yiddish, but they followed his movement and facial expressions fully enough to be thrown "into a frenzy of enthusiasm."[25] Visual clues also would have been present in Granovsky's direction of the ensemble:

> Rich men moved with their limbs drooping down. The movement of the laborers flowed in a symmetrical opposition, always upwards. . . . [I]n tailors's shops, the workers had straight backs, . . . their arms were vigorously lifted up in choreographed movements as they sewed. . . . The low-paid tailors—those who did not win the lottery—were shown to be physically as well as morally upright in Granovsky's production.[26]

Cutting all but forty lines of Aleichem's original script for *200,000,* the Soviet director made it easier for other components to take on equal or greater significance in his staging.[27]

Granovsky's 1923 approach to Sholem Aleichem, and Artef's later approach with movement as "half-dance," made the plays more accessible to non-Yiddish-speaking audiences in New York as well as Moscow. With so much physical comedy and nonverbal acting, was it necessary to hear Aleichem's Yiddish text at all? Moishe Nadir came to the author's defense in this regard, when he compared different productions of *200,000.* He preferred to see "the director interfere as little as possible," and found Aleichem's characters "uncomfortable" in the "stiff garments of sophisticated stylization."[28] A playwright himself, Nadir wanted to hear Aleichem's lines of dialogue, and not have them dispersed during acrobatic feats. He thought of Sholem Aleichem opening his eyes, coming back to life in Moscow, and wondering whether Granovsky is good for his plays. In Nadir's imaginary monologue for Aleichem, the resurrected writer asks about Granovksy: "For what shouldn't he be good?" and answers himself: "Only for my plays he is not good. That is to say, he would have been good for my plays, only what he wants will not let *me* be in my plays."[29]

Nadir also wrote that Schneider had given the Artef production "not one soul, but two: the author's and his own," and the division troubled him.[30] That very division, between older and modern versions of Alei-chem, others found intriguing and timely in the productions, as the directors joined the popular Yiddish comedy of Sholem Aleichem to experimental, nonrealistic performance styles at Goset and Artef.

Granovsky's *200,000* also suffered from "excessive Chagallism," said Nadir, in an allusion to the beautiful dream-like set design Marc Chagall created for the 1921 Moscow production,[31] but this too might be seen as an asset, not a fault. Without question, Chagall's beautiful, dreamlike imagery, including a fiddler on the roof, influenced the nonrealistic act-ing style of the Goset production. Mikhoels later recalled, "On the day of the premiere, Chagall walked into my dressing room. After preparing his colors, he set to work. He divided my face into two parts. One he painted green, the other yellow (as they say, 'green and yellow' [pale, downcast]). Chagall lifted my right eyebrow two centimeters higher than the left. The wrinkles around my nose and lips spread all over my face. These wrinkle lines highlighted Menakhem-Mendel's tragic lot."[32] The actor began to look like a Chagall painting, and Granovsky's crowd scenes had some of the same fantastical, grotesque style about them.

Soviet writer Abram Efros reports Chagall "hated real objects as ille-gitimate disturbers of his cosmos and furiously hurled them off the stage. . . . With his own hands, he painted every costume, turning it into a complex combination of blots, stripes, dots, and scattering over them various muzzles, animals and doodles. . . . He did not look for types or images—he simply took them from his paintings."[33] Chagall wanted to immerse the play's characters in his world—to situate them in a moving painting, perhaps, as staged by Granovsky with colors and shapes by Chagall. In this sense, the stage exhibited a new world, one with memo-ries preserved and dreams celebrated through remarkable visual art. The old *shtetl* world of poverty and persecution did not disappear completely. Onstage, both worlds existed at once, but the *shtetl* survived as theatre, and was inseparable from the spirit of transformation and modernity that gave it theatrical form.

Aleichem's Messiahs

Aleichem's ideological and religious tendencies were radical before Artef or Goset adapted his writing. Half a century before Benjamin developed theses of history that connected the utopian promises of messianism to those of Marxism, Sholem Aleichem anticipated those connections. The language of his characters, particularly Tevye the dairyman's speeches, includes colloquial references to the arrival of the Messiah and the removal of poverty from East European life. The promise of a better life gives these characters hope, and their hope surfaces daily in folkloric, comic expressions about the Messiah. At one point Tevye speaks of summer customers in dachas looking forward to his delivery of fresh butter and cheese: they "wait for me as though I were the Messiah."[34] Menachem Mendel, advising Tevye that a business investment will benefit both of them, says: "You . . . have a chance not only to make a nice killing, but also to help save my life, I mean literally to raise me from the dead!"[35] Tevye is not the Messiah, as it turns out—he is only joking about it—and he cannot raise the dead; but does think himself capable of small miracles: delicious butter, cheese, and a financial fortune from partnership with Mendel.

During one installment of Aleichem's epistolary novel about Menachem Mendel and his wife, the bumbling investor informs his spouse, Sheyne-Shendl, that "the market has crashed just as futures, God help us, were being called. I'll see the Messiah before I see my money again."[36] That line would have resonated with some survivors of the Great Depression in America. Even if it doesn't appear in an Artef play, the sentiment about great loss and small prospects of redemption reflects experiences that Menachem Mendel, his investor Tevye, and the tailor Shimele Saroker expressed in stage adaptations.

Sholem Aleichem stood in the back of the theatre in Moscow, quietly asking himself, "Is it my fault, tell me, is it my fault that Communists and revolutionaries come here every night?" Moishe Nadir, standing next to him, whispered, "Yes. If only it were mine."

12

The *Anti-Milkhome Zamlung* of 1937

The Yiddish Anti-War Catalogue Reconsidered

Out of print and almost forgotten, the twenty-one-page booklet that lists a collection of anti-war plays still can be read in the New York Public Library by those who read Yiddish.[1] First mimeographed in July 1937, the faded words of the *Anti-Milkhome Zamlung* testify to a period in American history when Yiddish plays critical of war had both an attentive audience and promoters within the Federal Theatre Project, which published the booklet. At a time when the United States and other nations built arsenals and prepared for new wars, the messianic longing for a world at peace remained alive in Yiddish culture.

In October of 1934, the Yiddish theatre collective Artef staged to great acclaim Lipe Resnick's *Recruits, or, That's How It Was,* one of the plays listed in the booklet. The production was so widely praised in New York that actors, directors, and theatre critics who could not speak Yiddish attended and lauded it too. Its portrayal of Eastern European *shtetl* residents who force a Jewish tailor to enter the Tsar's army against his will evoked other, later objections to conscription and war. *Recruits* "became a major hit and began to attract the attention of the English-speaking theatre community," Nahshon reports.[2] Its success represented an all too brief triumph of anti-militarist tendencies in Yiddish theatre. A few years later, closer to the beginning of World War II, Artef staged *The Good Soldier Schweik,* based on Yaroslav Hasek's Czech novel, which Brecht and Piscator earlier adapted in Germany. *Morgn Frayhayt* critic M. Ring praised "the Artefniks" for turning themselves into "a gang of clowns" for this "anti-war comedy."[3] The July 1937 catalogue of anti-war plays omitted *Schweik,* possibly because the play was not staged in Yiddish until December of that year. The satire should be listed in the next edition of the *Anti-Milkhome Zamlung,* which is to say, the second edition.

The National Play Bureau, an office of the Federal Theatre Project, created the first edition of the catalogue. While the Federal Theatre Project's primary goal was to provide employment for artists in need of economic relief during the Depression, its subsidiary goals included the fostering of new theatre. As Leo Schmeltsman noted in his 1937 report on the Yiddish theatre of the Federal Theatre Project, the staff "prepares Yiddish and Yiddish-English play catalogues, bulletins, and news letters containing the latest information about developments in the theatre. These publications are distributed to Yiddish and other projects. They are also sold to professional and amateur groups, colleges, civic and cultural organizations."[4] Another official description of the Bureau's functions that year announced plans for "the issuance of a holiday list of Jewish one-actors; a list of full-length and one-act Anti-War plays; mimeographed both in Yiddish and in English; the preparation of several other lists, namely—full-length and one-act professional plays and a religious (royalty) list."[5]

Exactly who edited the anti-war play catalogue remains a mystery. The booklet's unsigned preface explains that the document is not the last word on the subject, as it surveys the best plays on war written by Jewish authors. (Fifteen different authors are listed in the *zamlung.*) The anonymous preface writer sees a general increase of public interest in anti-war literature, but makes no connection between that and the increasing dangers of another war in Europe, or the military buildups overseen by Hitler, Mussolini, and Hirohito in the thirties. Free of topical references to contemporary military dictators and current events, the preface leaves the reader wondering if the compilers saw the dangers of war ahead. The introductory page notes that the Anglo-Yiddish Play Bureau provides translations of plays to the Federal Theatre Project and other theatre groups, and this catalogue constitutes one means of letting others know about the available scripts; but the author carefully avoids suggesting that these plays might increase public concern about war, or constitute an anti-war protest.

The No-Conscription League

Were the compilers of the catalogue protecting themselves against accusations (which had already begun, and were directed at the entire Federal Theatre Project) of political bias, Communism, and un-American activities? It is not currently illegal to voice opposition to war or promote anti-war plays, but at times in American history, speeches against war and conscription led to the speakers' arrest and deportation. In 1917 when anarchists Emma Goldman and Alexander Berkman spoke on behalf of the No-Conscription League, they were arrested by a federal marshal and charged with "conspiracy against the draft." Goldman noted in her autobiography, *Living My Life,* that when Berkman was still in prison after she had been released, the Yiddish Left united in his defense. "In fact, everyone in the radical Jewish circles heartily co-operated with us. A special group to aid our efforts was composed of Yiddish writers and poets, among them Abraham Raisin [sic], Nadir, and Sholom Asch."[6] The arresting officer, Marshal Thomas McCarthy, simply followed federal orders when he incarcerated Goldman and Berkman; but he deserves some small praise for bringing Reisen, Nadir, Asch, and the editors of the socialist *Forward* and the anarchist *Freie Arbeiter Stimme* together in a movement for free speech against militarism. These Yiddish writers and editors were not often in agreement.

Nadir had previously published satiric Yiddish feuilletons about the nonsense of nationalism and militarism. In 1916 he wrote an imaginary dialogue with a character named Lazer-Elya, whom he said had developed "patents against war." Lazer-Elya had a "patent" "that the soldiers of both sides should exchange uniforms. . . . When the Germans see the Frenchmen in German uniforms, they'll think they are Germans and they won't shoot. The same with the French and all the others. In that way, the wars will be abolished."[7]

In response, Nadir reminded his imaginary colleague that if the German dressed in French clothes "looks at himself in the mirror he'll think he's a Frenchman, and he'll shoot himself as his own enemy. That's something you forgot completely, Lazer-Elya." Only briefly deterred, Nadir's friend soon proposed another "patent." Instead of shooting "bullets and shrapnel and all the other things and [making] wounds which . . . have to be bandaged up with cotton . . . better [to] shoot cotton in the first place and be done with it!" President Wilson never took up Lazer-Elya's suggestion, and Nadir subsequently had to join the committee defending the No-Conscription League speakers.

The next edition of the anti-war *zamlung* should list one of Nadir's plays (more about that in a moment), and offer a more substantial introduction to the topic of Yiddish anti-war plays. If the creators of the first *Anti-Milkhome Zamlung* read a few of the plays on their list, they surely knew and neglected to say that Yiddish theatre questioned the need for conscription and militarism from its beginnings. Even before the so-called father of Yiddish theatre, Avrom Goldfaden, wrote his play *The Recruits* in 1877, and the great Yiddish novelist Mendele wrote his play *The Draft* in 1884, Israel Axenfeld's play, *The First Yiddish Recruit in Russia*, was published in 1861. (*Recruits*, which Artef staged in 1934, was an adaptation of Axenfeld's play.) All three of these early Yiddish plays responded to the dangers of military conscription and war that Jews faced in Tsarist Russia. Many nineteenth- and early twentieth-century Eastern European Jews (including one of my grandfathers) fled the region to avoid service in the Tsar's army, in which anti-Semitism was rife, and soldiers on their own side might harm Jews when not at war with another enemy. After the Tsar banned all Yiddish theatre in 1887, the anti-militarist plays became dangerous to Jews too.

The Most Anti-Militaristic People in the World

Yiddish playwrights like Axenfeld and his twentieth-century adaptor Resnick poetically recapitulate the East European Yiddish community's history of anti-militarism. That history accelerated as nineteenth-century threats of conscription led to noncooperation and flight by Jews, and continued for a long time, over a wide geographic area. Joseph Roth wrote in his book, *The Wandering Jews*, that if "Eastern Jews weren't quite so timorous, they could take justifiable pride in being the most antimilitaristic people in the world. . . . They did not want to serve. They did not want to lose their lives. . . . The Eastern Jews were the most heroic of pacifists."[8] The plays pay tribute to these heroes without necessarily showing them triumphant.

While the Yiddish anti-military tradition developed in Eastern Europe, immigrants carried it with them as they took refuge in America. Irving Howe quotes a Lower East Side New York café habitué from 1905 saying, "Everywhere you meet people who are ready to fight for what they believe in and who do not believe in fighting."[9] The actors who performed *Recruits* and *The Good Soldier Schweik* at Artef kept those beliefs alive on stage in the 1930s.

Goldfaden's musical, *The Recruits,* was not listed in the 1937 anti-war catalogue, but it should be included in the next edition. The play portrays two Jewish soldiers whom the army dismisses after it has trouble with them. When they are learning to fire rifles, the Yiddish recruits dive for cover after the first shot. Nahma Sandrow writes that at the time Goldfaden staged the play, he hired local Romanian soldiers to join the chorus and march to his play's music, "because they could provide their own impressive costumes."[10] Another source reports that Goldfaden wrote the play while he and some cast members hid in an attic to avoid military recruiters.[11]

Goldfaden's comedy about Jews unfit for military service has some resemblance to a scene in Mendele's 1878 novel, *The Travels of Benjamin III,* in which a scoundrel tricks two Jews, Senderl and Benjamin, into joining the army. Promised free food and baths, the two naïve men have no idea they are enlisting. They soon prove to be physically and psychologically incapable of following orders, which would make them dangerous to their fellow soldiers in wartime, and leads to their discharge. (A similar incapacity to follow orders surfaces in the Good Soldier Schweik's military career.)

Aderabe, ver iz meshuge?

Discussing Senderl and Benjamin's inability to obey instructions in the army, Aaron Lansky notes in his book, *Outwitting History,*

> Militarism lies outside their cognition: beyond their interest, their ability, or their comprehension. Their position . . . is radical to the core, for it challenges not only the legitimacy but the very *premise* of military culture. And the incredible thing is that they [Benjamin and Senderl] get away with it. Roaring with laughter, the assembled officers set our Jewish heroes free on grounds of insanity. . . . To quote the title of another of Mendele's works, *"Aderabe, ver iz meshuge?"* ("On the Contrary, Who Is Really Crazy?").[12]

Mendele's novel about Benjamin III was adapted for the Yiddish stage by Moishe Nadir in 1929, but his version leaves out the military training episode. (In Nadir's version, Benjamin and Senderl fire rifles when asked by "Little Red Jew," a Communist who gives them bread, a sickle, and a pick-ax—if not a hammer—on their journey.[13] Their preparedness to fight a windmill and their encounter with a dragon also recall scenes in the Cervantes novel, *Don Quixote,* from which Nadir borrows, but the wandering Jews in his play never join an army.) The dragon appears again, and the military episode disappears again, in the Yiddish adaptation of Mendele's novel that was staged in Moscow by the State Yiddish Theatre in 1927. A new adaptation, with the anti-military satire included, should be added to the *anti-milkhome* play catalogue.

Another play not listed is *The Straw Hero* (also known as *The Straw Soldier*), by Isidor Friedman, and influenced by Hasek's *Schweik.* Menasha Skulnik performed the title role when the play opened in 1934.[14] Still untranslated and unpublished, the script can be found in the Library of Congress's Marwick Collection. An excerpt from the opening scene, which takes place during a World War I battle, includes this dialogue:

> MEYERSON (*sighs*): God only knows if I'll still be alive when my parents get my letter.
>
> CHARLIE: Well, if the Fritzis don't have your number you'll live, and if they do, it'll be your hard luck. (*To everyone.*) Am I right, boys, or am I right?
>
> ALL: Oh, right Charlie. (*Loud shooting is heard outside.*)
>
> CHARLIE: Oho! Things are heating up already.
>
> MEYERSON: Oh my God! (*groans*) I'm dying.
>
> CHARLIE: Are you wounded, or what?
>
> MEYERSON: No. I'm just scared that I'll die of fright.
>
> CHARLIE: You'll die of death.[15]

The play was well received with Skulnik in the role of the "straw" or vulnerable protagonist Meyerson. Its critique of war includes some gallows humor that Friedman probably wrote specifically for the popular actor Skulnik. Theatre historian Nahma Sandrow describes the Skulnik role as "his famous characterization of an inept army recruit—a stock comic figure on the Yiddish stage since a Goldfadn sketch of the 1880s."[16] (The Goldfaden sketch became the basis for his play, *The Recruits.*)

Compilers of the 1937 catalogue found some of the plays published in Yiddish; others were available only in German or English. Their list was not limited to plays originally written in Yiddish; its purpose was to introduce anti-war plays to Yiddish readers and theatre artists.[17] The list of full-length plays included the following:

Hinkeman	by Ernst Toller
Frederick's Family	by Ernst Toller
The God of War	by Israel Zangwell
60,000 Heroes	by Benjamin Ressler
The Sailors of Cattaro	by Friedrich Wolf
Walls	by F. Bimko
When Luck Runs Out	by Morris Cohn
Journey's End	by R. C. Sherriff
Walls	by F. Bimko
The Enemy	by Channing Pollock
Peace on Earth	by George Sklar and Albert Maltz

The following one-act anti-war plays were on the 1937 list:

Bury the Dead	by Irwin Shaw
The World	by Alvin Davis
Diplomacy	by David Pinski
Little Heroes	by David Pinski
They Went Out	by H. F. Rubinstein
For All Eternity	by Jack Lande

The revised, second edition of the Yiddish anti-war catalogue, like the first edition, ought to include plays already available in Yiddish, as well as some that need to be translated into Yiddish. A few readers may argue that too few Americans read or speak Yiddish to warrant a translation or staging of plays in that language today. But a Yiddish translation will confer on some plays new, additional significance, as noted earlier in the discussion of Sinclair Lewis's *It Can't Happen Here*, another play that should be added to the list. Lewis and co-author Moffitt left no doubt in their script that they objected to the fascist army that serves American President Buzz Windrip, and holds his enemies in a concentration camp. (Lewis and other playwrights I propose to add to the second edition of the catalogue may not be Jewish, but their anti-war plays were performed in Yiddish, which should be sufficient to qualify them for inclusion in an *Anti-Milkhome Zamlung*.)

Brecht's Jewish Mother

The next anti-war catalogue also ought to include Brecht's *Mother Courage*, which was performed in Yiddish by the great Polish actress Ida Kaminska in 1957. Her character became a Jewish mother by virtue of the language she spoke. The mother protective of her grown children in Brecht's play never claims to be a Jew. But Brecht's portrait of a woman who wants to keep her daughter and two sons out of danger in wartime recalls the early Yiddish plays of Goldfaden and Axenfeld in which characters want to avoid military service. The fact that Mother Courage keeps her religious affiliation quiet, and changes it to help her survive in wartime, also recalls the dangers Jewish identity posed for many European Jews. Kaminska's postwar Yiddish production of *Mother Courage* was doubly tragic, because many Yiddish theatregoers did not survive the war. After watching Kaminska perform Brecht's play in Warsaw, Polish critic Jan Kott lamented that hardly anyone in the audience understood Yiddish. War losses could be seen not only on stage but also in the audience, or rather, in the loss of an audience.[18]

Karl Kraus's gargantuan anti-war play, *The Last Days of Mankind*, should be listed in the next *zamlung*.[19] Kraus, an Austrian Jew who converted to Catholicism, wrote in German with great wit and carefully chosen words. His vision of twentieth-century war's cruelty and its outrageous self-justifications remains prophetic. Reports of genocidal and suicidal carnage continuing to this day echo the scenes he recorded during World War I and published in a book in 1922. Kraus's vocal rejection of war and his commitment to the survival of the human race despite its stupidity and prejudices make him a precursor of the Yiddish speakers who survived war atrocities and wrote about them (though not in theatre texts) later in the century.

At the same time Kraus was completing his play on mankind's last days, Maurice Schwartz staged Moishe Nadir's play, *The Last Jew*, in New York in 1921. (Nadir surely knew Viennese culture and wit, and may have read installments of Kraus's anti-war writings published before 1921 in the journal, *Die Fackel* [*The Torch*].) Scenes in Nadir's play, still untranslated, show military leaders consulting with Europe's last Jew, a survivor they imagine has a special understanding of warfare.[20] Nadir's Last Jew, like the Grumbler, Karl Kraus's spokesperson in *The Last Days of Mankind*, becomes an authority about war by virtue of being a survivor.

Finally I would propose listing in the next anti-war catalogue a partially Yiddish version of the opera *Hydrogen Jukebox,* with music composed by Philip Glass and a libretto by Allen Ginsberg. Ginsberg's poetic critique of American life, set to Glass's experimental compositions, was first recorded in 1993. Both artists were practicing Buddhists at the time; but you don't have to be Jewish to oppose war. (Ginsberg acknowledged his Jewish ancestry in a number of poems, notably *Yiddishe Kopf* and *Kaddish.*) One song in *Hydrogen Jukebox* includes a compelling declaration of an end to war, with words excerpted from Ginsberg's long poem, "Wichita Vortex Sutra."

> *I lift my voice aloud,*
> *Make Mantra of American language now,*
> *I here declare the end of the War!*

> *Let the States tremble,*
> *Let the Nation weep,*
> *Let Congress legislate its own delight . . .*[21]

Rhythms in some of Ginsberg's poetry recall the chants of synagogue prayers; many Jews on the Lower East Side, where he lived for decades, shared his concerns about war, illegitimate government authority, loneliness, and lost generations. A few of his opera's lines could justifiably be delivered in Yiddish, taking a cue from a stanza in the libretto where the poet writes, "I search for the language / that is also yours— / almost all our language has been taxed by war." (The recital of Yiddish in a largely English-language performance has a wonderful precedent in Jacob Adler's 1903 Broadway performance of the role of Shylock, with the rest of the cast speaking Shakespeare's English in *The Merchant of Venice*; the effect was to render Shylock more of an outsider, a man who retains his own language, culture, and identity even if it means he is misunderstood and despised as an alien. One critic at the time, writing for the *Public Ledger* in Philadelphia, remarked that "it seemed as though this must have been the great poet's [Shakespeare's] thought in writing the play."[22])

In another context, Ginsberg once inadvertently explained why plays and other writing against war could be among Yiddish artists' most important contributions to literature. He said, "Yiddish can speak for all species that are being wiped out and for all cultures that are being wiped out. Here's a very active, alert international culture that may not survive another couple of hundred years except as a literary language."[23] Since its start in the nineteenth century, Yiddish theatre has continued to offer the artistic testimony of an endangered species; for better or worse, the Yiddish-speaking world's experience of persecution, war, exile, and its need to survive anticipated the experience and needs of many other ethnic and regional communities over the past century. In this regard Yiddish can indeed "speak for all species that are being wiped out and for all cultures that are being wiped out." It would be best if the other endangered cultures also speak out against war, until Yiddish becomes more widely spoken.

13

Conclusion

Still Waiting for the Messiah

The Messiah will come only when he is no longer necessary; he will come only on the day after his arrival.

—Franz Kafka, *Parables and Paradoxes*[1]

The messianic satire created by politically conscious theatre artists in the thirties has not entirely disappeared. Traces survive in play texts, program notes, reviews, memoirs, and photographs. The social and artistic conditions that led to the creation of the plays still exist too, though the Great Depression has ended. Other immigrant groups and indigenous populations now face variations of the displacement, sweatshops, inequality, and militarism once widely known to Jews newly arrived in America. In our time the most prominent false messiahs no longer wear white beards or ride motorcycles, as did Nadir's characters; instead they wear expensive suits and ties, hold press conferences, call for national prayer and pre-emptive wars, and promise to serve their constituents if elected.

The decline of messianic Yiddish theatre began before World War II, and its diminution cannot be attributed simply to losses in the war. Before the end of the thirties, Artef had lost its momentum. Its innovative director, Benno Schneider, moved to Hollywood. Yosl Cutler died in a car accident in 1935, and Modicut ceased to perform its puppet plays. The Federal Theatre Project's funding ended after Congress investigated its alleged un-American activities; the Yiddish Unit and all other units closed in 1939.

Leftist Yiddish theatre of the thirties was not alone in its losses, which took place, as Edna Nahshon notes, in "the context of the overall decline of the American theatre of the far left during the second half of the 1930s."[2] That decline was accelerated by congressional persecution of Communists, and the Hitler-Stalin nonaggression pact of 1939. The pact was particularly disturbing to pro-Soviet Jews who were asked by Moscow to accept Stalin's alliance with the Nazis.

Questions raised during the thirties in some of the most humorous Yiddish stage satire, including *Messiah in America, The Crisis Dybbuk,* and *We Live and Laugh,* still need to be asked, but the old answers no longer serve. A Roosevelt wonder rabbi is not likely to arrive again, with a new program for relief, as he did in Cutler's *Crisis Dybbuk.* Politicians are still dismantling the relief programs of the thirties. The chance that a new Federal Theatre Project will fund more Yiddish satire remains remote. The actor who complained in *We Live and Laugh* that no stars had "suggested how to save the Yiddish theatre from destruction" in 1937 would hear few actors proposing to save Yiddish theatre today.

To keep Yiddish theatre alive in its original language, and not simply offer a few museum-like productions on stage each year, would require thousands if not tens of thousands of Yiddish theatregoers. It would require teaching Yiddish to actors and directors, as well as audiences. The messiah who could do this, and alter Jewish cultural assimilation accordingly, has yet to arrive.

The 1937 revue actor's plea for plays that "portray truthfully the present-day fight for existence . . . plays with a social background . . . anti-war plays, plays against Fascism, pictures of working-class life, strikes, Capitalism in its true form," still could be issued today; such plays remain scarce, at least among newly written stage works in English and Yiddish. Plays along those lines in Yiddish theatre archives provide a basis for recovery and renewal of interests in the social justice, satire, and *Yiddishkayt* that animated Artef, the Federal Theatre Project's Yiddish Unit, the Modicut puppeteers, Leo Fuchs in "Trouble," and Menasha Skulnik in *Getzel Becomes a Bridegroom.*

It is not necessary to read Yiddish, or have a Yiddish acting ensemble, to return to the cultural activism and campaigns for social justice with which plays from the thirties were concerned. Conversing mostly in English, members of the Workmen's Circle branches in Los Angeles, Boston, San Francisco, and New York and the journal *Jewish Currents,* under the editorship of Lawrence Bush, sustain a consciousness of radical Jewish history through their current activism, as do the groups Jewish Voice for Peace, and Jews for Racial and Economic Justice. Socially engaged and popular Yiddish culture has become better known through the songs of the Klezmatics, Adrienne Cooper, Gerry Tenney, and Zalmon Mlotek, among others; through the Klez Camps guided by Henry Sapoznik; through the Yiddish puppetry of Jenny Romaine and Great Small Works; through publications by Zachary Baker, Joel Berkowitz, Robert Brustein, Paul Buhle, Jeremy Dauber, Harvey Fink, Amelia Glaser, Itche Goldberg, Mel Gordon, Itzik Gottesman, Kathryn Hellerstein, J. Hoberman, Rokhl Kafrissen, Stefan Kanfer, Dovid Katz, Tony Kushner, Aaron Lansky, Catherine Marsden, Tony Michels, Edna Nahshon, Edward Portnoy, David Roskies, Aaron Rubenstein, Nahma Sandrow, Naomi Seidman, Jeffrey Shandler, Nancy Sherman, David Shneer, Alisa Solomon, Ilan Stavans, Jeffrey Veidlinger, Nina Warnke, Ruth Wisse, and Michael Wex, to name only some contributors. The YIVO Institute for Jewish Research, Yiddishkayt Los Angeles, and the National Yiddish Book Center creatively encourage Americans to return to Yiddish literature in translation and its original forms. Sharon Rivo and the National Center for Jewish Film prevent Yiddish acting from disappearing by restoring and distributing classic examples on film.

These gifted writers, musicians, performers, and cultural activists have renewed some of the radical political and cultural impulses fostered by Yiddish theatre in the thirties and other decades. Still, many of the innovative stage texts developed by Nadir, Cutler, Maud, Pinski, and the Federal Theatre's Yiddish Unit in the Thirties remain unavailable to English-language readers and actors. A few translations from the period's plays exist. More English versions could be completed, and discussed in print, to make the works known to a larger public. The plays and the progressive views they offer might then more fully enter the repertoire of American theatre, where they rarely receive recognition. We will know the times have changed when anthologies of American drama and theatre seasons include a play by Nadir or Pinski. But their legacy deserves more than that.

"In Every Jew Resides the Dybbuk of a Messiah"

One model for the further development of radical Yiddish culture in English can be found in the career of Isaac Bashevis Singer. Although Singer kept his distance from most Yiddish leftists, his attitude toward translation led to more widely accessible literature. As the critic Joseph Sherman explained, "In America, Bashevis realized that he would have no future if his work were to be published only in Yiddish, a language with a steadily diminishing readership. Emulating Sholem Asch (1880–1957), the first Yiddish writer to gain international recognition, Bashevis encouraged those English translations of his work through which he progressively achieved worldwide celebrity."[3]

It could be argued that Sholem Aleichem gained international recognition before Asch, and without translation; he was read in Yiddish throughout Europe, Russia, and the Americas. But as Sherman astutely observes in his tribute to Singer, the novelist created more than translations of Yiddish fiction with his collaborators:

> [W]e confront texts that are not simply "translation" but works sometimes conceptually recast by the author; and Englished by teams of collaborators. . . . However, even as Bashevis broke with his Yiddish contemporaries, he remained rooted in the Yiddish literary tradition. No one could mistake his work for "American" literature; thematically and stylistically, it remained quintessentially Yiddish. For zealots determined to see Yiddish as sacred, of course, Bashevis [with his endorsement of English language versions of his work] was a betrayer; for everyone else he revitalized both the language and its literature through the medium, ironically, of English.[4]

Singer also probably attracted some readers because he avoided endorsing radical Yiddish political positions, although Communists and false messiahs occasionally appear in his fiction. One of Singer's characters in the novel *Meshugah* acknowledges the messianic promise within every Jew. "In every Jew resides the dybbuk of a messiah," Max Aberdam informs us.[5] But I. B. Singer himself expressed serious reservations about Jewish writers who sought a more just world. He said in a conversation that some Yiddish authors "were both sentimental and social. . . . They constantly fought for what they thought was a just world. They scolded the rich and praised the poor. I never felt this was my function in literature. I was interested in specific stories and exceptional people."[6] Today, Yiddish novelists and playwrights seeking social justice, satirizing the rich and praising the poor, can be found almost nowhere except in archives and libraries. Their world of Coney Island messiahs, singing sweatshop tailors, and unions for chicken-flickers seems almost as distant from mainstream America as the East European *shtetls* that Singer recreated in his fiction. Nadir, Pinski, and Modicut, like Singer, might attract more attention if more of their "exceptional" literature could be read in English.

Yiddish radicalism's advance, particularly its cultural momentum, has never become widely known through translations. Some of the movement fell victim to Europe's false messiahs—Hitler, Stalin, and Mussolini— and to anti-Communism in America. But some of the Yiddish Left's achievements, particularly those of its leading writers, were lost in translation, which is to say, in the absence of translation. That loss is reversible. Returns to earlier Yiddish radicalism, and beginnings of its renewal, can be glimpsed in klezmer music camps, where songs by the sweatshop poets are heard once in a while; in the new staging of plays and adaptations; in the publication of new translations; in national conferences involving the groups and individuals mentioned earlier and others, at which Yiddish literature and history are often discussed in English.

A return, with translators, historians, and directors as guides, to repressed and neglected American Yiddish theatre might qualify as one of the "postvernacular" cultural excursions Jeffrey Shandler describes in his fascinating book, *Adventures in Yiddishland*. Shandler sees that while there has been a decline in the number of speakers for whom Yiddish is a primary vernacular, the language has acquired new significance as a kind of "performance art," in which "utterance is enveloped in a performative aura, freighted with a significance as a *Yiddish* speech act quite apart from the meaning of whatever words are spoken."[7] This change, which shifts emphasis in performance from understanding the Yiddish language to an appreciation of Yiddish culture, may enhance the activities of artists who choose to present Yiddish theatre in translation, as Shandler himself suggests when he writes the following:

> Performances of plays, poems, songs, folktales, and the like are mainstays of contemporary Yiddish cultural events, but in these venues, Yiddish-language texts seldom stand on their own. As a rule, their presentation entails translation into a local vernacular by means of a variety of devices: explanatory comments delivered during the performance or in program notes, wholesale translation of Yiddish . . . or bilingual performance of texts originally written only in Yiddish. Translation has thus become intrinsic to postvernacular Yiddish performance.[8]

Shandler does not discuss the Yiddish plays of the thirties in his study, but "postvernacular" performances of such works—new translations, adaptations, and extensions of their political and social consciousness, as well as their language—could give them a new, first hearing by contemporary American audiences.

There is another, more troubling model for making Yiddish-derived theatre available in English, and that is the transformation of Sholem Aleichem's Tevye stories into a musical comedy. As Irving Howe and Robert Brustein observed after the musical *Fiddler on the Roof* opened in 1964, the Broadway play distorted and betrayed authentic Yiddish culture. Brustein warned against confusing the appeal of such works

> with serious revival of interest in Yiddish culture ... they are popular by virtue of being inauthentic. Trading on the exotic, romanticizing Jewish history for the sake of an easy nostalgia, such Broadway plays are always invested with a trace of condescension. The laughter that invariably greets a pair of hunched shoulders and an upward inflection springs less from racial or religious pride than from a very comfortable assimilation.[9]

Even misrepresentation of Yiddish culture and history provides an occasion—every time *Fiddler on the Roof* reopens, for example—to reconsider and renew the legacy of Sholem Aleichem's fiction and theatre. The renewal might begin with questions raised by Howe and Brustein and then follow with study of the productions through which Artef, Goset, Nadir, and Chaver Paver looked without nostalgia at Aleichem's world, and saw the dreams and miscalculations of his characters anew, filtered through their own political and artistic sensibilities.

The reconsideration of cultural history and the innovative staging and translation of plays pioneered by Artef, Goset, Nadir, Chaver Paver, Yosl Cutler, Benson Inge, Hallie Flanagan, and the Federal Theatre's Yiddish Unit represent viable models for the creation of new American theatre and new Yiddish theatre out of the old. Benson Inge contended that the Federal Theatre Project Anglo-Jewish Play Department's presentation of *It Can't Happen Here* in Yiddish "proved conclusively the manner in which universal material may be altered, translated or adapted to suit Jewish needs."[10] Similarly, Yiddish material can be altered, translated, or adapted to suit an American-language audience's needs. Theatre offers the opportunity for new "translation" of a text not only by changing its language but also through the visual and aural amplifications that actors, designers, musicians, and stage directors add to the performance.

Moishe Nadir once joked that Yiddish theatre doesn't have the strength to die. But it may live again in revivals, as Aleichem's writing did through the stage direction of Benno Schneider, and in parodies, as Ansky's *Dybbuk* did through Modicut's puppetry. It may also live in American-language versions like Tony Kushner's *A Dybbuk,* and Donald Margulies' new adaptation of Sholem Asch's *God of Vengeance.* Caraid O'Brien's recent translations have brought other Asch plays, such as *Motke Thief,* back to the public.

At the same time, a loss of the momentum for social change, social justice, and satire embodied by radical American Yiddish theatre of the thirties must be acknowledged. Perhaps the full impact made by that theatre, and by the political activism and secular messianism within which it arose, can be known only by listening to what Rebecca Solnit calls "the Angel of Alternate History." A successor to Walter Benjamin's Angel of History, Solnit's imaginary messenger tells us that "our acts count, that we are making history all the time, because of what doesn't happen as well as what does." Alternate History's Angel pays tribute to unacknowledged and unrecorded accomplishments in history, the protests and campaigns for change that sometimes deter war and other disasters without the protesters knowing it. Where Walter Benjamin's Angel of History sees only ruins in the storm of progress, Solnit's Angel of Alternate History says, "'Could be worse.' They're both right, but the latter angel gives us grounds to act."[11] Perhaps just as we need an Angel of Alternate History, a witness who sees the radical course of events that others missed, we also need to speak of an alternate Yiddish theatre, to acknowledge those who inaugurated in artistic form their visions of justice, mutual aid, and satire in a time of adversity. The secular and comic testament of a messianic theatre, separate from Second Avenue's more conventional musicals and melodramas, also gives us grounds to act.

A few years ago, Hillel Halkin proposed that his translation of Peretz's 1909 play, *A Night in the Old Marketplace,* should be staged on Broadway.[12] He compared the expressionistic Yiddish text's challenges to those posed by Broadway musicals like *Cats* and *Les Miserables.* Here too, recourse to an alternate Yiddish theatre would be advisable. Rather than follow Halkin's plan and turn the Peretz play into a Broadway sequel to *Cats* or even *Fiddler on the Roof,* I would prefer to see the play directed by Robert Wilson, Peter Sellars, or Anne Bogart—noncommercial experimenters whose remarkable stagings of operas in foreign languages, and of American texts, display qualities that would better serve Peretz's poetic, dreamlike writing. New music based on traditional klezmer tunes, performed by the Klezmatics, might give the presentation additional contemporaneity. Projection of supertitle translations from the original text would make the play accessible to American audiences. What could be more fitting to inaugurate a new period of Yiddish theatre than an operatic production of *A Night in the Old Marketplace*, featuring the dance of the dead who arise from an Old World Jewish cemetery and recall their lost culture? We would hear the play's wedding jester predict in Yiddish (and read in translation) that a messiah will blow his horn (a shofar) after a pious couple gives birth: "They shall bring forth the Messiah!"[13] Once again the stage would prepare spectators for a messiah's arrival, with new music and theatre.

Peretz includes a small tribute to the Yiddish Left in his play. Responding to the wedding jester's warning that he should "be prepared for anything" when the dead return, the character known as the Worker answers:

> He thinks we're easy to scare.
> Doesn't he know we're Reds?[14]

At least one Yiddish-speaking Communist would return to the stage with these lines. And even if the messiah's shofar is not heard, through the lively dialogue, song, and dance of productions drawing on the plays of Peretz, Nadir, Chaver Paver, Pinski, and Modicut, Yiddish theatre's voices for social change, justice, and satire will again be available to help an audience "be prepared for anything."

Perhaps the best reason to hear once more from Yiddish theatre the voices of the thirties in Yiddish, in translation, or in an adaptation can be found in Nadir's epic, *Rivington Street*, where the street peddler asks

> What is it they sing in the Yiddish theatre?
> "Oy, po-ver-ty,
> how I love you from a distance.
> Oy, po-ver-ty,
> Remind me please of better times."

Appendix

I. Menachem Mendel and Menasha Skulnik

Sholem Aleichem's popular character, Menachem Mendel, wouldn't leave the stage. In addition to the ensembles of Goset and Artef, which placed the character onstage, Aleichem's dreamer attracted several popular American Yiddish comedians, who also took on the role. Records of their performances are scarce, but Sholem Aleichem's own text offers clues to the kinds of humor and physical behavior with which the actors could have endowed the famous *luftmentsch*.

In September of 1933, comedian Menasha Skulnik performed the title role in a new musical version of *Menachem Mendel* at the Hopkinson Theatre in Brownsville, New York. The Yiddish cast featured other gifted actors, including Seymour Rechtzeit, Yetta Zwerling, Betty Budanov, Sara Skulnik, and Itzik Friedman. The text was written by William Siegal and Israel Rosenberg, with songs by Isidor Lillian and music by B. Blank. Sholem Aleichem received no acknowledgment as the source of the book, at least not in the advertisements for the play, which, regrettably, are almost the only record that survives.[1]

Without a copy of the play's text or its songs, and with few reviews, it is difficult to say how Skulnik and his collaborators approached the story of Menachem Mendel. One brief reference to the play suggests it focused on a period when Mendel was in the United States over "the last few years." Assuming the text's lines had some resemblance to those given Menachem Mendel by Sholem Aleichem, the depiction of activities might have resonated with the concerns of the 1930s. Aleichem's Mendel tries and fails to become wealthy in the stock exchange early in his career. Some of Aleichem's original lines for Mendel would quite readily transfer to a *schlemiel* portrayed by Skulnik. "No one knows when his luck will look up. It's bound to happen if you wait long enough," says Aleichem's character.[2] "I'm still waiting," Skulnik's Mendel might add in 1933. Aleichem had his creation admit, "The harder I try, the less it works out." Skulnik might have shrugged and continued, "If I don't try so hard, it still doesn't work out." His hard luck might continue; but he would continue too, and survive for another day, as *schlemiels* usually do.

Given that Mendel almost always needs money and a job, he still might have been seeking overnight wealth in 1933. "I can get in at the ground level, market prices have fallen so low even I can almost afford them," the speculator would have told his wife. His wife, Sheyne-Shendl, still had good reason to ask him, "Who ever heard of a grown man playing in a market?" And where she once said, "Mark my words, Mendel, all your overnight tycoons will soon by the grace of God be the same beggars they were before," she could now say, "I told you, Mendel, all your overnight tycoons would soon by the grace of God be the same beggars they were before."

Yetta Zwerling once again could have portrayed a wealthy widow, only now she could be a formerly wealthy widow, a victim of the market crash in search of a new husband to keep her in luxury. She might mistake Menachem Mendel for such a man. Mendel could tell her he was in the insurance business again, which would bring him into the wealthiest circles: "the richer you are, the more you need insurance, because an old age lived in poverty is harder on a rich man."

Sholem Aleichem's jokes about wealth, poverty, tycoons, and beggars still would have resonance in 1933, and Skulnik as an optimistic *schlemiel* might have given these jokes just the kind of hesitant, naïve delivery they need to sound misinformed. Audience members might have identified with Skulnik's Mendel, the man who dreams of wealth in the New World, and loses his shirt. Whatever else he loses, Skulnik's Mendel on stage could keep his sense of humor, and share it.

II. Leo Fuchs's Menachem Mendel

In 1940 Yiddish actor Leo Fuchs also portrayed Sholem Aleichem's Menachem Mendel, or a variation of the character. Originally Maurice Schwartz planned to play the role in his own production, *If I Were a Rothschild,* inspired by a story with the same title. Illness forced Schwartz to replace himself with Fuchs before the play opened at the end of 1939. *New York Times* critic William Schack wrote that Fuchs performed the lead role "nimbly, inventively and with gusto," but the play as a whole was less enticing. Schack found that the adaptation with music by Sholem Secunda, produced at the Yiddish Art Theatre, fell "considerably short of its objective because it lacks a clear-cut point of view."[3]

Schwartz's and Fuchs's approach to the story differed from Sholem Aleichem's, first of all because Menachem Mendel never appears in the original story, "If I Were a Rothschild." It would take considerable invention to transform that short story into a full-length play; the original tale is only a few pages in length, and consists largely of a stream of consciousness dream about wealth and philanthropy. Subtitled "Soliloquy of a Kasrilovka Melamed," the teacher who has no name in the story imagines how he would spend a fortune, if he had one.[4] (Some of *Fiddler on the Roof*'s song, "If I Were a Rich Man," came from the same source.) The underpaid man cannot afford to give his wife money for the Sabbath meal she wants to prepare. Still, once he starts daydreaming, there is almost no limit to the *melamed*'s imagined philanthropy. After attending to the needs of his own home, he plans to endow his town with an old age home, an interest-free loan program, free clothing, dowries for poor girls, and subsidies for learning. His generosity leads the teacher to think that with enough money he could also end wars. He would loan billions to the Turks, the English, whichever nations engaged in territorial disputes. His philanthropy would stop war and initiate the arrival of the Messiah, creating a paradisiacal world where the *melamed* could live without money—almost the situation he finds himself in at the end of the dream, when he remembers he is penniless and can't give his wife money for the Sabbath meal.

Aleichem wrote a wonderful, comic excursion into economic theory; without overtly saying that the wealthy could reduce war instead of profiting from it, the monologue contemplates that possibility and also modestly questions the credibility of such a plan by having a poor man without any resources propose it.

Menachem Mendel enters this dream in the Schwartz production. Exactly how he enters can only be reconstructed from reviews of the play, since the manuscript of the play itself has not been found. In one review, H. Rogoff states that in Act Two, the teacher dreams of a world peace conference, and Menchem Mendel appears in the dream as the teacher's minister of finance.[5] (Since the teacher dreams he is Rothschild, his finance minister controls myriad banks.) Mendel wants justice, world peace, and a rescue of the Jews from Germany; world leaders come to him because he has money. Mendel's interests in justice and peace seem somewhat out of character, given that in Sholem Aleichem's own writings, Mendel the *luftmentsch* lives on air, mismatches prospective spouses, and seeks personal profit rather than improvement of humanity's welfare. His crusade for world peace and justice could hardly be expected to end happily, if his earlier miscalculations are any indication. In fact, it is surprising he does not start World War II in Schwartz's version of the story. Leo Fuchs in the Mendel role might have undercut his own character's delusions through humorous acting, which usually made him look like a *schlemiel*; Rogoff praised the comic actor's consistent character. Schwartz's addition of Menachem Mendel as financier of peace was an inspired idea, even if the play itself was not well received.

The larger plot, involving the schoolteacher's fantasy of an international peace conference, was not so satiric, according to the *Times,* because "the author [Schwartz] has not thought seriously enough of the causes and possible cures of war. He also straddles the Jewish problem disingenuously, with vague overtures." Sholem Aleichem's own writing rarely devoted itself to "serious" thought, and it may well be that Schwartz was right to avoid seriousness. Rogoff in his review found only the characters of Himmler and Stalin clearly defined. Roosevelt and Chaim Weitzman were less coherent in character and statement; they didn't know what they wanted, and no one could understand what they said, according to Rogoff, whose comments echo the *Times* reference to "vague overtures." In any case, the play's utopian dream of a world peace conference rescuing Jews in Europe was far removed from reality. A number of leading European statesmen, deadly serious at the time, were not about to give or accept large sums of money to achieve peace and avert violence. They would spend it on armaments. Poland had already been invaded by Hitler before Schwartz's play opened; the urgency of talk about war and peace outside the theatre could not easily be matched on stage late in 1939. Perhaps Schwartz was taken in by Menachem Mendel himself; the character once wrote in a letter to his wife: "P.S.—I forgot to tell you where I'm going. I'm off to America, my dear wife. . . . The streets, they say, are paved with gold and money is dished out by the plateful. Why, a day's work is worth a whole dollar there! . . . Everyone says that in America, God willing, I'll be a big hit." The man who thought he would be "a big hit" in America kept returning to the New York stage, in the company of Artef, Skulnik, Schwartz, and Fuchs.

III. Walter Benjamin's Yiddish Theatre

Walter Benjamin (1892–1940) never wrote about Yiddish theatre. The German Jewish critic was celebrated for discussions of Brecht, Kafka, surrealism, the Messiah, and Paris in the nineteenth century, and his essays continue to influence radical interpretations of literature and drama. Benjamin's exemplary writings call for artistic and political resistance to authoritarian government, and for historical memory of oppressed cultures. As he observed in 1939, the "courage, humor, cunning, and fortitude" displayed by those struggling against oppression "have retroactive force and will constantly call in question every victory, past and present, of the rulers."[6]

Some of the courage, humor, cunning, and fortitude expressed by the past century's Yiddish theatre might have been noted by Benjamin, had he seen the Communist puppeteers Maud and Cutler portray a rent strike on their small New York Yiddish stage in 1934; watched the Federal Theatre Project's anti-fascist play, *It Can't Happen Here* in Yiddish in 1936; or heard Leo Fuchs jubilantly sing about surviving "Trouble" (his song's title) in 1937. Benjamin might have greeted this genre of theatre with enthusiasm, just as he welcomed the socially engaged plays of his friend, Bertolt Brecht.

Benjamin's essay on Yiddish theatre, composed after a visit New York's Lower East Side in the thirties, could have opened by stating that Yiddish is a language without a country. Its exiled speakers assemble in Manhattan and Brooklyn theatres to hear Old World expressions in a new context. The audiences laugh and weep at Yiddish actors as if they had never left Poland, Russia, or Romania—or because they had to leave those countries in the face of continuing persecution and poverty. The language spoken by Jewish women in East European tenements and small towns (*shtetls*)—by wives and daughters left behind when husbands and sons went to the prayer house to speak Hebrew—Yiddish is a language born in practicality; it resides not in unanswered prayers, but in recipes for bread, in the songs of a labor chorus, in the plays of Sholem Aleichem, and in everyday acts of survival about which Aleichem writes with great humor.

In New York, an economically troubled metropolis still rich in museums, libraries, universities, theatres, and cafés, the language of East European ghettos acquires a new, popular existence as entertainment—but this entertainment practiced by Moishe Nadir, Zuni Maud, Yosl Cutler, Leo Fuchs, and the great comedienne Yetta Zwerling celebrates social change and elusive justice, as well as the pleasures of daily life.

On the stages of New York's Yiddish theatres, Benjamin's essay would conclude, the exiles still dream of a promised land. Forty years of wandering are not so bad, when Moses has been replaced by comedians who perform Sholem Aleichem at Artef. One can imagine the Yiddish humorist still alive, watching his play in New York and asking, "Is it my fault, I ask you, is it my fault if I'm applauded by Communists and other radicals?" Sholem Aleichem, in his own satiric way a great critic of poverty and oppression, still speaks Yiddish today, through his revived plays, and his successors. The Old World's resistance to persecution lives on in a new country.

Acknowledgments

I am grateful to many individuals and organizations for the support and encouragement they offered while I was writing this book. Thanks are due to Fred Astren, Zachary Baker, Bolerium, Lorraine Brown, Robert Brustein, Roy Conboy, Adrienne Cooper, R. G. Davis, Larry Eilenberg, Sara Felder, Irv Fishman, Yuki Goto, Joan Holden, Henry Hollander, Ron Jenkins, Rose Katz, Stanley Kauffmann, Klez California, Mohammad Kowsar, Fishl Kutner, Alan Lew, Frank London, Florentina Mocanu-Schendel, Yeshia Metal, Eugene Morris, Edna Nahshon, Caraid O'Brien, Tom Oppenheim, Edward Portnoy, Aaron Rubenstein, Nahma Sandrow, Bernard Schechter, Laurence Senelick, Jeffrey Shandler, Gerry Tenney, Peter Thomson, Elise Thoron, Robin Titelbaum, Harvey Varga, Barry Witham, and the Workmen's Circle.

Special thanks to Diana Scott, who attended many Yiddish plays and concerts with me; Harvey Fink and Nahma Sandrow, who translated Nadir's writings and shared their unpublished pages with me; Spain Rodriguez, for his wonderful illustrations; Larry Bush and Paul Buhle for their own writing on *Yiddishkayt,* and advice on mine; Gail Naron Chalew for copyediting; San Francisco State University, which granted me a sabbatical to conduct research and welcomed my classes on Yiddish theatre; the librarians and curators at YIVO, the Dorot Reading Room of the New York Public Library, the National Archives in Adelphi, Maryland, the National Yiddish Book Center, and the Jewish Community Library of San Francisco; and Elena Coler and Micah Kleit, my editors at Temple University Press, who made this publication possible.

Finally, a few words of gratitude to A. J. Liebling, whom I never met. In 1938 he expressed a wish "to write a history of the laughing Jew, which would establish Noah, the bad kings of Israel and Harpo Marx as the authentic leaders of Jewish thought." I have not written the volume he proposed nor did he, but I share his interest in the subject.

Fragments of this book previously appeared, in different form, in the anthology, *Extraordinary Actors,* and the journal, *Studies in Theatre and Performance.* The illustrations by Spain Rodriguez were first published in *Jewish Currents,* and the stories I wrote for his comic strips include fiction as well as facts of history. Permission from the editors to reprint these materials is gratefully acknowledged.

Permission for use of photographs has been generously granted by the *Forward* Association, the National Archives, the National Center for Jewish Film, and the Archives of the YIVO Institute for Jewish Research, New York.

Notes

CHAPTER 1: MESSIAHS OF 1933

1. Throughout this study I am indebted to David Lifson's book, *The Yiddish Theatre in America,* and to Edna Nahshon's book, *The Yiddish Proletarian Theatre: The Arts and Politics of the Artef, 1925–1940,* for their information about Artef. Both volumes discuss Artef's major accomplishments; however, many of the plays I consider, particularly Nadir's stage works, are not discussed in detail by these pioneering earlier studies.

2. Cutler, *The Dybbuk in the Form of a Crisis* published in two parts in the periodicals *Der Hamer,* June 1936, 11–15, and *Der Signal,* June, 1936, 11–12. Chapter 8 on Cutler and Maud offers a more complete discussion. I am indebted to Edward Portnoy for calling this play to my attention, and to his essay cited later in the chapter on Modicut's puppetry. Yosl Cutler, as Edna Nahshon has noted, was one of the original founding board members of Artef (Nahshon, 21). His puppet theatre, Modicut, was created as a separate artistic entity in 1926.

The dream of a "united front" in this scene could well be a passing reference to the Popular Front, a coalition against fascism for which Moscow began to call in 1934. The scene was written before the 1937 founding of YKUF, the Yiddish Kultur Foundation created to build Yiddish arts-based coalitions in efforts parallel to those of the Popular Front.

3. Nadir, *Messiah in America,* translated by Nahma Sandrow. Translations from this unpublished English version of the play are used throughout

the chapter. Permission for use and Nahma Sandrow's advice are gratefully acknowledged.

4. The cost of admission to Artef's performance of *Messiah in America* for May 17, 1933, is noted in a press announcement published in *Morgn Frayhayt,* May 13, 1933. The May 17th performance took place at Webster Hall, a space now used for rock music concerts and earlier in its history home to special balls for artists featuring the likes of Marcel Duchamp. Emma Goldman lectured there, according to the current management's history of the theatre. The hall accommodates as many as 2,500 spectators today. Perhaps Jack the Bluffer's calculation that an audience of 2,000 spectators would see the messiah each night was not so far away from the capacity Webster Hall held for Nadir's audience.

5. Lifson, *The Yiddish Theatre in America,* 441.

6. Sandrow, *Vagabond Stars,* 62–63, and Kanfer. *Stardust Lost: The Triumph, Tragedy, and Mishugas of the Yiddish Theatre in America,* 100–101.

7. Kafka, *Parables and Paradoxes,* 81.

8. Adler, *Celia Adler Dertzeilt (Celia Adler Story)*, Volume II, 577–78. Other information on Nadir is derived from his biography in *Lexicon of Yiddish Theatre,* Volume II, columns 1389–93. Sources for biographical information earlier in this section include *The Norton Anthology of Jewish American Literature,* 230, and comments from Harvey Fink.

9. Nadir recalls his need for disguise in *Teg Fun Mayne Teg (Days of My Days)*, published in 1935. The inside cover of the book says its stories were all printed in the *Frayhayt* in the years 1925–28. I am grateful to Harvey Fink for this information, as well as his translation of the sequence in which Nadir writes, "Maurice Schwartz is the 'guy' who disguises me, dresses me . . . I let it be known through the *Groyser Kundes* that comes out on *Shabes* (where I write my column 'Theatre Things') that . . . this coming Friday night, God willing, I'll be in such-and-such theatre in the Bowery and be reviewing their play. And so my enemies will increase their 'guard.' . . . The cashier has all his eyes out. He is so flustered he gives back more change than he should. It's a frenzy of activity! But it doesn't help. Because I've already seen the play (if you understand me) last week!" Nadir clearly had no fondness for producers, and this also led him to write a comic article about the 1926 death of the famous Yiddish stage actor Jacob P. Adler. Nadir speculated that some producers would have liked to sell tickets to Adler's funeral. His premise was based on the fact that while Adler was alive but infirm, audiences would pay two or three dollars to see the ailing popular actor stand onstage. The satirist clearly had no fondness for producers like those who sold tickets to Adler's last live appearance; their exploitation of abnormality might have been a source of inspiration for the infirm old man who was proclaimed savior in *Messiah in America* (Nadir, *Nadirgang,* 229–30).

10. Nadir, *Teg Fun Mayne Teg* (*Days of My Days*), 1935. The statistics in this section come from David Passow, *The Prime of Yiddish*, 24, and from Lifson, *The Yiddish Theatre in America*, 538.

11. Shapiro in "The Writer in Kheyder," translated by Harvey Fink, whose discovery of this passage is greatly appreciated. The performance Shapiro witnessed at the Civic Repertory Theatre in 1929 presented only Act One of *Messiah in America*, and should not be confused with the May 1933 Artef production discussed elsewhere in the chapter.

12. Buhle, "The Prince of Satire: Moishe Nadir," *Shmate*, 1978, 8. The reference to his "break with the Party" does not necessarily mean that Nadir joined the Communist Party. He never formally joined, but supported Party decisions until 1939, it seems; "although embracing Soviet support for Yiddish culture and institutions, he did not in the end join the Communist Party," according to the *Norton Anthology of Jewish American Literature* (230). In any case, Nadir stayed in the Soviet Union for nine months in 1926, and expressed admiration for the Soviets upon his return to the United States.

He continued to support Communist Party policies after a 1929 conflict between Jews and Arabs in Palestine, despite protests at the *Frayhayt* by other progressive Yiddish writers. At one point the *Frayhayt*, for which Nadir wrote, described the conflict in Palestine as an anti-Semitic pogrom and said it originated in "economic exploitation of Arabian peasantry, whose land has been expropriated by British imperialism through the reactionary Jewish Zionism," and in the "land-grabbing aggression" of the British "to which the Zionist movement is willingly and knowingly lending itself" (Source: *Jews and the Left* by Arthur Liebman, 348). The 1929 denunciation of Zionists by the Communist Party's Yiddish newspaper led other prominent writers such as Avrom Reisen and H. Leivick to resign from the *Frayhayt* in protest. The debate over "land-grabbing" in the Mideast still rages in the twenty-first century, in new forms, as questions arise over the right of return to Israel's land by Palestinians who lived there before Israel became a state.

Nadir continued to write for the *Frayhayt* after this controversy, and opened a September 14, 1929 column by addressing those ready to throw stones at him. In the course of the essay, he noted that the Communist Party had weaknesses that needed to be strengthened. The satirist's polemic left at least a little space between him and the Party. In the same essay he made it clear that he favored Yiddish culture, particularly its secular East European and American achievements, over Zionist tendencies and traditions within Judaism. Not interested in the "Judaizing" of culture, he wrote more affirmatively of his support for Yiddish language and its literary achievements: "We are for culture in Yiddish, with all the beauty, vitality and richness of our cultural treasures" (translation by Harvey Fink).

Nadir may have found it possible to support American Yiddish Communist positions more readily than Moscow's positions. Bat-Ami Zucker notes in the periodical *Modern Judaism,* no. 14, 1994, that the Yiddish Bureau of the Communist Party was "a separate Jewish organization" within the American Communist Party, and its press, educational network, and social and cultural circles, including Artef, fostered "a secular leftist Jewish culture" that was "based upon Jewish experience, used familiar Jewish expressions, and drew upon its images from Jewish folklore." In the twenties and thirties, Nadir became a prime source of the culture Zucker describes here; in a sense, the satirist had his own Yiddish literary branch within the Party. That branch became more exclusive when other Yiddish writers resigned from the *Frayhayt* in 1929.

13. Fiedler, *Freaks,* 89–90. Edward Portnoy informs me that many of the performers in one Coney Island sideshow were Jewish. Perhaps Nadir knew them.

14. The play was staged in the Studio Theatre at San Francisco State University, May 17–20, 2001, directed by Joel Schechter, co-directed by Florentina Mocanu-Schendel, with musical direction by Gerry Tenney, set and costume design by Irisa Tekerian, additional text by Sara Felder, and translation by Nahma Sandrow.

15. Brecht, "Emphasis on Sport" in *Brecht on Theatre,* 6–7. Bakhtin, *Rabelais and His World,* 33–49.

16. Benjamin, "Brecht's *Threepenny Novel*" in *Understanding Brecht,* 84.

17. Benjamin, "Theses on the Philosophy of History" in *Illuminations,* 254.

18. Ibid., 264.

19. Ansky, *The Dybbuk,* translated by Joseph C. Landis, 43.

20. The different versions of Maud and Cutler's parody are discussed in Chapter 8.

21. Brecht, *Brecht on Theatre,* 98. Brecht called Artef "a highly progressive theatre," but objected to the staging of a scene in which "a cry" was spoken "as if it were perfectly natural." His objection here was mild, compared to his critique of the left-wing artists in the Theatre Union who staged his play, *The Mother,* in English. Writing to Erwin Piscator about his Theatre Union experience, in which Brecht was denied entry to rehearsals of his own play, and the script was cut without his approval, he said: "The upshot of the whole thing is one conclusion: have absolutely no dealings with the so-called left theatres. They are dominated by small cliques in which hack playwrights rule the roost." He subsequently pursued commercial Broadway productions in New York. The experience did not deter Brecht from founding a "left theatre" in Berlin, and dominating it himself (Klaus Volker, *Brecht Chronicle,* 76).

22. Kushner, *Angels in America, Perestroika,* 136–38. Toward the end of Tony Kushner's epic play, *Angels in America,* characters who have moved on to the afterlife play pinochle and converse in Yiddish. While their scene is hardly the

culmination of the play, Kushner writes at least a few lines of it in Yiddish, adding the language and its culture to his theatrical vision of American diversity. In Kushner's own humorous vision of Gan Eden, the Yiddish Paradise, a deceased grandmother meets her grandson Louis's lover, Prior Walter, after he dies of AIDS. Prior Walter wants to return to life on earth, and his Yiddish-speaking hosts simply and adeptly perform a Kabbalistic ritual that restores life to him. The card-playing Jews show no ill will toward Prior, even though he briefly interrupts their game. At one point he is described as "fegeyle" (gay), and as "a bissele farblonjet" (a little mixed-up). One of several comic, surreal fantasies about the afterlife that Kushner creates in the closing section of his play, this sequence briefly pays homage to the language and perseverance (beyond life) of East European Jews, from whose culture Prior Walter benefits.

23. I. B. Singer, quoted in "365 Days of Yiddish," a calendar published by Workman Publishing, 2001.

24. Miron, *Tales of Mendele the Book Peddler*, lxv.

25. Buhle, "Jews and American Communism," 20. Buhle also traces the impact of Yiddish culture on popular American culture in his book, *From the Lower East Side to Hollywood: Jews in American Popular Culture*.

26. "Today 'Artef'-Nadir Satire Evening," a short news article, announces the play's performance as a benefit in the May 17, 1933, issue of *Morgn Frayhayt*, my translation.

27. Benjamin, "Theses on the Philosophy of History" in *Illuminations*, 253.

28. Eleanor Gordon Mlotek and Joseph Mlotek, *Pearls of Yiddish Song*, 170–71.

29. Sapoznik, *Klezmer!*, 82. One of the most recent performances of a Messiah song by the Klezmatics offers a new lyric; instead of saying that the Messiah "will come," the popular klezmer group now sings, "We need the Messiah," on their album, *Brother Moses Smote the Water* (2004).

30. Seidman, *A Marriage Made in Heaven: The Sexual Politics of Hebrew and Yiddish*, 15.

31. Lifson, *The Yiddish Theatre in America*, 446.

32. Zinn, *Artists in Time of War*, 50.

33. Harley Erdman, "Jewish Anxiety in 'Days of Judgement.'"

34. Eisenberg, *Ten Years Artef*, 10.

35. The Group Theatre has some interesting links to Artef, but probably should not be regarded as its successor. Lifson describes one of the links when he writes that Artef's studios "provided the inspiration for . . . the Theatre Guild's Studio which became the Group Theatre" (574). Also, Group Theatre co-founder Harold Clurman and the distinguished actress Stella Adler both knew New York's Yiddish theatre scene before the Group Theatre began. (Stella Adler was the daughter of two Yiddish actors.) However, Clurman expressed considerable disapproval of Artef in 1933, and placed some distance between

his view of theatre and Artef's, in an article he wrote for the *Daily Worker.* Writing under the pseudonym of Harold Edgar, Clurman reviewed Artef's production of *The Third Parade,* and objected to Benno Schneider's direction of the play (a story about the 1932 march by American veterans seeking a bonus payment in Washington, D.C.). Edgar questioned the portrayal of workers by Artef's actors and subsequently debated in print with Artef proponent Nathaniel Buchwald. In the debate, Clurman suggested that Broadway, not the theatre of Stanislavsky or Meyerhold, was Buchwald's model, and Broadway acting (by extension, Artef's) was "based on a thin imitation of actuality which is the theatrical equivalent of capitalist showiness" (Nahshon, 105–08). Given the tenor of Clurman's objections to Artef in this debate, it is doubtful he regarded his own Group Theatre as a successor to the Yiddish ensemble. The Group Theatre achieved some of its best productions a few years later, when Clurman directed *Awake and Sing* and other plays by Clifford Odets. Subsequently, artists who left Artef (Lydia Slava, Jacob Mestel) became involved in the Federal Theatre Project's 1938 Yiddish production of *Awake and Sing,* discussed elsewhere in this volume. So it could be argued that the Group Theatre's artists influenced those formerly in Artef.

36. Wex, *Born to Kvetch,* 23.

37. Nadir, "The Average Theater Goer," viii.

38. For a recent, lively account of this story, see Stefan Kanfer's *Stardust Lost: The Triumph, Tragedy, and Mishugas of the Yiddish Theatre in America,* 41–46.

39. The printed card advertising (in Yiddish) a May 27,1933, reading by the "Yiddish Workers' Art Theatre" of Nadir's play at the Worker's Club, 608 Cleveland Street, New York, is on file in YIVO's archive of Artef materials.

40. Nahshon, *Yiddish Proletarian Theatre,* 76.

41. Ibid., 37.

42. Lifson, *The Yiddish Theatre in America,* 472.

43. Buchwald, "The Artef on Broadway," 8.

44. Lifson, 464.

45. Ibid., 574. Whether Artef actually inspired the Group Theatre is debatable. See note 35 above.

46. Lifson, 438–39.

47. Howe and Greenberg, *A Treasury of Yiddish Poetry,* 12.

48. Nadir, *Moide Ani (Confession),* 23–36.

49. Fink, Introduction to his translation of *From Man to Man,* iv–v.

50. Lifson, 446–48.

51. Nadir, *Peh-El-Peh (Face to Face),* 53–54.

52. Rubenstein, "Devils and Pranksters: *Der Groyser Kundes* and the Lower East Side," *Pakn Treger* (Spring 2005), 17–18.

53. Roth quoted in the introduction to *The Jackpot* by Sholem Aleichem, translated by Kobi Weitzner and Barnett Zumoff, 12. Another commentary on

the iconoclasm of such Yiddish theatre can be found in Stefan Kanfer's book, *Stardust Lost*, where he writes of the "irony" that Artef's "innovative group could defy any convention and any leader save for the one who lived six thousand miles from New York" (155). But judging the collective by its Yiddish plays, rather than its extra-theatrical discussions, it could be argued that Goset, the Moscow State Yiddish Theatre, and not Stalin was the "leader" Artef followed, as it selected plays previously staged by Goset. Kanfer's critique of Artef is offered without any mention of Nadir's contributions to the collective. He refers to Artef's staging of Aleichem's Kassirovka hotel stories, "done as a group recitation, [with] the comrades delivering their lines by popping their faces out in large placards" (157), but neglects to say that Nadir wrote that 1928 adaptation of Sholem Aleichem's stories.

54. Golden, *Enjoy, Enjoy!*, 156.

55. Leo Weiner in his 1899 book *Yiddish Literature*: "It is very doubtful whether the Jewish theatre can subsist in America another ten years" (242). There are already special courses, lectures, and symposia on the history of Yiddish theatre. Golden's prediction has proven accurate, as a few actors from Yiddish theatre's past have in recent years delivered their reminiscences in public. Among the theatres that continue to stage Yiddish plays are the Folksbiene in New York City, the Yiddish Theatre of the Saidye Bronfman Centre for the Arts in Montreal, and the Jewish Theatre in Bucharest.

56. Benjamin, *Illuminations*, 260.

CHAPTER 2: NADIR'S *RIVINGTON STREET*

1. Nadir, *Rivington Street*. Translation by Harvey Fink used with permission throughout the chapter.

2. Boyarin, "The Lower East Side: A Place of Forgetting," in *Storm from Paradise*, 7.

3. Zylberzweig, *Lexicon of Yiddish Theatre*, Vol. II, column 1390. The entry for Moishe Nadir notes that on March 20, 1932, the Artef actor Gendl read the poem for the sixth jubilee of Artef and afterward at various Communist events. Gendl's brief biography in *Ten Years Artef* (1937, pp. 45–46) reports that the actor performed solo shows and toured extensively.

4. Notices for the readings can be found in the *Morgn Frayhayt* of May 19, 1932, and April 6, 1933. The Chicago tour dates of February 16 and 18, 1934, are listed on a playbill for the event filed in the Artef archive at YIVO, Box 4, RG 531; no cast is listed in the playbill, which credits performances to the "Artef Actors Collective." Nadir's "most-often-produced play" was *Rivington Street*, according to a biography for the author in the *Norton Anthology of Jewish American Literature*, 230.

5. Buchwald, "The Artef on Broadway," 8–9.

6. Fo, "Les Intellectuels et La Culture," 64–67.

7. Bakhtin, *Rabelais and His World*, 167. S. D. Singer offers a very different view of the language here; instead of seeing collective, street life origins in such speech, he describes the poem as "one more chapter of recollections from [Nadir's] unfinished autobiography. The young Nadir speaks through the words of the Jew with the peddler basket, crying through laughter at all that is past and gone." Singer seems to have been aware of the poem's presentation on stage; although he does not refer to its staging, he calls *Rivington Street* "a dramatic word-spectacle," and also acknowledges that in the poem "an entire generation, with its joys and its sorrows, steps up onto the stage of life and is portrayed in its naïve-comic aspect" (Singer, *Poets and Prose Writers*, Yiddish translated by Harvey Fink). In June of 2002, when I interviewed Itche Goldberg, who knew Nadir personally, he told me that *Rivington Street* was written "in two solid days," which would suggest Nadir had lived with these memories and voices for years, and knew them well.

8. Howe, *World of Our Fathers*, 458–59. In fairness to Howe, it should be noted he wrote about "defiance of history" as "the central premise of Jewish history" in 1976, and took the Holocaust and other losses into account when referring to "the cost, beyond measure." Those losses were unknown to Nadir when he wrote his poem to remember past history in New York, and to revive its radical momentum, rather than defy history.

9. *Morgn Frayhayt*, May 4, 1933, 1–3.

10. Benjamin, "Theses on the Philosophy of History" in *Illuminations*, 255.

CHAPTER 3: PRAYER BOXES AS PRECIOUS AS DIAMONDS

1. Olgin quoted in *Lexicon of Yiddish Theatre*, Vol. VI, column 5800, my translation.

2. Veidlinger, *The Moscow State Yiddish Theatre: Jewish Culture on the Soviet Stage*, 75.

3. Buchwald quoted by Nahshon, *Yiddish Proletarian Theatre*, 71.

4. Nadir's comments on the play can be found in the *Lexicon of Yiddish Theatre*, Vol. VI, column 5800, my translation. Incidentally, the title given to the play in New York differed from its original Moscow title; although this hardly explains the warmer reception of the play in New York, the new title, *Diamonds*, was far more lively (sparkling, even) than its ponderous Soviet name, *137 Children's Homes*.

5. Veviorka, *Diamonds*, my translation from the Yiddish. *Dramatic Works of A. Veviorka*, Vol. I, 164. Copy provided by YIVO in New York.

6. Litvakov quoted by Veidlinger, 75–76. The Russian revolution inspired more than one satire involving a search for diamonds. Ilf and Petrov's 1928 novel, *The Twelve Chairs*, another Soviet satire of corruption and greed revolving

around a search for missing diamonds, was quite popular among Russian readers, and later became the source for an American film directed by Mel Brooks.

7. Veidlinger, 75.

8. Ibid.

9. "Artef-Jewish Workers Conference plans important work for the coming season." Excerpted from a "Worker's Theatre" report dated May–June 1933. Located in Box 5 of 5, RG53, 325 in Artef Archive at YIVO, New York.

10. *Ten Years Artef* (list of repertoire), 133–35.

11. Veidlinger, 111.

12. Ibid., 192, 213, 259–60.

13. Houghton, *Moscow Rehearsals,* 219.

CHAPTER 4: THE FEDERAL THEATRE PROJECT IN YIDDISH

1. Flanagan, *Arena,* 75.

2. Schack, *New York Times,* May 9, 1936, 10.

3. Buchwald and Mukdoiny quotations are reprinted in the Federal Theatre's playbill for the revue, on file in the Federal Theatre Project papers at the National Archives.

4. Flanagan, *Arena,* 124. Jacob Mestel offers another favorable view of the Lewis play, and a possible source for its volubility and gesticulation, in his book *Our Theatre* (1943). Mestel praises both the Yiddish production of *It Can't Happen Here,* produced by Bleich, Schooler, and Barzell, and his own Yiddish Unit production of Odets' *Awake and Sing,* in which press and public particularly admired the zeal shown by "old timers" who formerly performed Yiddish vaudeville and melodrama (Mestel, 179, my translation). Yiddish actors' proficiency in melodrama and vaudeville may have augmented their performance in the plays by Lewis and Odets.

5. Schmeltsman, "The Yiddish Theatre of the Federal Theatre Project," unpaged 1937 report.

6. Excerpt from an unsigned document titled "Anglo-Jewish Play Department," probably written by Benson Inge, or approved by him, since he was the department supervisor. Found in the National Archive's collection of Federal Theatre Project papers. Box 161, RG69, File of National Service Bureau, 1935–39. Inge's title within the Federal Theatre Project changed several times, although his promotion of Yiddish theatre continued after the changes. In 1936 he was supervisor of the Anglo-Jewish Play Department, which in 1937 merged with the Translations Department, where he also served as supervisor, under Emmet Lavery, who headed the Play Department of the National Service Bureau (NSB) in 1937 and became head of the NSB in 1938. (Budget cuts and reorganization within the Federal Theatre Project led to these almost comical changes, several of which Inge acknowledged in a 1937 explanation: "The

Anglo-Jewish Department has since been merged with the Foreign Play and is known as the Translations Department.") These departments were housed within Federal Theatre Project offices initially known as the National Play Bureau, which merged with the Play Policy Board to become the National Service Bureau. Both entities provided units of the Federal Theatre with new play scripts and translations, and arranged for rights and royalties. Inge helped the "Yiddish Unit" of the Federal Theatre secure plays and translations. Hallie Flanagan refers to Inge a few times in her book *Arena,* noting that he was head of translation and co-editor of *The Theatre Abroad,* a digest of foreign theatre news published by the National Service Bureau. The National Service Bureau was in Flanagan's view "the greatest power in Federal Theatre." She qualified that by adding, "I am using the word 'power' definitively: 'the ability to act so as to produce some change'" (*Arena,* 265, 267).

Benson Inge died in New York in 1970 at the age of 61. When not employed by the Federal Theatre Project, Inge wrote plays, served as drama critic for the *New York World Telegram,* and worked for a few decades in advertising after 1941.

7. Gray Brechin, "Keeping the Faith." The letters from Inge discussed here, and some replies to them, are preserved in the National Archives II in Adelphi, Maryland, among the Federal Theatre Project papers—RG 69, Works Progress Administration Records of the Federal Theatre Project, Correspondence of the Translations Department, 1935–39. Letters are filed alphabetically by the last name of the author to whom the letter is addressed.

8. Inge, letters to Mack and Schorr both dated March 11, 1937, on file in Federal Theatre Project papers.

9. Inge's letter, dated June 18, 1937, indicates that Odets not only consented to the translation of *Awake and Sing!* into Yiddish, but also commissioned it.

10. Ellen Schiff discusses the Yiddish qualities of the first American-language version of the play in her essay, "Taking the Heat," 22–23.

11. Flanagan, *Arena,* 389.

12. Berson, "Can *Awake and Sing!* Still Sing?," 56.

13. Friedrick's Wolf's German play, *Profesor Mamlock,* was staged in English in New York by the Federal Theatre Project's Anglo-Yiddish group, which felt that the anti-Nazi play needed to be shown by them, even if it was not originally written in Yiddish. Its depiction of a German doctor persecuted simply because he is a Jew opened on April 12, 1937, and ran for 67 performances. My source here is George Medovoy's unpublished dissertation, *The Federal Theatre Project Yiddish Troupes,* 112–42.

14. Inge, Foreword to *Anglo-Jewish Plays: In English and Yiddish,* Federal Theatre Project, New York, 1938. The copy I read was provided by the Dorot Reading Room of the New York Public Library, whose assistance I appreciate.

15. Medovoy, 176.

16. Ibid.

17. Nahshon, 189.

18. Lifson, 476.

19. Ibid.

20. Ibid., 453.

21. Federal Theatre, I, no. 2, November 25, 1935, issued by Bureau of Research and Publication for all workers of the Federal Theatre Project, New York, unpaged. The announcement neglects to mention that Schooler, Barzell, and Bleich had previously produced other Yiddish cabaret evenings in New York. The three collaborators presented in their Federal Theatre Project cabaret some of the same sketches and actors they featured in *Die Boyes* (*The Boys*), *Zalts un Feffer* (*Salt and Pepper*), and *Die Tskulakhnekes* (*In Spite of All the Hardships*), as George Medovoy notes in his unpublished dissertation, *The Federal Theatre Project Yiddish Troupes,* 92. The Yiddish Unit's backing enabled the existing collaboration to continue until Schooler was fired and federal funds were cut in June 1937. Medovoy discusses only the first edition of *We Live and Laugh* in his study, and seems unaware of the second edition discussed later in my survey. Reference to the preparation of a new humorous revue can be found in the last line of the June 25, 1937, Yiddish *Forward* account of the FTP cabaret group's last days (p. 3), discussed further in note 24.

Medovoy mentions two sketches I did not find in the Yiddish copy of the first edition, and I regret not finding them: *Betlehrs oif Delancey Street* (*Beggars on Delancey Street*) portrayed four Lower East Side beggars complaining about how the 1929 stock market crash harmed their profession; in *Bai dos Bargeh* (*In the Mountains*), women discussed the weight they lost in a mountain resort (Medovoy, 101).

The poster for the revue *We Live and Laugh* advertised "Cast of 100," and "Skits and Lyrics by Famous Authors." (A copy of the poster can be found in the FTP archive at George Mason University.) The production traveled to different locations in New York. By the end of its 1937 run, the revue had been seen by 31,990 spectators, in a total of ninety-five performances at theatres that included the Public, the Adelphi, and the Parkway (in Brooklyn). After visiting these theatres, the company was divided in two parts, which toured other area locations (Medovoy, 103–04). This tour created accessible theatre much like the Artef's "mobile theatre" offering of *Rivington Street.*

22. All translations of the first edition of the revue are my own, based on the Yiddish manuscript of *We Live and Laugh* in the Federal Theatre Project papers of the National Archives II, Adelphi, Maryland. The script remains unpublished.

23. Schack, op. cit.

24. Nadir, "Troops on the March." All English translations here come from the version by Julius Schmerler and Isidore Edelman, Federal Theatre Project

text provided by the archive at George Mason University. The text was translated in 1937 under the auspices of the FTP's Anglo-Jewish Play Department.
As noted above (in note 21), reference to a new 1937 edition of the revue can
be found in the June 25, 1937, Yiddish *Forward* account of the FTP Yiddish
vaudeville group's last days (p. 3). It is possible that Nadir's poem and other
sketches discussed here were rehearsed but not widely performed (if performed
at all) that year, because budget cuts prevented continuation of the revue. No
newspaper reviews of this material and no reference to performance of the
revue itself beyond March 1937 have been found. In a letter to Morris Schorr
dated April 13, 1937, Anglo-Jewish Play Department Supervisor Benson Inge
cites *We Live and Laugh* as "an excellent example of a revue which ran for a long
time in New York"—implying the run has ended; and an appendix in Hallie
Flanagan's memoir lists the revue's end date as March 6, 1937 (*Arena*, 389). The
Yiddish *Forward* for March 5, 1937, includes a theatre announcement (p. 3) that
We Live and Laugh will perform at the Middle Bronx Jewish Center (432 Clare-
mont Parkway, Bronx, New York) on March 5, and at the Hebrew Center (276
Commonwealth Avenue, Bronx) on March 6. These would have been the last
performances of the revue, if Flanagan's memoir list of dates is accurate. As
noted above, Medovoy reports that the show closed on March 6 after 95 performances (103–04). However, the June 25, 1937, Yiddish *Forward* column indicates that the Yiddish vaudeville group had prepared a new humorous revue
around that date. A Federal Theatre Project report from the Anglo-Jewish Play
Department covering its work for the first nine months of 1937 remarks that
"two editions of *We Live and Laugh*" were translated during that year, and refers
to the New York Unit "rehearsing *We Live and Laugh*, 1937 Version" ("Survey of
the Anglo-Jewish Play Department," unpaginated Activity Report section of
National Play Bureau files, National Archives II). The reference to rehearsal of
the revue's second version suggests that after the vaudeville ensemble's actors
were given pink slips in June and Zvee Schooler was fired in July 1937, the new
sketches never reached the public.

25. Lifson, 382.
26. Adler, *The Celia Adler Story*, Volume II, 422–23.
27. Sholem Secunda, *Memoirs of the Yiddish Stage*, 151.
28. Earlier in theatre history, one Yiddish actor audaciously cast himself
as the Messiah. Celia Adler recounts this audacious episode in her memoir,
Celia Adler's Story. During Passover feasts, the front doors of Jewish houses are
opened to welcome the prophet Elijah, should he choose to arrive. Just as the
door opened at one such feast, the handsome, charming young actor Jacob
Adler walked through the portal to visit his future wife's father (Celia Adler's
grandfather), and his future wife, Dina. Jacob Adler proceeded to tell Dina's
father why Dina should become an actress. Some of the greatest Jews in history
(Sarah Bernhardt, Rachelle) had been actors, who brought honor and pride to

their people, said Adler. Suffering Jews everywhere would benefit from the respect and pleasure a gifted actress brought them. He spoke as if an actor could in fact redeem the Jews from their suffering. His beautifully delivered oration won over the young woman's father. For a brief time, Jacob Adler, Celia's father-to-be, became the new Elijah. At least according to Celia's telling of the story, her father defended Yiddish theatre's role in history with all the eloquence and persuasion one might expect from a messianic leader. Her account of this episode has been published in English in *Memoirs of the Yiddish Stage*, edited by Joseph C. Landis, 66–68.

In the same memoir, Celia Adler offers a fascinating assessment of the damage that the "star" system (in which her family played a role) inflicted on Yiddish theatre. In an anecdotal recollection of stars abusing their top billing, and denying less well-known actors a chance to display talent, Adler suggests that Yiddish theatre's future, so much in question in the 1937 *We Live and Laugh* revue sketch, "Stars," was seriously endangered by the "stars" themselves.

29. Zvee Schooler, supervising director of the ensemble that created *We Live and Laugh*, was fired from the Federal Theatre Project on July 7, 1937, and his group was disbanded. The charge against him was "insubordination," after he refused to follow an order to cut the size of the Anglo-Yiddish unit in half. (The order to cut actors and reduce the budget was issued earlier that summer.) According to John O'Connor and Lorraine Brown, Schooler refused to follow the order "because he felt his supervisors were discriminating and because he did not want to be open to similar charges" (30). At the time rumors circulated that suspected Communists were being dismissed from the project. Higher officials never admitted staff cuts were made for that reason, at least not before Congress convened hearings on the Federal Theatre Project. The investigation, led by Congressman Martin Dies, began in August of 1938. Most of the witnesses testifying against the project had earlier been fired or refused promotions in the Federal Theatre Project, according to O'Connor and Brown (32). The primary accuser, Hazel Huffman, was a former WPA mail clerk, with little experience in theatre (32).

Schooler continued to work in the Yiddish theatre, including the Folksbiene in New York, where in 1977 he co-created (with Isaiah Sheffer) and performed in a musical based on Abe Cahan's novel, *The Rise of David Levinsky* (Sandrow, 394–95). In 1964 he performed in the original Broadway production of *Fiddler on the Roof*, in the company of the great, once-blacklisted actor, Zero Mostel.

CHAPTER 5: THE MESSIAH OF 1936

1. Sinclair Lewis referring to his novel, *It Can't Happen Here*, quoted by Richard Lingeman in *Sinclair Lewis: Rebel on Main Street*, 399.

2. Flanagan, *Arena*, 115–29, and O'Connor and Brown, *Free, Adult and Uncensored*, 59–61. The Lewis-Moffitt play was also briefly staged in Yiddish in Los Angeles, October 27 to November 3, 1936.

3. Flanagan, 124.

4. Schack, "Yiddish Version Given," *New York Times*, October 28, 1936, 2; Brooks Atkinson, untitled review, *New York Times*, October 28, 1936, 30.

5. Olgin, *Morgn Frayhayt*, October 30, 1936, 6. Oglin contrasts the English-language version of the play at the Adelphi, where the actors had thoroughly learned their roles and performed at a faster pace, with acting at the Biltmore, which was in his view melodramatic (my translation). George Medovoy reports that the Los Angeles Yiddish production "followed the English version closely, except that it was staged much more simply . . . and finally, from the evidence available, the production seems to have been melodramatic. On the last point, while melodrama may have been favored by Freedman's [Los Angeles Yiddish] group, Lewis and Moffitt's play itself was melodramatic" (Medovoy, *The Federal Theatre Project Yiddish Troupes*, 183). Both the English and Yiddish versions of the play in Los Angeles included the concentration camp scene discussed in this chapter.

6. Holden, "In Praise of Melodrama," in *Reimagining America*, 279.

7. Lewis quoted by an unsigned author in *New York Times*, October 28, 1936, 30.

8. O'Connor and Brown write that "Lewis charged that the studio considered the topic too controversial" (59). In *Arena*, Flanagan reprints a *Hollywood Citizen-News* report from October 26 1937, which noted, "Where the motion pictures feared to tread, the Federal Theatres tomorrow night will step boldly into the limelight of a controversial issue. . . . [T]he project has been the target of criticism from sources holding that the play will antagonize sympathizers of the Hitler and Mussolini regimes" (Flanagan, 117).

9. Flanagan, 117.

10. Flanagan, 127, 389.

11. Lewis and Moffitt, *It Can't Happen Here*, text courtesy of Federal Theatre Project archive at George Mason University. The Yiddish version of the text, translated from the English by Benson Inge and Benjamin Ressler, was provided to me by librarians at the Dorot Reading Room, Jewish Division, New York Public Library. Ressler also reportedly wrote a play that Artef considered for production in 1936 (Nahshon, 157).

The stage version of *It Can't Happen Here* includes less anti-Semitic language than the novel, in which Buzz Windrip's anti-Semitic policies are shaped with more complexity. In the book, dictator-President Windrip's platform promises that Jews "will continue to prosper and to be recognized as fully Americanized, though only so long as they continue to support our ideals." Those ideals include prohibition of Negro voting, and removal of women from all jobs "except in such peculiarly feminine spheres of activity as nursing and beauty parlors." The result, the novel reports, is that "Jews were no longer to be barred from fashionable hotels . . . but merely to be charged double rates. . . . Jews were never to be discouraged from trading but were merely to pay higher graft to commissioners and inspectors . . . [and] all Jews of all conditions were frequently to sound their ecstasy in having found in America a sanctuary, after their deplorable experiences among the prejudices of Europe." Lewis explores Windrip's allegedly populist policies with subtle irony in the prose of his novel. On stage, the melodramatic plot tends to overwhelm the ironies of the situation (*It Can't Happen Here,* 1935 edition of novel, pp. 77, 78, 190; other quotes from the novel are taken from the same edition).

12. Atkinson, *New York Times,* November 8, 1936, X:1.

13. Flanagan, 116.

14. Flanagan, 122.

15. Olgin, *Frayhayt,* October 30, 1936, 6. No metal cell bars are evident in photographs of the New York Yiddish production's prison camp scene. The comic strip image of the scene included in this chapter illustrates the play's text, not the Biltmore stage set.

16. Schack, *New York Times,* November 19, 1936, XII:3.

17. Fishel, quoted by Brown and O'Connor, 61.

18. Flanagan reports that during rehearsal and revision of the play, she received one telegram from San Francisco complaining, "Object to cutting White House scene only good scene Lewis play" (*Arena,* 117) She wondered at one point, "How would Buzz Windrip's campaign speech sound in Yiddish?" (120). On opening night she would have missed the Yiddish performance of the speech, delivered in scenes six and seven of Act One. She heard only Act Two at the Biltmore. She did not understand a word of Yiddish, according to Tony Buttitta and Barry Witham, in *Uncle Sam Presents* (89). But Flanagan knew the American-language version of the play quite well, and also probably knew that the Yiddish audience would share her alarm over Windrip's campaign speech, particularly his denunciation of "any money-wallowing international Jewish banker."

CHAPTER 6: PINSKI'S PRELUDE TO A GOLDEN AGE

1. Flanagan, *Arena,* 432–33, and *Brief Containing Detailed Answers to Charges Made by Witnesses Who Appeared Before the Special Committee to Investigate Un-American Activities, House of Representatives,* 6, 25, 30, 34. In her *Brief* defending the plays, Flanagan notes that they had been called "subversive" and "Communistic propaganda" by witnesses. The "honor" Pinski's play acquired lay in the distinguished company with which it was associated in the hearings. The witnesses naming such plays were not particularly astute critics of theatre, but at least they

named some gifted writers during their accusations. Brown and O'Connor note in their assessment of the hearings, led by Congressman Martin Dies in 1938, that most of the witnesses who spoke against Federal Theatre Project plays "had been fired or refused promotions" within the organization before they spoke against its work. The primary witness, Hazel Huffman, was a former WPA mail clerk, whose statements were "filled with hearsay evidence, conjecture, inconsistency, half-truths, and untruths" (Brown and O'Connor, 32). The inquiry into Communist influence on Federal Theatre Project activities ultimately led to a one-paragraph conclusion in the Dies Committee Report, filed January 3, 1939, that "a rather large number of employees on the Federal Theatre Project are either members of the Communist Party or are sympathetic with the Communist Party. It is also clear that certain employees felt under compulsion to join the Workers' Alliance in order to retain jobs" (*Arena*, 347). No specific allegation against any employee or artist was included. Earlier, in her refutation of such accusations, Hallie Flanagan had responded, "To the best of my knowledge, we have never done a play which was propaganda for communism; but we have done plays which were propaganda for democracy, for better housing . . ." (*Arena*, 342). Pinski's play fits none of these categories, but its pro-union satire might have been mistaken as propaganda by some conservatives and mail clerks.

Another Yiddish play that Flanagan defended against criticism was *Her Confession*. The play was criticized on the floor of the Senate, not in committee, and Flanagan responded by writing that the play, "pregnant with possibilities for senatorial humor, is a typical Yiddish drama which tells the tragic and highly moral story of the terrible price one woman pays for an indiscretion in her early life" (Flanagan papers in the Billy Rose Collection of the Lincoln Center Library for the Performing Arts, Series II, Federal Theatre Project file, document titled "Analysis of Federal Theatre Plays Criticized on the Floors of the U.S. Senate and House").

Hallie Flangan's *Brief*, nearly forgotten today, once meant a great deal to her. In 1938, she asked her friend Burns Mantle, "Please keep [a copy of] the Dies brief in case I am whisked away by the American Cheka on some dark night. It can happen here, but only after you and I and quite a few others have done all in our power" (*Hallie Flanagan* by Joanne Bentley, 329).

(Incidentally, the acronym HUAC was used later, to refer to a subsequent version of the 1938 committee led by Dies.)

2. Pinski, *The Tailor Becomes a Storekeeper* (*Der Schneider Vert a Kremer*), translated from the Yiddish by Elihu Winer. All quotations from the play are taken from this version, courteously provided by the archivist of the Federal Theatre Project papers at George Mason University.

3. Lifson, 85.

4. Schack, *New York Times*, April 14, 1938, 26. Schack's line praising the play as an "expressionistic romp" was quoted by Hallie Flanagan in her brief

defending Pinski's play against congressional witness charges that the work was "pro-union propaganda."

5. Edlin, *Der Tog,* April 23, 1938. My translation from the Yiddish. Flanagan, *Brief,* 34.

6. Zylberzweig, *Lexicon,* Vol. III, 1762 ff.; Sandrow, *God, Man and Devil,* 188–89; and Flanagan, *Arena,* 426. An unnamed source in Irving Howe's *World of Our Fathers* (491) claims Pinsky published fifty-six plays and no more than ten were produced. However, more than ten productions are noted by Zylberzweig.

7. Excerpt from an unsigned document titled "Anglo-Jewish Play Department," probably written by Benson Inge, or approved by him, since he was the department supervisor. Found in the National Archive's collection of Federal Theatre Project papers. Box 161, RG69, File of National Service Bureau, 1935–39. Evidence of Inge's interest in Pinski's play can be found in several letters preserved among Federal Theatre Project correspondence by Translations Department personnel. In a letter dated December 21, 1937, Inge thanked Pinski for a copy of the play *Gressa,* and added that "'*Tailor Becomes Store-Keeper*' seems the more desirable at the present time for any of our units, and I am holding all copies for further promotion." Evidently at that time the production had not yet been set. Earlier, on November 16, 1937, Inge wrote Chicago Yiddish theatre director Adolph Gardner (who directed the premiere of the play), "I am still trying to get for you, *Sodom and Gemorah* [by Leivick] and *The Tailor Becomes a Storekeeper,*" and in another letter dated December 7, 1937, Inge asked Pinski for copies of the *Tailor* play "both in English and Yiddish, if you have them, for typing and release to other units." He had received at least one copy of the Yiddish version by December 21st. These letters can be found in the files labeled "Correspondence of the Translations Department, 1935–39," RG 69, Works Progress Administration, Boxes 249–50, National Archives II.

8. Zylberzweig, *Lexicon of Yiddish Theatre,* Vol. I, columns 499–500.

9. Zylberzweig, *Lexicon of Yiddish Theatre,* Vol. IV, column 3208.

10. Zylberzweig, *Lexicon of Yiddish Theatre,* Vol. III, column 1648.

11. Zylberzweig, *Lexicon of Yiddish Theatre,* Vol. III, columns 1787–88.

12. Goldberg, *Three Plays by David Pinski,* vi.

13. Ibid., v.

14. Hapgood, *The Spirit of the Ghetto,* 198.

15. Sandrow, *God, Man and Devil,* 230. This and other excerpts from *The Treasure* are taken from Nahma Sandrow's translation. Comparing *The Treasure* and the 1938 *Tailor* play in an essay, B. Rivkin found the latter not achieving the earlier play's level in its fusion of realism and fantasy; but it is worth noting that the two plays briefly were compared in Rivkin's 1951 Yiddish essay, reprinted in the anthology, *David Pinski: Novels, Drama, Essay and Studies on Jewish Literature* (Congress of Jewish Culture, Buenos Aires, 1961, p. 325).

16. Sandrow, 186.

17. Bakhtin, 48. Pinski's *The Treasure* was rightly compared to Ben Jonson's *Volpone,* by no less an authority than Harvard's celebrated playwriting teacher, George Pierce Baker (Lifson, 86). The two plays share a richness of poetic language and a commonality of grotesque situations. Volpone lies in bed pretending to be dying, so prospective heirs will flatter him with gifts. Characters in *The Treasure* enter the town cemetery; their search for hidden gold frees most of them from inhibitions about trespassing on sacred burial grounds.

Pinski's *Tailor Becomes a Storekeeper* also displays the tendencies Mark Fearnow analyzes when he writes that the "grotesque" arises from "apprehension of an unresolved contradiction among two or more elements in an object, producing within one a sense of tension that nevertheless resolves into a limited pleasure in finding similar conflicts from life to have been 'named'" (Fearnow, *The American Stage and the Great Depression,* 12). Sam the Tailor faces unresolved contradictions as he seeks prosperity through private business at a time when businesses are failing. He finds security by returning to the needle trade and the union he left in search of greater security. "Thus reified," writes Feardon, "these cultural 'nightmares' are rendered less frightening but remain troubling and disruptive of an easy acceptance of 'reality.'"

18. Sandrow, 24.

19. Bakhtin, 48.

20. The Fair Labor Standards Act of 1938, as amended (referred to as "the Act" or "FLSA"), is published in sections 201–19 of title 29, United States Code and can be found at http://www.dol.gov/esa/whd/flsa/.

21. In 1998, a mere sixty years after Pinski's play opened, a movement of unemployed workers in France took the logic of the play further, as they spoke about "giving lessons in generosity to storekeepers" by taking from markets the groceries they could not afford. Their action had a precedent. In his book *Strike,* Jeremy Brecher reports, "By early 1932, according to New York newspapermen, groups of thirty or forty men would enter chain stores and ask for credit. When the clerk tells them business for cash only, they bid him stand aside; they don't want to harm him, but they must have things to eat. They load up and depart" (Brecher, 144). (Italian satirist Dario Fo based a farce on some similar actions, and titled it, *We Can't Pay, We Won't Pay.*) Brecher also discusses the Communist Unemployed Councils (mentioned in Chapter 8) that protested against evictions, and carried tenants' furniture back into an apartment after policemen placed it on the street.

Some of the unemployed in France also called for the abolition of wage labor and money in 1998, arguing that "the best way to abolish unemployment is to abolish the work and the money that are linked with it" (leaflet from the Bureau of Public Secrets, P.O. Box 1044, Berkeley, California, April 1998). If Pinski's play were staged today, a few of these ideas might be inserted into the union's song lyrics. The thirty-hour work week has yet to be tried in any country, as far as I know.

   22. Zylberzweig, *Lexicon of Yiddish Theatre*, Vol. IV, columns 3208–10.

CHAPTER 7: MENASHA SKULNIK BECOMES A BRIDEGROOM

   1. Buchwald, *Teater*, 305.

   2. Hapgood, *The Spirit of the Ghetto*, 173–74.

   3. Nadir, "The Average Theater Goer," viii.

   4. Nadir, *Tsutsik*, 1928.

   5. Lifson, *The Yiddish Theatre in America*, 335.

   6. Funke, "Molly Picon in Yiddish Musical Production, 'Sadie Is a Lady,' Again Charms Second Avenue," *New York Times,* January 28, 1950, 9.

   7. Irving Drutman, "Skulnik: Better than Sean Connery?" *New York Times,* November 7, 1965, X7.

   8. Lifson, 435.

   9. Leo Rosten, *The Joys of Yiddish,* 349.

   10. This and all later quotations from the play come from my translation of *Getzel Vert A Chusen* by Isidor Friedman and Isidor Rosenberg, unpublished manuscript in the Marwick Collection of the Library of Congress, Washington, DC, 1936.

   11. Arthur Gelb, "*The Fifth Season's* Happy Man," *New York Times,* June 14, 1953, 1.

   12. Herman Yablokoff, *Der Payatz* (*The Clown*), 311.

   13. William Shack, "*Schlemiehl* on Second Avenue," *New York Times,* September 19, 1936, 20.

   14. Skulnik recorded on audio tape, "Menasha Skulnik with Abe Ellstein's Orchestra," Banner Records, New York, 1996. Perhaps Skulnik's fame as a Yiddish Sultan of song led S. J. Perelman to jest once that he would write "a Pro-Semitic musical starring Menasha Skulnik, the title of which is to be *The Rape of the Lox*" (Perelman in *Don't Tread on Me,* edited by Prudence Crowther, 202).

   15. Said, *Orientalism,* 1978.

   16. Sholem Aleichem, "Homesick" in *My First Love Affair and Other Stories,* 223.

   17. Wisse, *The Schlemiel as Modern Hero.* Wisse made no reference to Skulnik when she wrote these words, and his role as Getzel does not fully conform to her observations.

   18. The anecdote about army service occurs when Getzel explains to Eva that he once was a soldier, "only they never gave me a rifle." Instead, Getzel spent his time in a hospital bed. "I was a soldier in bed." "You were ill?" she asks. He answers that in his family if you were going to be conscripted, you would make yourself ill. His Tsarist army career began when Getzel's relatives suggested

mutilating different parts of his body (his eye, his lung, his ear) in order to be rejected for military service. He took his mother's advice, punctured a hole in his ear, and as a result, "now, when I blow my nose, there's a whistling in my ear. You want to hear it? It's very interesting." The army still drafted him, and didn't notice the ear problem until he made himself deaf in the barracks. He didn't hear when they spoke to him. He used to hear only one thing—when he was called to meals—in the hospital, where he lay around for two years. Then they sent him home with a medal. Getzel's story suggests that his survival in military service was due to his rejection of the army, more than its rejection of him.

Another fascinating scene of social protest by Skulnik can be found not in the play, *Getzel Becomes a Bridegroom*, but in an undated photograph that shows the Yiddish comedian and the Hopkinson Theatre troupe under a Yiddish banner announcing, "Hopkinson Theatre Campaign Protesting Against Hitler's Barbarism." The photograph in the *Lexicon of Yiddish Theatre*, Vol. V, vi, 1967, was probably taken during the mid-thirties, when Skulnik played a number of lead comic roles at the Hopkinson. He clearly was capable of taking a stand against injustice both on stage and off.

19. Kobrin, quoted by Lifson, 126.

20. Even as the old system of matchmaking and arranged weddings portrayed in the play was yielding to newer methods of mating in the United States (such as Catskills resort weekends for single Jews), Yiddish *shund* in the 1930s and '40s preserved some functions of the *badchanim* through comic acting. Eventually comedians speaking the American language, and learning a few practices from Yiddish comics at Borscht Belt hotels, would create a new, American tradition of Jewish humor, moving from New York to Hollywood and other entertainment centers, where Mel Brooks, Danny Kaye, Lenny Bruce, Rob Reiner, Jerry Seinfeld, Nora Ephron, and Joan Rivers could joke about blind dates, mixed marriages, and "shiksa" (non-Jewish woman; as opposed to "sex") appeal.

Curiously, in 1976 when Irving Howe described Woody Allen as "a reincarnated Menashe Skulnik, quintessential *schlemiel* of the Yiddish theatre, but now a college graduate acquainted with the thoughts of Freud and recent numbers of *Commentary*," he neglected to mention that Allen performed in English, not Yiddish, aside from occasional Yiddishisms (*World of Our Fathers*, 571). Skulnik himself switched to English-language comedy during his long career, a change that acknowledged the new, assimilated American audience for *schlemiels*; but Menasha Skulnik's Yiddish-speaking world of *shund*, matchmakers, and militant kosher unions was far different from the postwar American society in which Allen "reincarnated" him.

CHAPTER 8: PROSPERITY'S CRISIS ON STAGE

1. Craig, "The Actor and the Über-Marionette," 90.

2. Cutler, *Der Dybuk in Crisis Gestalt* ("The Dybuk in the Form of a Crisis"), *Der Signal,* June 1936, 11.

3. Cutler's only film, "Yosl Cutler and His Puppets," courtesy of the National Jewish Film Center at Brandeis University. In the film, an English subtitle reference to the Unemployed Council translates the spoken Yiddish word as "office," when it should be "council." Discussion of this kind of political activism can be found in Brecher, *Strike!,* 144–45, and Folsom, *Impatient Armies of the Poor,* 261–76. Folsom quotes Carl Winter, a Communist leader of an Unemployed Council in New York, who recalls, "Squads of neighbors were organized to bar the way to the dispossessing officers. Whole neighborhoods were frequently mobilized to take part in this mutual assistance. Where superior police force prevailed, it became common practice for the Unemployed Councils to lead volunteer squads in carrying the displaced furniture and belongings back into the home after the police had departed" (Folsom, 268).

4. Cutler, "Out and In," *Muntergang,* 101–13.

5. Brecht, "Emphasis on Sport" and "Three Cheers for Shaw" in *Brecht on Theatre,* 6–13.

6. The *Purimshpil,* a festival play reenacting the biblical story of Queen Esther's triumph over the tyrant Haman, was one of the few theatrical activities in which European Jews engaged prior to the creation of Yiddish acting companies late in the nineteenth century. For a discussion of wedding jesters, see Chapter 7 on Menasha Skulnik. The first puppet play staged by Maud and Cutler in New York told the Purim story.

7. For much of the historical background and biographical information about Modicut, I am indebted to Edward Portnoy's essay, "Modicut Puppet Theatre: Modernism, Satire, and Yiddish Culture." In private correspondence, Portnoy also has noted that the first documented Yiddish puppet theatre was not Modicut, but rather Khadgadye, created by Moyshe Broderzon and Yosef Broyner, who performed in Lodz and Warsaw in 1923. Their puppetry caricatured Jewish political and cultural figures.

8. Katz in preface to *Proletpen: America's Rebel Yiddish Poets,* 10–11.

9. Portnoy, 117.

10. Tenenbaum, "Puppets that Speak Yiddish," *B'nai B'rith Magazine,* 1934.

11. Cutler, "He Wants to Know the Truth," in *Muntergang,* 125–28. The excerpts cited here are my own translation from the Yiddish.

12. Goldberg quoted by Paul Buhle in "Jews and American Communism," 26.

13. Cutler, "Nishka," from *Muntergang,* 189–90. The translation of excerpts here is my own, incorporating suggestions from Gerry Tenney. A complete and

more lyrical translation by Amelia Glaser can be found under the title of "Not-a" in her anthology of Yiddish poetry, *Proletpen,* 244–49.

14. This synopsis was published in a playbill for the Modicut production around 1927. I excerpt these lines from a copy in the Zuni Maud Archive in YIVO.

15. Portnoy, 113.

16. Ibid.

17. Katz, *Der Signal,* June 1936, 11.

18. The complete text of "The Dybuk in the Form of a Crisis" was published in two parts. Scenes I and II appeared in the June 1936 issue of *Der Hamer,* and Scenes III and IV appeared in the June 1936 issue of *Der Signal.* I read a copy of the first half in YIVO, the second half in the New York Public Library's Dorot Reading Room, and thank both libraries for assisting me in this research, and Edward Portnoy for telling me where to look for the text. It should be noted that while Maud and Cutler collaborated on several versions of their Dybbuk puppet play, the 1936 version is credited to Yosl Cutler alone ("not S. Ansky" he wrote on the first page), and was published after his 1935 death in an automobile accident. Translations from the 1936 version are my own.

19. Portnoy, 113. The waving of the eagle might also be regarded as a parody of *kapores,* the traditional Jewish practice of waving a rooster overheard before the Day of Atonement (Yom Kippur) to exorcise sins and pass them on to the sacrificial animal.

20. Ansky, *The Dybbuk,* translated by Joseph Landis, 34.

21. T. H. Watkins, "The Bird Did Its Part," *Smithsonian Magazine,* 1999.

22. This scene can be seen in the film, "Yosl Cutler and His Puppets."

23. Arendt, "Walter Benjamin," in *Men in Dark Times,* 164.

24. Nadir, *Marionette Play* in *Complete Works,* Vol. III, 155–61. The translation from the Yiddish is my own. Chaver Paver recalls a performance of this play in his autobiographical fiction titled *Gershon;* he states that Cutler's "cheery youthful voice" spoke for God, and Maud's "very resonant voice" spoke for Gabriel (Paver, 347–48); giving the angel the deeper voice and giving the voice of youth to the Eternal One comically went against preconceptions. A March 29, 1933, advertisement in *Morgn Frayhayt* announced an April 10th evening of "anti-religious satire" before Passover; the event featured presentations by Artef and Modicut. The ad doesn't name the plays Modicut performed, but perhaps one was *The Other World,* which remained in their repertoire of "anti-religious satire" for many years.

25. Groucho Marx, in *Flywheel, Shyster, and Flywheel,* 14.

26. Robert Yukelson, *Frayhayt,* April 16, 1926. Translation is my own.

27. Nadir, *Marionette Play (The Other World),* op. cit.

28. Benjamin, *Selected Writings,* Vol. II, 664. Walter Benjamin did not quote the Hasidim very often, but here he seems to have been amused, like

Nadir, by the possibility that the world to come will not differ so much from our own.

29. Paver, *Clinton Street,* 346.

30. Maud, song found among papers in the Zuni Maud archive, YIVO, New York, and attributed to *Business* by Edward Portnoy in his essay, mentioned above.

CHAPTER 9: LEO FUCHS, YIDDISH VAUDEVILLIAN IN "TROUBLE"

1. Yablokoff, *Der Payatz: Around the World With Yiddish Theatre,* 360. Fuchs evidently expressed his doubts to Yablokoff, despite the favorable reception he earlier received for his New York debut in the Yiddish play, *Lucky Boy.* In December 1935, *Times* critic William Schack welcomed "young Leo Fuchs, a newcomer from abroad" as an actor "every inch a one-man show . . . a nimble dancer, but he is not only a dancer. He can put over a song; he can fiddle, and he is a subtle character actor" (*New York Times,* December 2, 1935, 19:5).

2. Fuchs, "Der Millionaire Fun Delancey Street," recorded on "Leo Fuchs Sings Yiddish Theatre Favorites," Greater Recording Company, 1973.

3. Howe, *World of Our Fathers,* 558.

4. Goldberg, *Laughter Through Tears,* 93.

5. Yablokoff, 360.

6. Sapoznik, *Klezmer!,* 84.

7. Sandrow, *Vagabond Stars,* 127.

8. Shepard, untitled review in the *New York Times,* October, 21 1963, 39. As this review hints, Leo Fuchs also performed comic tricks with his fiddle. He played it while holding the instrument behind his back, for example. I learned this from his former stage colleague, the Yiddish actress Frances Wagenfeld (now known as Robin Tigelbaum) in a conversation in 2002.

9. All references to the film, and lines excerpted from its subtitles, are taken from the version released by the National Center for Jewish Film. Directed by Joseph Seiden, the film was completed in 1937. Critic Judith Goldberg writes that *I Want to Be a Boarder* "was made from the outtakes of *I Want to Be a Mother,*" and quotes Fuchs himself complaining that his songs were cut from one film and placed in others (Goldberg, 78). If that is the case, Seiden or his editor deserves praise for some masterful cutting and splicing. The song sequence in *I Want to Be a Boarder* occurs between shots of Fuchs's greenhorn character falling asleep and waking, and its presence as a dream needs no further explanation. I do not think that the creation of the film from outtakes in any way reduces its comedy or its impact. Fuchs almost certainly performed the song and dance live in vaudeville houses before it was filmed; Yablokoff describes the success of a similar dance number on stage (without naming the act's title).

10. Shepard and Levi, *Live and Be Well: A Celebration of Yiddish Culture in America,* 26.

11. Benjamin, "Surrealism," in *Selected Writings,* Vol. II, 217–18.

12. Howe, *World of Our Fathers,* 567.

13. Rosten, *The Joys of Yiddish,* 348.

14. Benjamin, "Ibizan Sequence," in *Selected Writings,* Vol. II, 590. Leo Fuchs wanted to perform another great *schlemiel* role, Gimpel the Fool, in his own adaptation of I. B. Singer's story, *Gimpel the Fool.* Yiddish actress Frances Wagenfeld told me in 2002 that Fuchs wanted her to play the role of Gimpel's wife, but the production was never realized. Singer's Gimpel, and Fuchs as *schlemiel,* bear some resemblances to the "messianic" fool Menasha Skulnik created (discussed in Chapter 7).

15. Sapoznik, 53.

16. For this understanding of *Yiddishkayt,* I am indebted to Paul Buhle's essay, "Tikkun— Shadows of Empire, Hopes of Redemption," 58.

17. I am indebted to Laurence Senelick, private correspondence, 2002, for this observation. Another comic dance by Fuchs was described to me by Yiddish actress Frances Wagenfeld, who performed the dance with him. In a parody of traditional dance partnerships, at a point where the audience expected the actress to leap gracefully into Fuchs's arms, he would jump into hers. Wagenfeld, who first performed in Yiddish theatre at the age of ten, and often portrayed young boys (as did Molly Picon), told me about this act and others in 2002.

18. Yablokoff, 379.

19. Peter Thomson, *Shakespeare's Professional Career,* 116, 139. This essay first appeared, in different form, in a book published to honor Thomson, and I am grateful to the editors and publisher (Exeter University Press) for permission to reprint the essay from *Extraordinary Actors.*

20. Hoberman, *Bridge of Light,* 219.

21. Schack, "Leo Fuchs Hit of Production—Musical Comedy Opens at the Public Theatre," *New York Times* (review signed by W.S.), December 2, 1935, 19.

22. Schack, "Musical Show on Second Ave.," *New York Times* (review signed by W.S.), October 4, 1937.

23. Dialogue excerpted from the film *Avalon,* directed by Barry Levinson (1990).

24. Fuchs, "Hop Along Knish," song recorded on "Leo Fuchs Sings Yiddish Theatre Favorites," Greater Recording Company, Brooklyn, 1973.

25. Margaret Harford reviewed the 1956 production at the site of the former Turnabout Theatre (renamed 716 N La Cienega Theatre) in Los Angeles for the *Mirror-News.* She noted that Tennessee Williams had protested the take-off titled *Katz on a Hot Tin Roof,* and said Fuchs "rides wildly through

his usual repertoire of corny puns and earthy jokes . . . throws in a couple of songs and some of his rubber-legged dance routines before bounding downstage to embrace several startled ladies in the first row of the audience." Once again the lead performer, not the play text, garnered the most attention from the critic.

26. For this information I am indebted to Hoberman, *Bridge of Light,* 321.
27. Shepard, untitled review in *New York Times,* October 29, 1962, 36.
28. Perelman, "The Sweet Chick Gone," in *Chicken Inspector No. 23,* 129.
29. Smith, *Fires in the Mirror,* xxxiii.

CHAPTER 10: YETTA ZWERLING'S COMIC DYBBUK

1. Sources for this essay include the Yiddish films mentioned here, in which Zwerling performs, and Zwerling's own memoir, published in the Yiddish *Forward,* in November and December of 1951. Reviews of the plays in which she performed rarely describe her acting in detail; they only offer an adjective ("madcap," for example) in front of her name. The films mentioned here are available from the National Center for Jewish Film. A Yiddish biography of Zwerling can be found in the *Lexicon of Yiddish Theatre,* Vol. III, columns 2276–77.

2. Young, "Two Theatres" in *The Flower in Drama,* 1923, 134–35.

3. Schack, *New York Times,* November 23, 1934, includes no assessment of Zwerling's role. The lines from Aleichem's play come from the Weitzner/Zumoff translation, titled *The Jackpot,* 42. In 1933, Zwerling also appeared with Menasha Skulnik in a stage play based on Aleichem's book about Menachem Mendel; I have been unable to find any information about her role in this production. Also, I never saw her lose her wig, but heard about it from a Yiddish theatregoer.

4. Schack, *New York Times,* January 24, 1936, 14:2.

5. Schack, *New York Times,* January 17, 1938, 11:2. Rendering the actress "eccentric" even after death, a brief *New York Times* obituary for Zwerling (January 19, 1982) noted that her "eccentric costumes" "included fruit and costume jewelry, which were her hallmark."

6. Brecht, *Brecht on Theatre,* "Short Organon," 202.

7. While Zwerling did not necessarily write her own dialogue in this scene or others, she was cast in a series of roles that either matched her comic propensity, and took shape through her art, or shaped her acting to a degree that the characters and their physical humor can be regarded as part of her own comic repertoire.

8. Brecht, op. cit., 194.

9. Aleichem, *The Great Fair: Scenes from My Childhood,* 276.

CHAPTER 11: MENACHEM MENDEL'S FALSE PROFITS

1. Aleichem, "Tevye Blows a Small Fortune," *Tevye the Dairyman and the Railroad Stories,* 33.

2. Hoberman, "Sholem Aleichm in the U.S.S.R.," 38.

3. Nahshon, *Yiddish Proletarian Theatre,* 47.

4. The stories combined and adapted in dramatic form are "Tevye Strikes It Rich," "Tevye Blows a Small Fortune," both from the Tevye stories, and "It's No Go: Menakhem-Mendl the Matchmaker," also translated as "You Can't Win," from *The Letters of Menakhem-Mendl and Sheyne-Sheyndl.* Paver's play, *Nisht Gefidelt,* can be found in the National Archive's collection of Yiddish plays from the Federal Theatre Project. The excerpt from it quoted here is my own translation from the Yiddish.

5. Rosenfeld, "The Sweatshop," in *A Treasury of Yiddish Poetry,* 78.

6. Buchward, *Lexicon of Yiddish Theatre,* Vol. VI, column 5873, my translation. The play itself, *Motl Paysee Dem Hazan in America,* can be found on pp. 157–74 of Chaver Paver's book, *Brownsville and Dramatisher Shpiln,* 1976. The lines quoted from it are my own translation.

7. Nashon, 190, provides this response and others in her summary of the production's reception.

8. Goldberg, *Clinton Street,* x.

9. Nahshon, 160.

10. Buchwald, *Teater,* 424–26. Some of the regrets he expressed in the 1943 book were anticipated by his article, "The Artef on Broadway," 9, in which Buchwald said Artef lacked "worth-while American plays in its repertory and . . . [it is] continuing to subsist on foreign plays alone." *New York Times* critic William Schack more or less agreed with Buchwald on the distance between *200,000* and contemporary political struggles; although he admired the "epic clowning" of the production, Schack found the Artef presentation "remote from rainbow shirts and fronts popular or patriotic, concerning itself with nothing more novel than the virtues of the poor and the ignobling influence of sudden wealth" (*New York Times,* November 29, 1936, XII:3:3).

11. Aleichem, "Tevye Blows a Small Fortune," in *Tevye the Dairyman and the Railroad Stories,* 33.

12. Ibid., 33–34.

13. Benjamin, "Theses on the Philosophy of History," *Illuminations,* 263.

14. Benjamin, "What Is Epic Theatre" in *Understanding Brecht,* 15–22.

15. Brecht, "Alienation Effects in Chinese Acting" in *Brecht on Theatre,* 98.

16. Efros, "The Artists of Granovskii's Theatre" in *Marc Chagall and the Jewish Theatre,* 156.

17. Nahshon, 158. Nahshon does not say that Schneider saw the Brooklyn production.

18. Mikhoels quoted by Benjamin Harshav in his essay, "Chagall: Postmodernism and Fictional Worlds in Painting," in *Marc Chagall and the Jewish Theatre*, 48.

19. *Jewish Luck,* film directed by Alexander Granovsky, Moscow, 1925. This silent film is available with subtitles in Yiddish and English.

20. Veidlinger, 48–49.

21. Schack, untitled review, *New York Times,* November 29, 1936, XII:3:3.

22. Nahshon, 160, also see Note 10 above.

23. Nadir, *Lexicon of Yiddish Theatre,* Vol. IV, columns 3432–33.

24. Efros, op. cit., 155.

25. Dennen quoted by Hoberman, op. cit., 40.

26. Weitzner, introduction to his translation of *The Jackpot,* 10.

27. Nahshon, 158. Nahshon only refers to the cut; I am speculating about its impact.

28. Nahshon, 161. The first quote is Nahshon's own view; the second, her translation of Nadir.

29. Nadir, *Lexicon of Yiddish Theatre,* Vol. IV, columns 3432–33, my translation.

30. Nahshon, 161.

31. Nadir in Zylberzweig's *Lexicon of Yiddish Theatre,* Vol. IV, Column 3433. My translation.

32. Yosef Schein quotes this statement in "Mikhoels and Chagall," *Marc Chagall and the Jewish Theatre,* 153.

33. Efros, op. cit., 156.

34. Aleichem, "Tevye Blows a Small Fortune" in *Tevye the Dairyman and the Railroad Stories,* 22.

35. Ibid., 26. And one place where the Messiah should appear, but does not: Zumoff and Weitzner in *The Jackpot,* their translation of the Aleichem play, change "Messiah" to "Devil" in Eti Meni's first act speech (24). In the original Yiddish, version, Shimele's wife says, "We should have mentioned the Messiah," just as her husband enters. The translators change her line to: "Here he comes, my breadwinner, speak of the Devil!" Then Shimele asks what she was saying about the Devil, instead of asking what she said about the Messiah. The change removes a comic reference to the messiah from the play's everyday conversation. Perhaps the translators felt an American audience would not appreciate the colloquial Yiddish expression.

36. Aleichem, *Letters of Menakhem-Mendl and Sheyne-Sheyndl,* translated by Hillel Halkin, 15.

CHAPTER 12: THE *ANTI-MILKHOME ZAMLUNG* OF 1937

1. *Anti-Milkhome Zamlung,* published by the National Play Bureau of the Federal Theatre Project, 1937. I found a copy in the Dorot Reading Room's

archive at the New York Public Library. Translations from the Yiddish in the booklet are my own. George Medovoy's unpublished dissertation, *The Federal Theatre Project Yiddish Troupes (1935–1939)*, briefly refers to the same document, and notes that the Anglo-Jewish Play Department of the National Service Bureau often recommended "anti-fascist, anti-war pieces." He is not referring to the catalogue when he writes this last statement, but suggests the Bureau's recommendation of such dramas to Yiddish theatres followed "Hallie Flanagan's advice to the Federal Summer Theatre in 1937, when she told delegates not to fear plays of protest" (Medovoy, 55, 62).

2. Nahshon, *Yiddish Proletarian Theatre*, 120–28.

3. Ring, *Frayhayt*, December 17, 1937, 6. My translation.

4. Schmeltsman, "The Yiddish Theatre of the Federal Theatre Project," unpaged 1937 report in the National Archive papers on the FTP.

5. "Survey of the Anglo-Jewish Play Department," 1937, unsigned, in the National Archive papers of the FTP.

6. Goldman, *Living My Life*, Vol. II, 634.

7. Nadir, in *Pushcarts and Dreamers*, 199–200.

8. Roth, *The Wandering Jews*, 93.

9. Howe, *World of Our Fathers*, 236.

10. Sandrow, *Vagabond Stars*, 52.

11. *Lexicon of Yiddish Theatre*, Vol. I, 284.

12. Lansky, *Outwitting History*, 163. Also deserving note in this context is I. B. Singer's statement, in his acceptance of the Nobel Prize for Literature, that Yiddish is "a language of exile, without a land, without frontiers, not supported by any government, a language which possesses no words for weapons."

13. Nadir, *Benjamin Quixote*, included in *Complete Works*, Vol. III, 109–52.

14. Sandrow, 292, and *Lexicon of Yiddish Theatre*, VI, column 6076.

15. Translation by Harvey Fink from the unpublished manuscript.

16. Sandrow, 292.

17. The translation of the titles in the Yiddish list is my own. Descriptions of these plays are included in Yiddish in the 1937 catalogue.

18. Jan Kott, *Theatre Notebook*, 103–5. A brief discussion of Kaminska's production can be found in her autobiography, *My Life, My Theatre* (1973). Also see Schechter and Spain on her *Mother Courage*, in a comic strip originally published in *Jewish Currents*, July 2005.

19. An abridged English translation of the gargantuan play can be found in Frederick Ungar's edition of *The Last Days of Mankind*, Ungar Publishing, New York, 1974.

20. Nadir's play remains unpublished, but a discussion of the text can be found in Noah Steinberg's 1926 book on Nadir, *A Moishe Nadir Book*, 93–96.

21. Ginsberg, libretto for *Hydrogen Jukebox*, unpaged, included with compact disc published by Elektra Nonesuch, 1993.

22. Adler, *A Life on the Stage,* translated by Lulla Rosenfeld, 348.

23. Ginsberg quoted by Corey Fisher in "Diamonds in the Dark," p. 5 of the program for a production by Traveling Jewish Theatre, San Francisco, December 1998.

CHAPTER 13: CONCLUSION: STILL WAITING FOR THE MESSIAH

1. Kafka, *Parables and Paradoxes,* 81.

2. Nahshon, 201. Artef did not completely vanish. Some of its members reorganized and started another company, the Yiddish Theatre Ensemble, in 1945. The Ensemble kept alive some of the spirit of Artef, but the body (of plays, that is) was diminished, as productions were less frequent and less celebrated than the pre-war work of Artef. Its plays included versions of *The Bloody Joke* (1945, based on Sholem Aleichem), *The Gold Grabbers* (Sholem Aleichem, 1948), *The Family Zanenberg* (by Leon Krutskovsky, 1951), and *The Devil in Boston* (by Leon Feuchtwanger, 1953).

An intriguing influence of radical Yiddish theatre on later culture surfaces in references to Camp Nitgedayget ("Don't Worry" in Yiddish), a Mid-Hudson Valley New York summer retreat for adults and children, where left-wing Yiddish plays were staged in the twenties and thirties. In the summer of 1927, for example, *Strike,* by Nathaniel Buchwald and Boruch Fenster, directed by Jacob Mestel, was staged at the camp, and later restaged at the Central Opera House in the Bronx (Nashon, 44). Mestel writes in his book *Our Theatre* about the camp's weekly plays, which educated actors politically as well as artistically. An ad for the camp in the 1937 Artef tenth-anniversary album advertises that "the Yiddish Worker's theatre was born on the stage of Camp Don't Worry" (my translation from the Yiddish). The camp name could be heard later in S. J. Perelman's 1936 parody of Odets' *Waiting for Lefty.* In a playlet titled *Waiting for Santy,* Perelman portrays elves at the North Pole protesting against exploitive working conditions they suffer under S. Claus. One elf in love with the boss's daughter, Stella Claus, praises the young woman as "a double malted with two scoops of whipped cream . . . the moon rising over Mosholu Parkway . . . a two weeks' vacation at Camp Nitgedaiget." *Mad* magazine writer Harvey Kurtzman included a comic reference to the camp in his mid-fifties parody of the comic strip "Mark Trail," in which Boy Scouts ask repeatedly to see "the habitat of Nit-ge-die-get the Girl Scout Camp." *Mad*'s motto, "What me worry? I read *Mad,*" transformed the Yiddish summer camp's name into a formula for nationwide comic relief from pressures to conform during the 1950s. Paul Buhle reports that Kurtzman attended Camp Nitgedayget in the thirties; perhaps this *Mad* man's satire of consumer culture and American icons was influenced by his summer days at Camp Don't Worry—certainly by the name of the camp (Buhle, *From the Lower East Side to Hollywood,* 194).

3. Sherman, "Revaluating Jewish Identity: A Centenary Tribute to Isaac Bashevis Singer (1904–1991)," 2, 6.

4. Ibid.

5. Singer, *Meshugah*, 20.

6. Singer, "The Yiddish Writer and His Audience" in *Creators and Disturbers*, 32.

7. Shandler, *Adventures in Yiddishland: Postvernacular Language and Culture*, 127.

8. Ibid., 139.

9. Brustein, *Seasons of Discontent*, 169. Also see Howe in *Commentary*, November 1964. Stefan Kanfer's amused response to the success of *Fiddler on the Roof*, and to Irving Howe's objections to the musical, points out that some Yiddish was spoken in the Broadway musical. Portraying Tevye in the American-language comedy, Zero Mostel occasionally "improvised in Yiddish, at once delighting and mystifying the onlookers—after all, the show was supposed to *be* in Yiddish, magically translated for American audiences." Kanfer also acknowledges a more progressive New York adaptation of Yiddish stories, *The World of Sholem Aleichem*, staged in 1953; there the formerly blacklisted actor Morris Carnovsky helped deliver a "message . . . of social agitation. He and other blacklistees identified with Aaron [a victim of anti-Semitism] from the first rehearsal" (Kanfer, 285, 273).

10. Inge or his staff wrote this in an unsigned statement quoted previously. The document titled "Anglo-Jewish Play Department" was found in Box 161, RG69, File of the National Service Bureau, 1935–39, Federal Theatre Project Papers, National Archives II. See Chapter 4 for additional discussion.

11. Solnit, *Hope in the Dark*, 75–76. Another consideration of the impact that Yiddish radicals had on our own culture can be found in Paul Buhle's book, *From the Lower East Side to Hollywood*.

12. Halkin writes, "Am I seriously proposing that *A Night in the Old Marketplace* should be produced as a Broadway musical? As a matter of fact, I am. Why not? After *Cats* and *Les Miserables*, it is a play whose time has come" (*The I. L. Peretz Reader*, 439). The gifted klezmer Frank London has already composed music for an adaptation of this play. But the new version differs considerably from the original, and sacrifices Peretz's complex poetic structure to a more conventional narrative line. As Rokhl Kafrissen astutely observes, the American adaptation with text by Glen Berger has been "created in the image of its producers—not in the apocalyptic spirit of 1925, but in the pragmatic yet revolutionary image of the Jewish avant garde of 2007. Much of the first act has been eliminated, along with the many layers of framing devices. A love story, which appears as just one of many ripples of drama among the original swarm of characters, has been moved to the top of the narrative. . . . It was the creators' intention to make a piece of Jewish art that was *not* about Jewishness"

(*Jewish Currents*, May 2007, 46). I still would like to see the original text staged by Wilson, Bogart, or Sellars, with music by London performed by his group, the Klezmatics.

13. Halkin translation, *A Night in the Old Marketplace* in *The I. L. Peretz Reader*, edited by Ruth R. Wisse, 389. Perhaps this is said in jest. David Roskies notes that the Jester in the play uses "the cover of night to ridicule all the redemptive schemes—whether sacred or secular—that once had vivified the Jewish body politic" ("Yiddish in the Twentieth Century," in *Yiddish Language and Culture, Then and Now*, Creighton University Press, 1998, 3).

14. Halkin, 403.

APPENDIX

1. A news item about Skulnik's Hopkinson Theatre production of *Menachem Mendel* in *Morgn Frayhayt*, September 24, 1933, lists the cast and reports that the play concerns "Yiddish life in America over the last few years." It adds, "You can't help yourself, you have to laugh." The notice sounds like part of a press release issued by the Hopkinson Theatre.

A performance based on the same Aleichem source was also presented by Yosl Cutler's Modicut in 1935, according to the *Lexicon of Yiddish Theatre*, Vol. IV, column 3348. While the text of the play seems lost, its lines may have been drawn directly from Aleichem's epistolary novel. The "cast" for the puppet theatre's presentation included Michael Rosenberg as narrator and Menachem Mendel, Al Harris as Sholem Aleichem, and Hannah Apel as Shayne-Sheyndl.

2. Aleichem, *Letters of Menakhem-Mendel and Sheyne-Sheyndl*, 7, 24, 100.

3. Schack, 'Yiddish Art Theatre Comedy," *New York Times*, January 1, 1940, 28:7.

4. Aleichem, "If I Were a Rothschild" in *Tevye the Dairyman and Other Stories*, 397–401.

5. Rogoff, *Lexicon of Yiddish Theatre*, Vol. IV, columns 3483–84 (my translation).

6. Benjamin, "Theses on the Philosophy of History" in *Illuminations*, 255. To avoid misunderstanding, it should be noted that the ideas about Yiddish theatre expressed in this section are my own, not Benjamin's. A few thoughts here were inspired by I. B. Singer's Nobel Prize acceptance speech and Michael Chabon's essay on an imaginary Yiddish-speaking homeland, titled "Guidebook to a Land of Ghosts," 67–69, with superb illustrations by Ben Katchor, including the design for a postage stamp honoring Moishe Nadir.

Bibliography

Adler, Celia. *Celia Adler Dertzeilt (Celia Adler Story)*. 2 vols. New York: Shulsinger Brothers Linotyping and Publishing Company, 1959.

Anti-Milkhome Zamlung. New York: WPA. Federal Theatre Project, July, 1937.

Ansky, S. *The Dybbuk*. In *The Dybbuk and Other Great Yiddish Plays,* translated and edited by Joseph C. Landis. New York: Bantam Books, 1960.

Arendt, Hannah. *Men in Dark Times*. New York: Harcourt, Brace & Company, 1968.

Bakhtin, Mikhail. *Rabelais and His World,* translated by Helene Iswolsky. Bloomington: Indiana University Press, 1984.

Barson, Michael, ed. *Flywheel, Shyster and Flywheel: The Marx Brothers' Lost Radio Show*. New York: Pantheon, 1988.

Benjamin, Walter. *Illuminations,* translated by Harry Zohn. New York: Schocken Books, 1968.

—— *Understanding Brecht,* translated by Anna Bostock. London: New Left Books, 1977.

—— *Selected Writings,* Vol. 2. Cambridge, MA: Belknap/Harvard, 1999.

Bentley, Joanne. *Hallie Flanagan*. New York: Knopf, 1988.

Berson, Misha. "Can *Awake and Sing!* Still Sing?" *American Theatre* (March 2005).

Boyarin, Jonathan. *Storm From Paradise*. Minneapolis: University of Minnesota Press, 1992.

Brecher, Jeremy. *Strike!* San Francisco: Straight Arrow Books, 1972.

Brecht, Bertolt. *Brecht on Theatre,* edited and translated by John Willett. New York: Hill and Wang, 1964.

Brechin, Gray. "Keeping the Faith." *San Francisco Chronicle,* December 27, 2005.

Brown, Lorraine and John O'Connor. *The Federal Theatre Project: Free, Adult and Uncensored.* London: Eyre Methuen, 1986.

Brown, Lorraine and others. *Cultural Diversity in the Federal Theatre Project (1935–1939).* Library of Congress Federal Theatre Project Collection at George Mason University, undated.

Buchwald, Nathaniel. "The Artef on Broadway." *New Theatre* (February 1935), 8–9.

—— *Teater.* New York: Farlag Committee, 1943.

Buhle, Paul. "Jews and American Communism." *Radical History Review* 23 (Spring 1980).

—— "The Prince of Satire: Moishe Nadir." *Shmate* 13 (Summer 1983), 8.

—— "Tikkun—Shadows of Empire, Hopes of Redemption." *Tikkun* 17 (January 2002).

—— *From the Lower East Side to Hollywood: Jews in American Popular Culture.* London: Verso, 2004.

Buttitta, Tony and Barry Witham. *Uncle Sam Presents: A Memoir of the Federal Theatre.* Philadelphia: University of Pennsylvania Press, 1982.

Chabon, Michael. "Guidebook to a Land of Ghosts." *Civilization* (June/July 1997), 67–69.

—— *The Yiddish Policemen's Union.* New York: Harper Collins, 2007.

Chametzky, Jules, ed. *Jewish American Literature: A Norton Anthology.* New York: W. W. Norton, 2001.

Chaver Paver (Gershon Einbinder). *Clinton Street and Other Stories,* trans. by Henry Goodman. New York: YKUF Publishers, 1974.

—— *Brownsville and One-Act Plays* (in Yiddish). Los Angeles: Chaver-Paver Book Committee, 1976.

Craig, Gordon. *On the Art of the Theatre.* London: Mercury Books, 1962.

Crowther, Prudence, ed. *Don't Tread on Me: The Selected Letters of S. J. Perelman.* New York: Penguin, 1987.

Cutler, Yosl. *Muntergang.* New York: Farlag Signal Bam Proletpen, 1934.

—— *Yosl Cutler and His Puppets* (film), 1935. Waltham, MA: National Center for Jewish Film.

—— *Der Dybuk in Crisis Gestalt* ("The Dybbuk in the Form of a Crisis" in Yiddish). *Der Hamer* (June 1936), 11–15 and *Der Signal* (June 1936), 11–12.

Drutman, Irving. "Skulnik: Better than Sean Connery?" *New York Times,* November 7, 1965, X7.

Epstein, Lawrence. *The Haunted Smile: The Story of Jewish Comedians in America.* New York: Public Affairs, 2001.

Epstein, Melech. *The Jews and Communism.* New York: Trade Union Sponsoring Committee, 1959.

Erdman, Harley, "Jewish Anxiety in 'Days of Judgement,'" *Theatre Survey* 40, no. 1 (May 1999), 51–74.

Fiedler, Leslie. *Freaks: Myths & Images of the Secret Self.* New York: Simon and Schuster, 1978.

Flanagan, Hallie. *Brief Containing Detailed Answers to Charges Made by Witnesses Who Appeared Before the Special Committee to Investigate Un-American Activities, House of Representatives.* Unpublished manuscript in National Archives, 1938.

—— *Arena.* New York: Duell, Sloan and Pearce, 1940.

Fo, Dario. "Les Intellectuels et la Culture." *Travail Theatral* (Paris) 31 (1978), 64–67.

Folsom, Frederick. *Impatient Armies of the Poor: The Story of Collective Action of the Unemployed.* Denver: University of Colorado Press, 1990.

Friedman, Isidor and Isidor Rosenberg. *Getzel Vert A Chusen (Getzel Becomes a Bridegroom).* Unpublished Yiddish manuscript in the Marwick Collection of the Library of Congress, Washington, DC, 1936.

Fuchs, Leo. "Leo Fuchs Sings Yiddish Theatre Favorites." Greater Recording Company, 1973. Audio tape.

Gelb, Arthur. *"The Fifth Season's* Happy Man." *New York Times,* June 14, 1953.

Glaser, Amelia and David Weintraub, eds. *Proletpen: American Rebel Yiddish Poets,* translated by Amelia Glaser. Madison: University of Wisconsin Press, 2005.

Goldberg, Itche. Interview with the author on Moishe Nadir. June 5, 2002.

Goldberg, Judith. *Laughter Through Tears.* Rutherford, NJ: Associated University Presses, 1983.

Golden Harry. *Enjoy, Enjoy!* Cleveland: World Publishing Company, 1960.

Goldman, Emma. *Living My Life.* 2 vols. New York: Dover, 1970.

Granovsky, Alexander. *Jewish Luck.* Silent film available on videotape, originally released in Moscow, 1925.

Hapgood, Hutchins. *The Spirit of the Ghetto,* edited by Moses Rischin. Cambridge, MA: Belknap/Harvard, 1967.

Hoberman, J. *Bridge of Light: Yiddish Film Between Two Worlds.* New York: Museum of Modern Art/Schocken Books, 1991.

—— "Sholem Aleichem in the U.S.S.R." *Pakn Treger* 22 (Summer 1996).

Holden, Joan. "In Praise of Melodrama." In *Reimagining America: The Arts of Social Change,* edited by Mark O'Brien and Craig Little. Philadelphia: New Society Publishers, 1989.

Howe, Irving. *World of Our Fathers.* New York: Simon and Schuster, 1976.

—— and Eliezer Greenberg. *A Treasury of Yiddish Poetry.* New York: Schocken, 1976.

Inge, Benson and staff. *Anglo-Jewish Plays: In English and Yiddish.* New York: Federal Theatre Project, 1938.

Kafka, Franz. *Parables and Paradoxes.* New York: Schocken Books, 1961.

Kaminska, Ida. *My Life, My Theater,* edited and translated by Curt Leviant. New York: Macmillan, 1973.

Kanfer, Stefan. *Stardust Lost: The Triumph, Tragedy, and Meshugas of the Yiddish Theatre in America.* New York: Knopf, 2006.

Kazacoff, George. *Dangerous Theatre: The Federal Theatre Projects as a Forum for New Plays.* New York: Peter Lang, 1989.

Kraus, Karl. *The Last Days of Mankind,* translated by Alexander Gode and Sue Ellen Wright. New York: Ungar Publishing, 1974.

Kurtzman, Harvey. *The Mad Reader.* New York: ibooks, inc., 2002.

Kushner, Tony. *Angels in America.* New York: Theatre Communications Group, 1994.

—— *A Dybbuk and Other Tales of the Supernatural,* translated by Joachim Neugroschel from S. Ansky. New York: Theatre Communications Group, 1998.

Lansky, Aaron. *Outwitting History.* Chapel Hill: Algonquin, 2004.

Lewis, Sinclair and John Moffitt. *It Can't Happen Here.* Unpublished manuscript of the play courtesy of George Mason University Federal Theatre Project Records, 1936.

Liebman, Arthur. *Jews and the Left.* New York: John Wiley and Sons, 1979.

Lifson, David. *The Yiddish Theatre in America.* New York: Thomas Yoseloff, 1965.

Lingeman, Richard. *Sinclair Lewis: Rebel on Main Street.* New York: Random House, 2002.

Marc Chagall and the Jewish Theater. New York: Guggenheim Museum, 1993. Includes essays by Abram Efros, Aleksei Granovsky, Benjamin Harshav, Yosef Schein, and others.

Medovoy, George. *The Federal Theatre Project Yiddish Troupes.* Unpublished dissertation, University of California at Davis, 1975.

Mendele Moykher Sforim (S. Y. Abramovitsh). *Tales of Mendele the Book Peddler,* edited by Dan Miron and Ken Frieden. New York: Schocken Books, 1996.

Mestel, Jacob. *Unzer teater.* New York: YCUF, 1943.

Miron, Dan. *A Traveler Disguised: The Rise of Modern Yiddish Fiction in the Nineteenth Century.* Syracuse, NY: Syracuse University Press, 1996.

Mlotek, Eleanor Gordon and Joseph Mlotek. *Pearls of Yiddish Song.* New York: Education Department of the Workmen's Circle, 1988.

Nadir, Moishe. *Peh-El-Peh (Face to Face),* translated by Joseph King. New York: Pagan Publishing, 1920.

—— "The Average Theater Goer," In *One-Act Plays From the Yiddish,* translated by Etta Bloch, Second Series. New York: Bloch Publishing Company, 1929, viii–xi.

—— *Rivington Striit* (in Yiddish). New York: Yidburo Publishers, 1932.

—— *Teaterteks.* In *Complete Works* (in Yiddish). Vol. III. *Theatre.* New York: Freiheit Publishing Company, 1932.

—— *Teg Fun Mayne Teg (Days of My Days).* New York: Freiheit Publishing Company, 1935.

—— *Polemic.* New York: Yidburo Publishers, 1936.

—— *Nadirgang.* New York: Posy-Shoulson Press, 1937.

—— *Moide Ani (Confession).* New York: Posy-Shoulson Press, 1944.

—— *From Man to Man.* Translated from the Yiddish by Harvey Fink. Ladysmith, BC, Canada: Windshift, 2006.

—— *Messiah in America.* Translated from the Yiddish by Nahma Sandrow. Unpublished manuscript loaned to the author.

—— *Rivington Street,* translated from the Yiddish by Harvey Fink. Unpublished manuscript loaned to the author.

Nahshon, Edna. *Yiddish Proletarian Theatre: The Art and Politics of the Artef, 1925–1940.* Westport: Greenwood Press, 1998.

Passow, David. *The Prime of Yiddish.* Jerusalem: Geffen Publishing House, 1996.

Perelman, S. J. *Chicken Inspector No. 23.* New York: Simon and Schuster, 1966.

Peretz, I. L. *The I. L. Peretz Reader,* edited and with an introduction by Ruth R. Wisse. New Haven: Yale University Press, 2002.

Pinski, David. *Oisgeklibene Shriftn (Selected Writings)* (in Yiddish). Buenos Aires: Congress of Jewish Culture, 1961.

Pinsky, David (sic). *The Tailor Becomes a Storekeeper.* Translated from the Yiddish by Elihu Winer Unpublished manuscript courtesy of George Mason University Federal Theatre Project Records, 1937.

Portnoy, Edward. "Modicut Puppet Theatre: Modernism, Satire, and Yiddish Culture." In *Puppets, Mask and Performing Objects,* edited by John Bell. Cambridge, MA: MIT Press, 2001.

Rosenfeld, Max, ed. and trans. *Pushcarts and Dreamers: Stories of Jewish Life in America.* Philadelphia: Sholem Aleichem Club Press, 1967.

Rosten, Leo. *The New Joys of Yiddish,* edited by Lawrence Bush. New York: Three River Press, 2001.

Roth, Joseph. *The Wandering Jews,* translated by Michael Hofmann. New York: Norton, 2001.

Said, Edward. *Orientalism.* New York: Pantheon, 1978.

Sandrow, Nahma. *Vagabond Stars: A World History of Yiddish Theatre.* New York: Harper and Row, 1977.

—— *God, Man, and Devil: Yiddish Plays in Translation.* Syracuse: Syracuse University Press, 1999.

Sapoznik, Henry. *Klezmer! Jewish Music From Old World to Our World.* New York: Schirmer Trade Books, 1999.

Schack, Willliam. "Leo Fuchs Hit of Production—Musical Comedy Opens at Public Theatre." *New York Times,* December 1, 1935, 9.

—— "Revue on East Side: *We Live and Laugh* Offered Under Federal Auspices." *New York Times,* May 9, 1936, 10:3.

—— "*Schlemiehl* on Second Avenue." *New York Times,* September 19, 1936, 20.

—— Essay on Yiddish production of *It Can't Happen Here* and Artef's *200,000. New York Times,* November 29, 1936, XII: 3:3.

—— "Musical Show on Second Ave." *New York Times,* October 4, 1937, 17.

—— "Yiddish Art Theatre Comedy." *New York Times,* January 1, 1940, 28:7.

Schechter, Joel. "Leo Fuchs, Yiddish Vaudevillian." In *Extraordinary Actors: Studies in Honor of Peter Thomson,* edited by Jane Milling and Martin Banham. Exeter: University of Exeter Press, 2004, 150–63.

—— "Messiahs of 1933: Radical Yiddish Theatre at Artef." *Studies in Theatre and Performance* 25, no. 1 (2005), 79–81.

—— "Nadir's Messiah in America." Illustrated by Spain. *Jewish Currents* (March/April 2005), 47.

Schiff, Ellen. "Taking the Heat." *Lincoln Center Theater Review* 42 (Spring 2006), 22–23. Special issue on Clifford Odets.

Schmeltsman, Leo. "The Yiddish Theatre of the Federal Theatre Project," Federal Theatre Project. Available in National Archive II, Adelphi, Maryland. Unpaged, 1937.

Secunda, Sholem. *Memoirs of the Yiddish Stage,* edited by Joseph C. Landis. New York: Queens College Press, 1984, 150–51.

Seiden, Joseph, director. *I Want to Be a Boarder.* Film in videotape form, National Center for Jewish Film, Brandeis University, Waltham, MA, 1937.

Seidman, Naomi. *A Marriage Made in Heaven: The Sexual Politics of Hebrew and Yiddish.* Berkeley: University of California, 1997.

Shandler, Jeffrey. *Adventures in Yiddishland: Postvernacular Language and Culture.* Berkeley: University of California Press, 2006.

Shapiro, Lamed. *Der Shrayber Geynt in Kheyder.* Los Angeles: Aleyn, 1945.

Shepard, Richard and Vicki Gold Levi. *Live and Be Well: A Celebration of Yiddish Culture in America.* New York: Ballantine Books, 1982.

Sherman, Joseph. "Revaluating Jewish Identity: A Centenary Tribute to Isaac Bashevis Singer (1904–1991)." *Midstream* (July/August 2004), 2–6.

Sholem Aleichem. *The Great Fair: Scenes From My Childhood,* translated by Tamara Kahana. New York: Noonday Press, 1955.

—— *Tevye the Dairyman and the Railroad Stories,* translated and with an introduction by Hillel Halkin. New York: Schocken Books, 1987.

—— *The Jackpot: A Folk-Play in Four Acts,* translated by Kobi Weitzner and Barnett Zumoff. New York: Workmen's Circle Education Department, 1989.

—— *The Letters of Menakhem-Mendl & Sheyne-Sheyndl* and *Motl, the Cantor's Son,* translated and with an introduction by Hillel Halkin. New Haven: Yale University Press, 2002.

—— *My First Love Affair and Other Stories,* translated by Curt Leviant. New York: Dover, 2002.

Singer, I. B. "Yiddish Theater Lives, Despite the Past." *Yiddish* (I. B. Singer issue) 6, nos. 2–3 (Summer–Fall 1985), 149–55.

—— "The Yiddish Writer and His Audience." In *Creators and Disturbers,* drawn from conversations by Bernard Rosenberg and Ernest Goldstein. New York: Columbia University Press, 1982.

—— *Meshugah.* New York: Farrar Straus Giroux, 1994.

Skulnik, Menasha. "Menasha Skulnik with Abe Ellstein's Orchestra." Banner Records, 1996. Audio tape.

Solnit, Rebecca. *Hope in the Dark: Untold Histories, Wild Possibilities.* New York: Nation Books, 2006.

Smith, Anna Deavere. *Fires in the Mirror.* New York: Anchor Doubleday, 1993.

Steinberg, Noah. *A Bukh Moishe Nadir.* New York: Leben, 1926.

Tennenbaum, Samuel. "Puppets that Speak Yiddish." *B'nai B'rith Magazine,* 1934.

Thomson, Peter. *Shakespeare's Professional Career.* Cambridge: Cambridge University Press, 1991.

Tsen yor Artef. New York: Artef, 1937.

Veidlinger, Jeffrey. *The Moscow State Yiddish Theater: Jewish Culture on the Soviet Stage.* Bloomington: Indiana University Press, 2000.

Veviorka, A. *Dramatic Works of A. Veviorka* (in Yiddish), Vol. I (with text of *Diamonds* in Yiddish). New York: YIVO.

Watkins, T. H. "The Bird Did Its Part." *Smithsonian Magazine* (May 1991).

We Live and Laugh Revue, 1937 Edition. Unpublished manuscript translated from the Yiddish by Julius Schmerler and Isidore Edelman. Courtesy of George Mason University Federal Theatre Project Records, 1937.

Weiner, Leo. *The History of Yiddish Literature in the Nineteenth Century.* New York: Charles Scribner's Sons, 1899.

Wex, Michael. *Born to Kvetch: Yiddish Language and Culture in All of Its Moods.* New York: St. Martin's Press, 2005.

Wisse, Ruth. *The Schlemiel as Modern Hero.* Chicago: University of Chicago Press, 1971.

Yablokoff, Herman. *Der Payatz: Around the World With Yiddish Theater.* Silver Spring, MD: Bartleby Press, 1955.

Young, Stark. *The Flower in Drama.* New York: Charles Scribner's Sons, 1925.

Zinn, Howard, *Artists in Time of War.* New York: Seven Stories Press, 2003.

Zucker, Bat-Ami. "American Jewish Communists and Jewish Culture in the 1930s." *Modern Judaism* 14 (1994), 175–85.

Zwerling, Yetta. "Yetta Zwerling Tells How She Traveled to America" and other memoirs in Yiddish, *Forward,* New York, November 6, 10, 13, 17, 20, 24, 27, and December 1, 1951.

Zylberzweig, Zalmen. *Leksikon fun yidishn teater.* Volumes 1 and 2: New York, assisted by Jacob Mestel, Hebrew Actors Union of America, 1931. Volume 3: New York, assisted by Jacob Mestel, Hebrew Actors Union of America, Farlag Elisheva, 1959. Volume 4: New York, Hebrew Actors Union of America, Farlag Elisheva, 1963. Volume 5: Mexico City, Hebrew Actors Union of America, 1967. Volume 6: Hebrew Actors Union of America, Mexico, 1969.

Index

Joel Schechter is Professor of Theatre Arts at San Francisco State University. He has written a number of books about satirists and circus clowns, and served as Editor of the Yale School of Drama's magazine, *Theater.* He also created a series of comic strips with the illustrator Spain, and currently writes a column, "Radical Yiddish," for the journal *Jewish Currents.*